BONDAGE

Anti-Blackness and Ancestrality

OSMUNDO PINHO

Translated from Brazilian Portuguese by Ayala Tude

AMÉFRICA
PRESS

ISBN: 979-8-9872776-6-9 (Paperback)
ISBN: 979-8-9872776-7-68 (eBook)

First English Translation, Printed Edition 2025

Améfrica Press
P.O. Box 24647
Baltimore, MD 21214 USA
www.amefricapress.com

First Published in Portuguese in São Paulo, Brazil in 2021 as:
Cativeiro: antinegritude e ancestralidade by Osmundo Pinho
ISBN 978-65-86754-13-1
Publisher: Editora Segundo Selo
Rua da Gengibirra do meio, nº 16-B Liberdade
Salvador/BA CEP: 40370-600
(Escritório Virtual)
contato@editorasegundoselo.com.br
https://editorasegundoselo.com.br/
This is an authorized translation from the Portuguese language edition published by Segundo Selo.

This book is dedicated to the memory of my grandparents,
Dona Regina and Seu Moreno.

CONTENTS

TRANSLATOR'S NOTE

Ayala Tude

As I sit with this completed translation of this book, I realize that it has presented me with challenges and insights that have deepened my translational practice, forcing me to confront not only the limits of language but also the political dimensions inherent in every choice of word and phrase.

Along this journey, I have found myself repeatedly returning to Beatriz Nascimento's conceptualization of "the person of the slave", a formulation that Osmundo Pinho identifies as central to understanding the persistence of anti-Black violence and dehumanization in contemporary Brazil. As Pinho examines in Chapter 1, "The Person of the Slave: Social Death and Political Imaginaries of the African Diaspora in Brazil", Nascimento's critique emerged during the Black Fortnight at USP in 1977, where she challenged academic historiography's obsession with slavery and proposed Africa and the quilombo as imaginative paradigms for Black political subjectivity. Her analysis reveals how the colonial construction of enslaved Africans as non-persons continues to structure Brazilian social relations, creating what she understood as an ongoing condition of social death that extends far beyond the formal abolition of slavery.

As I worked through passages discussing this concept, I was struck by how translation itself becomes implicated in questions of personhood and recognition. Each word choice in English carries an embedded question: how could I translate the untranslatable violence of reducing human beings to property without reducing them to the linguistic traces of bondage that persist in contemporary discourse? This question haunted every page, reminding me that translation, like the social relations it seeks to convey, is never neutral terrain.

In this sense, as you read, you will find terms in Portuguese that have resisted my attempts at easy equivalence, each carrying within it the weight of history, the specificity of place, and the complexity of lived experience. For instance, "quilombos", those spaces of resistance originally formed by escaped enslaved Africans, cannot be merely translated as settlements or communities without losing their revolutionary essence, their character as territories of cultural preservation and autonomous becoming. As I thought of how I could convey the meaning of this term in English, I found myself thinking of Nascimento's understanding of quilombos as spaces where "the person of the slave" could be reconstituted as simply "person", where the violent interpellation of enslavement could be refused, and alternative forms of sociality could emerge.

Similarly, "terreiros", the sacred spaces of Afro-Brazilian religious practice, particularly Candomblé and Umbanda, demanded my recognition not as simple "temples" but as cosmological centers where the sacred and secular intermingle in ways that European-derived languages struggle to articulate. Working with these terms, I began to understand my role less as translator and more as cultural mediator, attempting to create bridges of understanding while preserving alterity.

It was also a challenge when I encountered terms like "rolezinhos"—those gatherings of predominantly young, Black, and working-class Brazilians in shopping malls and public spaces. Here, I found myself grappling not only with linguistic difference but with the sociopolitical context that gives these events their meaning as challenges to spatial segregation and manifestations of racial and economic inequalities. Words like "biqueiras", those informal spaces for drug commerce controlled by trafficking organizations—and "paredões", the towering sound systems that create literal walls of sound during street parties, especially in the city of Salvador, each represent nodes in a complex urban ecology that defies simple categorical translation. There are many cultural specificities throughout this work that require constant negotiation between explanation and preservation of mystery.

As you go through these pages, you will find words like "pardas", "pardos", "crioula", and "crioulo"—terms referring to individuals of mixed racial or ethnic ancestry within Brazil's official classification system. Such words bear connotations that shift across temporal and social contexts, requiring constant vigilance regarding their contemporary reception. Working with these terms, I was repeatedly confronted with how racial classification systems attempt to fragment and hierarchize shared experiences of racialization. Whenever you encounter them, I advise you to read the footnotes for further contextualization.

This note serves as invitation and warning: to read this work is to encounter not merely translated content but a collaborative creation born from the meeting of Portuguese and English, local and global ways of knowing. I write this text in the first person intentionally, as a recognition that translation is always already interpretation, and that readers deserve to understand the interpretive choices that have shaped their encounter with the text. So, the work of translation lies not in the achievement of perfect equivalence, an impossible goal, but in the discovery of creative possibilities that emerge when languages meet, resist, and embrace each other.

FOREWORD

ONTOLOGICAL VOID AND (-) BLACK EXISTENCE IN THE BRAZILIAN POLITY

Jaime Amparo Alves
Department of Black Studies
University of California, Santa Barbara

I could start by referencing the tragic murders of Emilly and Rebecca, two Black little girls shot dead in a favela of Rio de Janeiro, the lynching of João Alberto, a Black man beaten to death in a supermarket in the southern part of the country, the anguish of Rute Fiúza, who has spent years searching for the mutilated and missing body of her son, Davi, or the premature death of Grandma Aurora, one of the many Black women whose lives have been shortened by medical racism. However, selectively highlighting these ordinary encounters risks turning ontological annihilation into the palatable liberal label of human rights violation. Human: the Brazilian dictionary of Portuguese language defines the adjective form of the word as "relating to man or proper to his nature."[1] How can the "proper nature" of being human be inscribed to Blackness when the gender, sexual, and racial marks on Black bodies exclude us from the white, property-owning, masculine, cisgender framework of Humanity?

One could argue, following Calvin Warren's steps, that the imagined white community, and the Rule of Law that demarks and polices its boundaries, is a biopolitical domain where the Black nonbeing becomes

---

[1] E.N.: In the initial Portuguese version, the following citation was used: Dicio. *Dicionário Online de Português*. Humano [adj.]. Available at: https://www.dicio.com.br/aurelio-2/. The link for this citation is no longer active as it pertains to the word *Humano* as an adjective. We did, however, upon an internet search using the quoted part of the definition of *human* as an adjective, find other links to dictionaries, research papers, texts, and books in Portuguese that used this definition of Human. Human is also sometimes used interchangeably with the term *humanitarian*, which is also defined exactly the same way. One example is this https://ciberduvidas-ql.iscte-iul.pt/consultorio/perguntas/humanitario-e-humano/30510

an *equipment* for the making of the world of Being.[2] In our times, this or-
derly biopolitical space is characterized by infinite possibilities of political
participation and the exercise of rights, even if such 'democratic' engagement sometimes crashes with hierarchies of Beings. Within the Brazilian
polity, the deaths of Emilly, Rebecca, Davi, Alberto, and Aurora, alongside
the deaths yet to come, may ignite protests and provoke token humanist
responses— an open letter, a report on police violence, or even a taskforce
for diversity promotion in state apparatuses—but ultimately, these reac-
tions fail to alter the trans-historical reality bound to the insurmountable
condition of *nonexistence*. To evoke philosopher Denise Ferreira da Silva's
critical discussion on the racial logic of obliteration that governs Brazil,
the Black subject is a subject devoid of a body, as her juridical condition
is one of (-) *negativization* [negative accumulation]. If on the one hand her
existence is *accumulated* as raw material for the making of modernity, on
the other, her body is a frontier where the negation of her existence other
than as a biological asset demarks the ethic-juridical terrain of political
belonging. Thus, the *minus* of existence calls attention not only to the unpayable and unquantifiable labor Black people have continued performing
for centuries, hence an unpayable debt, but also to the *property* of being
human and thus a subject of rights.[3]

   Bondage: Antiblackness and Ancestrality echoes much of the critiques
outlined above by addressing a central question: what happens when
the Slave engages and refuses *cativeiro* [bondage] as a totality? To do so,
Osmundo Pinho joins the project of destabilizing the Human, an endeavor
championed by, and rooted in, a Black feminist intellectual tradition that
positions the gendered bodies of Black women as the "interstice" between
the realms of the human and non-human, the body and the flesh, freedom
and slavery.[4] While firmly positioned in this tradition and carefully engaging with the Afro-pessimism and Black optimism debate,[5] the book expands the interpretive possibilities of locating Black diaspora as a geography of bondage and as a territory of freedom. To an international audience
unaware of the geographic context, Pinho theorizes from the rich tradition

---

[2] Calvin Warren. *Ontological terror: Blackness, nihilism and emancipation*. Duke University Press, 2018.

[3] Denise Ferreira da Silva. *Unpayable debt*. London: Sternberg Press, 2022.

[4] I have in mind here Sylvia Wynter, Sueli Carneiro, Lelia Gonzalez, Hortense Spillers and Saidiya Hartman, among others.

[5] The key figures in this debate are adequately examined by Pinho in the subsequent pages, rendering a detailed review in this preface unnecessary. For essential conceptual referenc-es, see Saidiya Hartman, Frank Wilderson, Jared Sexton, João Costa Vargas, Fred Moten, Christina Sharpe, and Cavil Warren, among others.

of marronage in the Bahian region called Recôncavo Bahiano. Place matters here for dislodging Salvador as the primary reference of theorizing on Blackness in northeast Brazil and for repositioning the unsettled territory of Cachoeira[6] as a permanent threat to the Brazilian state project of racial erasure. Indeed, Cachoeira embodies this book's apparent double bind: bondage and ancestrality.[7] The city and its surroundings figure as one of the most concentrated areas of homicidal violence against Black youth, and one of the most vibrant spaces of Black cultural resistance in Brazil. In this context, I can risk affirming that, as a site of cultural critique, the *city* holds the promise of a new reference point of academic intellectual production (the Escola do Recôncavo?) that Pinho forcefully brings to the international circuit.

Pinho does not take shortcuts nor shies away from the urgent challenge presented by the Afro-pessimist key contention on the Slave position Black people inhabit in the antiblack world, while also tuned to the Black optimist propositions on *lives self-stolen* from the domains of white sovereignty.[8] Rejecting the dichotomy that has often characterized this debate, Pinho illustrates that, on the one hand, what defines contemporary Brazil is colonial violence, notwithstanding celebratory approaches of a supposed benign Brazilian mode of sociability. The Black body is fungible, not only within the realm of political economy but also within an ontological economy that perpetually sustains dispossession and affirmation (thus highlighting the incommensurability of the Black experience). Because *cativeiro* persists as the *nomos* in democratic Brazil, Black inclusion is Black evisceration.

On the other hand, the book effectively resists nihilism and repositions the object of injury as an insurgent subject. Instead of the slave ship, Pinho reclaims the *quilombo*[9]*, the encruzinhada* (crossroad), and the *terreiro*[10] as

---

[6] Cachoeira is a historic city located in the state of Bahia, Brazil.

[7] T.N.: Cachoeira is a historic city located in the state of Bahia, Brazil. The city is part of the "Recôncavo Baiano" and was founded in the early 17th century. The city is also a central site for Candomblé, the Afro-Brazilian religion, and hosts "The Sisterhood of the Good Death" (Irmandade da Boa Morte), a historic Afro-Catholic confraternity. This organization, founded in the early 19th century, is one of the oldest groups of its kind in Brazil and is composed entirely of Black women, many of whom are descendants of former enslaved Africans who work to keep their heritage and memory alive.

[8] Fred Moten. *Stolen life.* Duke University Press, 2018.

[9] T.N.: A *quilombo* is a community originally formed by escaped enslaved Africans in Brazil, serving as spaces of resistance, cultural preservation, and autonomy. Today, quilombos symbolize broader struggles for land rights and cultural recognition.

[10] *Terreiro* refers to sacred spaces for Afro-Brazilian religious practices, particularly candomblé and umbanda.

alternative spatial references for conceptualizing a Black identity that questions the political utility of confining Black existence to the horrors of slavery and limiting Black subjectivity to realms of death. While it may be an oversimplification to reduce the Afro-pessimist project to an obsession with death—a misreading Moten himself acknowledges—as I have insisted elsewhere, these two propositions come together in a Black subject that is socially dead and politically alive. If we were to entertain the idea that Black life in urban contexts of precarity, as in Cachoeira, is only achievable through *cativeiro's* refusals—whether it manifests through "stealing" oneself away or stealing from a supermarket, occupying public land or engaging with the criminal world of micro-trafficking—we could embrace both positions within this intellectual debate without contradiction. That is why encruzilhada (crossroad) takes such a meaningful form here: in the candomblé, it is the site of an ancestral undoing of injury. In the book, it is also an escape route from *cativeiro*. It is not mutually exclusive to denounce historical trauma and contemporary racial terror, while also recognizing the rebellion ethos that gave birth to quilombos. We were defeated. Palmares was annihilated, but as Afro-Brazilian writer José Carlos Limeira has poetically noted, "even if they silence our story, I can't forget our people. If Palmares no longer exists, we'll reinvent it anew".[11]

Where to locate this insurgent tradition in a Brazilian context saturated by granting cultural rights and denying the right to live? Although I would rather focus on other outlawed acts of refusal by Black people when confronting racial terror in Bahia, by viewing Black performance as an ontological resistance (rightfully, Pinho insists life itself is the stage of an antiblack war and yet Black people refuse defeat), the book provides a nuanced analysis of the rebellious potential of Black cultural practices. I say 'potential' because these practices can easily be cannibalized (and Bahia is perhaps the most pronounced example of it) by the white gaze as just a street party. This insurgent being, whose practices many of us have located in diffuse repertoires of fugitivity —including centuries-long quilombos, the Black mothers' movement against police terror, the everyday self-and collective reinventions of the hoods, the underground economy of the biqueiras[12] and the ungovernable space of the favela—is articulated here

---

[11] Quilombos. Poet José Carlos Limeira. Repertório, Salvador, no. 17, pp. 195-197, 2011. Available at: https://periodicos.ufba.br/index.php/revteatro/article/viewFile/5741/4147
[12] T.N.: "Biqueiras" are informal locations used for the sale and distribution of drugs, typically controlled by local drug trafficking organizations. Often found in peripheral neighborhoods or slums, these spots serve as points of retail where dealers, known as "aviõezinhos" (mostly unemployed young Black men), sell drugs directly to users.

through the deviant and defiant methods of young Black men and women reclaiming their autonomous sexual selves in Cachoeira's public spaces.

To Pinho, race and sexuality are *loci* of a Black agency in the refusal of white morality. As Pinho argues, the "dirty" and "unruly" bodies of Black Brazilians embrace abjection as an "alternative mode of sociality," which establishes the groundwork for an epistemic rebellion against the colonization of bodies and peoples (p. 57). While policing and other strains of everyday life aim at restricting Blackness within ontological bondages, the occupation of public space by bodies unbound to any regime of morality manifests a bold refusal to blackness-as-captivity.

Thus, one way to approach "Bondage: Antiblackness and Ancestrality" is to view it as an invitation to embrace what Pinho describes as an "ontological void"—a void that is both daunting and disheartening, yet a place from which one can simultaneously lay the groundwork for alternative Black livelihoods. In Brazil, this alternative project is articulated by Black activism as quilombo, blackpolis, cidade negra, endeavoring to reposition the Black subject within the geo-ontological landscape of the nation. Given the dire context of the book (Brazil is the country with the highest rates of lynching by the police in the world), exploring these imaginaries of rebellion is a moral imperative. Coming from Brazil, one can only hope that such an invitation finds receptive ears in an Anglophonic field of Black Studies, its strange trajectory from fierce struggles and insurgent critiques of the racial order of empire, to redemptive celebrations of Black inclusion within the imperial machine. Pinho reminds us that the battle is not for identity but rather for ancestrality. I cannot agree more, if by that he means to criticize the cosmetic embracing of identity devoid of political commitments to (and practical engagement with) the work of liberation. Reclaiming ancestrality is reclaiming the roots of a radical tradition that refuses *cativeiro* as a totality.[13]

In the next pages, the reader is invited to explore the meanings of a centuries-old ritual performed in the streets of Cachoeira. The Nêgo Fugido (The Runaway Slave) ritual reenacts the history of Black resistance in the sugar plantations of the Recôncavo region of Bahia. With their bodies painted in blood color, the performers take the streets under the sound of drums. They are pursued, captured, gagged and collectively punished by the overseer clothed in police uniform. The unfortunate runaway slaves, now dragged in the streets by the police, are rescued by a Black mother. The spectacle of pain is momentarily interrupted and softened by her

---

[13] On the Black radical tradition as an ontological totality, see Cedric Robinson. Black Marxism: the making of a Black radical tradition. North Carolina University Press, 2008.

patching up their wounds while evoking the Orixás, the goddess and gods of Candomblé. The Negro Fugido performance engages with racial interpellation and ancestrality to deliver the message that Black lives are collectively owned (by the street spectators and by the nation's Beings), that Black suffering is an *equipment* for nation-making, and that Brazil is a plantation. This denunciation of injury did not stay there, however. By the end of the ritual, the audience is confronted with their own reckoning with the past and repositioning themselves as Negro Fugido. If the popular saying "in Brazil everyone has black blood, the rich in their hands and the poor in their veins" is correct, then by inviting the poor of all colors to embrace blackness as abjection, the runaway slave strikes back twice: calls into question the panacea of racial democracy and restates the terms of our freedom. Blackness is offered as a generous practice of freedom for Black people and for all.

REFERENCES

ALVES, Jaime. *The anti-Black city: Police terror and Black urban life in Brazil.* Minneapolis: University of Minnesota Press, 2018.

_____. VARGAS, João Costa. The specter of Haiti: Structural antiblackness, the far-right backlash and the fear of a Black majority in Brazil." *Third World Quarterly*, v. 41, n. 4, p. 645–662, 2020.

DAMATTA, Roberto. O que Faz o Brasil, Brasil?, Rio de Janeiro, 1994.

DAMATTA, Roberto. Carnavais, Malandros e Heróis. Para uma sociologia do dilema brasileiro. Rio de Janeiro. Zahar Editores. 3ª Edição. 1981.

DA SILVA, Denise Ferreira. No-bodies: Law, raciality, and the territory of justice. *Griffith Law Review*, v. 18, n. 2, p. 213–236, 2009.

_____. *Toward a global idea of race.* Minneapolis: University of Minnesota Press, 2007.

HARTMAN, Saidiya. *Scenes of subjection: Slavery and self-making in 19th century America.* Oxford: Oxford University Press, 1997, p. 17–79.

JAMES, Joy. *States of confinement: Policing, detention and prisons.* New York: St. Martin's Press, 2000.

MOTEN, Fred. The case of Blackness. *Criticism*, v. 50, n. 2, p. 177–218, 2008.

SPILLERS, Hortense. Interstices: A small drama of words. In: VANCE, Carole S. (Ed.). *Pleasure and danger: Exploring female sexuality.* Boston: Routledge, 1984, p. 73–100.

WINK, Georg. Jeitinho revisited. In: BRANDELLERO, Sara; PARDUE, Derek; WINK, Georg (Eds.). *Living (il)legalities in Brazil: Practices, narratives and institutions in a country on the edge.* London: Routledge, 2020.

WYNTER, Sylvia. Unsettling the coloniality of being/power/truth/freedom: Towards the human, after man, its overrepresentation—an argument." *The New Centennial Review,* v. 3, n. 3, p. 257–337, 2003.

INTRODUCTION

"Eu sou um velho
Filho de um guerreiro e curandeiro
Pelo Sertão da Bahia
Pelo Chapadão Mineiro
É Dandá, eu vivi
Os tempos do Cativeiro"
— Seu Marujo[14]

"I am an old man
The son of a warrior healer
Through the Sertão of Bahia
Through the Chapadão Mineiro
Oh Dandá, I lived
During the times of Bondage"
— Seu Marujo

THE WHIRLWIND AT THE CROSSROADS

"After my enemies are satisfied, in life or death I shall come back to you
to serve even as I have served before. In life I shall be the same; in death
I shall be the terror to the foes of Negro Liberty. If death has power, then
count me in death to be the real Marcus Garvey I would like to be. (…)
Look for me in the whirlwind."
— MARCUS GARVEY, "First Message to the Negros of the World from
Atlanta Prison", 1925

---

[14] See: https://www.youtube.com/watch?v=Ze-b2_3FGEw last accessed August 5, 2025
at 1:38 pm EST.

This book project was conceived shortly after my return in December 2014 from a period of 13 months at the University of Texas, in Austin, specifically within the African and African Diaspora Studies Department (AADS). Supported by a Senior Postdoctoral scholarship from the Brazilian Federal Government's Coordination for the Improvement of Higher Education Personnel (CAPES), I researched Black masculinities in collaboration with the project "Brincadeira de Negão: Subjetividade e Identidade de Jovens Homens Negros" (BN)— [Black Men's Play: Subjectivity and Identity of Young Black Men]. At that time, this initiative was being undertaken by a team of undergraduate and graduate students at the Federal University of Recôncavo da Bahia in Cachoeira, Bahia.

As I discuss in greater detail in the following chapters, I was profoundly struck not only by the segregated and barren landscape of the Southern city (my memory of that first winter is faded, much like the gray sky framing the twisted branches of leafless trees, under the shrill cries of crows and the somber hum of cars on deserted streets) but, more importantly, by my engagement with the works of authors such as Frank Wilderson III, Jared Sexton, Lewis Gordon, Fred Moten, Hortense Spillers, Saidiya Hartman, and João H. C. Vargas, who hosted me in Austin and with whom I co-edited the 2016 collection "Antinegritude: O Impossível Sujeito Negro na Formação Social Brasleira" [Antiblackness: The Impossible Black Subject in Brazilian Social Formation] (Pinho & Vargas, 2016). These authors, along with others more or less aligned with Afropessimism, most explicitly advocated by Wilderson, shook my imagination with a set of explosive categories and an intellectual approach that made tremendous sense, given the prevailing understanding in Brazil, which had already been integrated into our own reflections in Cachoeira, regarding the political and heuristic centrality of anti-Black state violence, Black genocide, and the political role that the death of Black people plays in stabilizing the Brazilian national project. The Black social movement and the movement of those affected by state violence, along with, primarily, the work of Abdias do Nascimento on one hand, and Achille Mbembe on the other, had already called my attention to the significance of violence in shaping Black subjectivity and politics in Western modernity and Brazil. My interactions with students in Cachoeira—many of whom come from communities marked by violence, dispossession, and death, whether in urban peripheries or rural quilombos, while others are actively engaged with the Black movement and hip-hop culture—along with, of course, my personal experiences and the shaping of my own subjectivity, forged in the social margins and urban interstices of the racial-sexual ghettos of Brazilian cities like Salvador, Recife, Campinas, and Rio de Janeiro, may have, I might say, prepared me prospectively for the Afropessimist shock.

It is indeed a shock, as we will see, since Wilderson's interpretation of Frantz Fanon and Orlando Patterson positions social death as a central category for the political imagination of Blackness (initially within the North American context), along with its corollaries, the exclusion of Black people from the world and the public sphere, and anti-Blackness, the overarching antagonism that sustains the incompatibility of Blackness with the world as we know it. This world, shaped by European expansion, colonialism, and modernity, leaves no place for Black people, and Blackness can only embody the most radical negativity, which, as we will frequently discuss in this book, fundamentally defines the Black condition as aligned with the positionality of the slave. This, of course, was the major shock. Because everything that the extensive political, critical, historiographical, aesthetic, and cultural mobilization promoted by the leading protagonists of Black resistance, not only in Brazil but also in other parts of Latin America, had always strongly rejected was precisely this identification between the Black individual and the slave. This is akin to the often-repeated assertion of Makota Valdina,[15] an Afro-Brazilian religious leader: "I am not a descendant of slaves, but of human beings who were enslaved." It is similar to Beatriz Nascimento's claim, discussed in Chapter 1, and her discomfort with the historiographical fixation on the slave and slavery. Afro-pessimism, however, not only sustains the identity between Blackness and slavery, but also establishes this identity as the foundation for an ontology defined, as in Saidiya Hartman's work, by the lash, by pure violence, by identification with the commodity, and by depersonalization. I later understood that, in the North American context, the memory of slavery and the insistence on placing side by side the conditions of life, or death, with slavery, are recurrent elements in the common experience and Afro-American sensibility, which is quite different from what happens in Brazil, where Africanity [*africanidade*] forms the historical-subjective-political matrix of Blackness or Afro-Brazilian identity, and this is part of the daily life experience of Black Brazilians. I recall a discussion with a group of African American intellectuals about the significance of slavery and the importance of preserving the memory of this peculiar institution, something that seemed obvious to all of them but was, in fact, disconcerting to me.

---

[15] Valdina de Oliveira Pinto, who passed away in 2019, was a religious leader, anti-racist educator, and makota (assistant to the mãe-de-santo, or priestess) of the Angola Tanusi Junsara terreiro (Afro-Brazilian religious temple), located in Engenho Velho da Federação, a community in Salvador.

From this shock arises a series of questions that shape the project of this book. It represents an effort not only to examine the (in)commensurability of Black experiences in the two largest slave societies in the Americas but also to establish critical categories within a comparative framework that reflects the historical nature of the subject formation, sensibilities, aesthetic forms, narrative structures, and social landscapes. On one side is the Afropessimism found in the African American context, and on the other, what I am naming in this book as the thought of *ancestrality* in the Brazilian context. In the latter, ancestrality appears to be the central category of political imagination, rather than social death.

From an Afropessimist perspective, or within the framework of antiblackness theory, the Black man is viewed as a slave, and the Black woman is similarly seen as a slave. Here, "being" means existing "like something among other things", since, according to this perspective, we remain suspended, suffering, above an ontological void. In contrast, when seen through the lens of ancestrality, the Black man is recognized as African, and the Black woman as African as well. Therefore, Afropessimism adopts the standpoint of an antiblack world to define our identity as enslaved people, while the perspective of ancestrality embraces the Black world, thus encompassing candomblés, batuques, and the quilombo to affirm that our subjective and political foundation is rooted in our African heritage.

With the contradictions, mediations, and nuances that I discuss in the subsequent chapters. It is almost as if Africans do not live in an antiblack world, built around colonialism, slavery, and white supremacy. As if this were not our world. However, as seen in the works of Denise Ferreira da Silva, Sylvia Wynter, and other authors (Silva, 2019; Wynter, 2003), the Western thought (and its war machine) produced/demanded the Black individual, or how the Black subject (a thing/nothing) is dependent on Western thought and white supremacy, becomes evident in the analysis of slave narratives that I develop in Chapter 5. In contrast, within ancestral thought, the Black ontology is already given and is independent of the West—the African preexists the colonial encounter, and enslavement and colonization are seen as transitory and non-essential contingencies. We can thus see that this presents a sociological and historical, aesthetic, ethical, and political problem. At the risk of an overly simplified summary, one could say that Afropessimism adopts the viewpoint of the slave ship's hold, while ancestrality adopts the perspective of the quilombo and the terreiro.

It is within this context that I use "bondage" and its associated categories. Bondage is the vernacular, traditional, and emic term employed by the enslaved and their descendants to denote the institution of slavery and, more specifically, the lived reality of enslavement. This term not only appears in the epigraph of this book but is also recurrent in numerous samba lyrics, capoeira chants, and macumba songs [pontos de macumba]. It is the term that historically enslaved individuals themselves used to refer to slavery. Accordingly, in this work, I endeavor to adopt a perspective that aligns with this experience that, in a profoundly unsettling way, I also share. Here, bondage means the condition imposed through the Middle Passage and the transatlantic journey in the holds of slave ships, a condition that encompassed both African subjects and ancestral knowledge. As a conceptual category, it aims to capture this passage, as well as the incomplete and reversible (due to its transtemporal nature) oscillation between the figure of the enslaved individual and the African. Throughout this book, I seek to expand the analytical scope of bondage by integrating it with other categories, which are applied across multiple dimensions.

First, there is the concept articulated by Fred Moten of the resistance of the object, a perspective that, while related to Afropessimism, is not fully identical to it. This approach recognizes slave fungibility in its identification with the commodity as a locus for the political ontology of Blackness. However, this identification does not wholly preclude resistance, subversion, invention, or objection, as explored by Harney and Moten (2013) in "The Undercommons". The notion of the resistance of the object, as well as objection, prompts an examination of the historical, sociological, and formal structures of resistance, which are primarily configured through the dominance of performance as a privileged cultural form, in contrast to other representational, "logocentric", or Cartesian modes of life and meaning production. Performance, understood as a non-representational and immanent form, allows for the resistance of the object without reverting to or reproducing Western, antiblack structures and epistemologies. It creates a scene—mediated by the "repertoire", experience, transcendence, and epistemological dissent—that responds to, and challenges institutionalized scenarios created by the "archive", which seeks to fixate, empty, and codify the transhistorical experience of Black objection. Between the scene and the scenario of Black objection, within—or against—the antiblack world, social death moves through its various metamorphoses: from the structured field of genocidal social patterns to colonial representational allegories, as well as in performative acts that exorcize the Middle Passage and slavery, such as the *Nego Fugido* in Acupe or the Mardi Gras Indians in New Orleans. In opposition to social death, objection invokes the ancestors and the concept of "good death" as a way of imposing ancestral symbolism upon that which would otherwise remain devoid of meaning, like a wild ghost. Black culture, as performed within the scene of objection, remains unrepresentable; as Lewis Gordon (1999) argues, we can find reasons to reject metaphor and insist on the irrepresentability of Black culture and Blackness itself.

These categories permeate this book in multiple forms and across the subsequent chapters. While the structure or rhythm may at times appear repetitive or redundant, it is intentionally designed to be fractal and spiral. The goal is to revisit and recontextualize concepts and authors within diverse settings, thereby expanding and testing the conceptual and critical efficacy of this framework through its recurrence. As Fredric Jameson notes, in a similar vein:

> ...at a certain level of concreteness, the thing itself...—whether it be a literary structure, a lived truth of a particular social organization, a specific type of subject–object relationship, a certain distance between language and its object, a particular mode of specialization or division of labor, or an implicit relationship between classes—can be described in any of a number of alternative codes, can be rearticulated in any of the numerous different dimensions. (Jameson, 1985, p. 270)

The "thing" in question here, in this context, is social death—and its transformations—as a central category.

In this sense, in Chapter 1, "The Person of the Slave: Social Death and Political Imaginaries of the African Diaspora in Brazil", I examine the critique presented by historian and activist Beatriz Nascimento during the Black Fortnight at USP (Quinzena do Negro, University of São Paulo), held in 1977 and documented in the film "Ori—Cabeça e Consciência" [Ori—Head and Black Consciousness] by Raquel Guerber. Nascimento critiques the academic historiography's obsession with slavery and proposes Africa and the quilombo as imaginative paradigms for Black political subjectivity in Brazil. This perspective is closely linked to the invention of "Black culture" as African culture, creatively and politically processed through the "Africa-Sign" within the context of re-Africanizing traditions in Afro-Bahian settings of the 1970s and 1980s. This process had a profound impact on the political imagination of the African Diasporic activism in Brazil, shaping associated subjectivities and sensibilities.

As Beatriz refers to the "the person of the Black man", I critically retrace the genealogy of the "person" as discussed in classical anthropology, confronting it with the colonial "space of death", which serves as the foundation or horizon from which colonial positionalities—marked by social death, paroxysmal violence, and slavery—emerge. I thus define social death in its connection to the erasure of the enslaved person as being, situated within a field of critical thought shaped by antiblackness, as an element of the broader antiblack antagonism. I identify, in parallel, an alternative field of critical thought rooted in the Afro-Brazilian tradition, which I term the thought of *ancestrality*. In this sense, the transitions between the "slave" and the "African" emerge as metamorphoses, rather than being framed as dualities.

In Chapter 2, "Arrastão: Decolonizing Gender and Sexuality in Pagode Baiano", I have the opportunity to discuss the prerogative of performance within the critical theorization of Blackness as a social, historical, and vernacular phenomenon. Building on Diana Taylor's (2003) established distinction between the repertoire (embodied and performative) and the archive (textual and institutional), which I reinterpret as the dichotomy between the scene, characterized by its immanence and irreproducibility, and the scenario, marked by its fixity and centralization as a strategy of power—I aim to engage with Moten's notion of the scene of objection (2003). The focal point of this analysis is pagode baiano, conceived as a performative ensemble of practices, categories, and aesthetic forms developed throughout the history of objection and resistance by racialized and gendered subjects within the Brazilian colonial environment. This chapter first delves into the colonial context, analyzing its entanglement with subjection processes rooted in the racialized production of gender and sexuality, framed by colonial moralities and the ideology of miscegenation, which operates as a central discourse in the construction of national culture as a heteropatriarchal apparatus of power. In this chapter I also rely on the ethnographic corpus developed within the Brincadeira de Negão Project to investigate, from the standpoint of the subjects, the categories and structures of feeling that emerge establishing a relationship with (a) state violence or "shootouts", (b) subjectivation mechanisms, such as the paredão de pagode, and (c) masculine performances like "botando a base".[16] This analysis then seeks to theorize the production of a scene of rebellion encompassing gender, race, and sexuality—within pagode baiano.

---

[16] T.N.: *Botar a base* is a colloquial term from pagode baiano—a popular Afro-Brazilian musical genre from Salvador, Bahia—referring to a dance movement often performed by men. This dance involves a grounded, rhythmic swaying of the hips, which is usually synchronized with the beats of the music.

In Chapter 3, titled "Black Border: Body and Struggle in Black Audiovisual Scene", the concept of "border", as originally proposed by Paula von Gleich (2017), is examined to probe the possibilities and challenges of representing Blackness and Black culture. This analysis draws upon the extensive discussions of reification and the consequent unrepresentability of Blackness and the Black subject, as articulated by Lewis Gordon and Frantz Fanon (Gleich, 2017; Fanon, 1983; Gordon, 1999). If the Black individual is, by one's very nature, non-symbolic, then what can Black culture convey? This debate is situated within the context of Black audiovisual media, where I explore ethical and aesthetic dilemmas making an analysis of four films. These include the classics "Soul in the Eye" by Zózimo Bulbul and "Now!" by Santiago Alvarez, both of which strain the formal nature of visual representation through the interplay between specific content and the proposed visual grammars. Additionally, I discuss two contemporary works or records, "Notícias de uma Guerra Racial Subnotificada" by the Reaja ou Será Morta, Reaja ou Será Morto Campaign, and "Experimentando o Dilúvio em Vermelho" by Musa Matiuzzi, where ethical boundaries are reshaped by the materiality of Black flesh. From a more radical Fanonian and phenomenological perspective, the reification or "nothingness" of Blackness, which impedes symbolization, finds a temporary yet precarious escape in the fugitivity of the undercommons, as described by Harney and Moten (2013). It is precisely through recognizing this insurmountable yet manageable limit or border that the potential for a viable Black representational—and ethical—content appears attainable within these unstable and radical forms.

In Chapter 4, "'Atlantic Blood': Social Death and Ancestrality in Albert Eckhout and Ayrson Heráclito", I continue to explore Black art or representation, under the sign of a fundamental categorical impossibility established by the Middle Passage as a historical-structural event that mediates between positionalities associated with social death and/or Africanity. Here, I analyze visual representations defined in two very distinct moments by two different artists: the Dutch painter Albert Eckhout, a member of Maurice of Nassau-Siegen's entourage during the 17th-century Dutch rule in Brazil, and Ayrson Heráclito, one of the most successful contemporary Afro-Brazilian artists. While Eckhout, in producing his ethnological series on the racial types of the colony, particularly in the striking painting "African Warrior", produces representations of race and gender in the allegorical records through a colonial visual epistemology, not only due to its content, but based on representation. Heráclito, rejecting mimetic art and the metaphorical politics of representation marked by coloniality, proposes his work as a material intervention. His art is based not on symbol, representation, or metaphor but on the immanent manipulation of materials such as dendê oil (palm oil), reconfiguring the relationship between the sacred, art, and life through the recognition of the agency, as Alfred Gell suggests, art objects akin to fetishes, as proposed by J. Lorand Matory (Gell, 2018; Matory, 2018). The comparative analysis of these two artists allows us to address two epistemological forms for producing Black art, in its ambiguity as both art by Black people and art *about* Black people: one based on representation, and thus alienated, allegorical, and colonial; and the other based on immanence, and thus coherent with epistemological dissent, removing Blackness from the space of Western death and assuming ancestrality as an epistemological/cosmological paradigm.

Finally, in Chapter 5, "The Scene of Objection: Narrative, Political Economy, and Performance", I return to the Black men's personhood (person/pessoa), explored in dialogue with various fields and other categories, such as personhood and subjectivity. To this end, I examine three areas or *corpus*: first, a selection of some of the most renowned and influential slave autobiographies or narratives, like those of Frederick Douglass and Harriet Jacobs, discussed alongside fictional texts, since imagination and historical imagination represent ways to situate the Black subject within antiblack modernity. Second, I delve into the problematic historiography of Black people in Brazil, notably the debate on the social being of the enslaved, contested between the perspectives of colonial slavery by Jacob Gorender and established academic readings by figures like Florestan Fernandes and Roberto Slenes, who specifically discuss the meaning of the slave's personhood, agency, historical capacity, and cultural continuity. In theory, this would be denied by the definitions of slavery found in Orlando Patterson (2008) and Claude Meillassoux (1995). In the fourth section of the chapter, I revisit the debate on performance and the scene of objection, arguing that if the Black person can be a subject of their own representation within the antiblack world, that place is socially instituted by the performance. To substantiate this claim, I briefly discuss two performative traditions of the Black diaspora: the Nego Fugido of Acupe in the Recôncavo of Bahia and the Mardi Gras Indians in New Orleans. If, in the case of narratives, the Black subject requires the white mask of literary conventions and the intercession of white mediators; if, within the spectrum of the slave-based political economy, the Black individual could only exercise subjective agency amidst established contradictions, through their reduction to the status of a commodity; in the realm of performance, within the scene of objection, the Black individual can reject the Western resources and epistemologies to constitute themselves within the transtemporal and mythopoetic space of the street and the crossroads, domesticating social death through the symbolic and material means available within the tradition.

As summarized above, the chapters of this book have heterogeneous origins, and describing them will allow me to express gratitude to the people and institutions that, in various ways, facilitated the achievement of my objectives outlined eleven years ago.

Chapter 1 was initially written as a paper for a presentation at the Tepoztlán Institute for Transnational History of the Americas, a multidisciplinary seminar that takes place annually in the beautiful town of Tepoztlán, in the Mexican state of Morelos. Over the years I have participated, the institute has become a fundamental space for critical reflection, engaged multidisciplinary and transnational dialogue, in an intensive, democratic, and rich environment. I owe my experience at Tepoztlán to contact with various authors who became fundamental references in developing the ideas gathered in this book. The paper was presented in 2018, and I am particularly grateful to Micol Siegel, who first introduced me to the Institute in 2015; to David Kazanjian, the dominatrix (that is, the coordinator, in Tepoztlán's terminology) of the session where I presented; and to Megan Spencer and Tito Mitjans Alayón, who were the discussants in that same session.

Chapter 2 has a longer and more heteroclite history. The first section was originally written for this book, though it references work published in English about the "rolezinho", unpublished in Portuguese (2018), and presented in 2014 at the New Sexualities Seminar of the Interdisciplinary Humanities Center at the University of California, Santa Barbara, and at the Global Moral Panics Symposium in 2014 at Indiana University, Bloomington. I am grateful to Paul Amar, Mireille Miller-Young, Justin Perez, Steven Osuna, Jennifer Tyburczy, and Micol Seigel for the invitations, comments, and suggestions. The second section is a significantly revised version of an unpublished essay that formed the basis for a conference delivered at the International Congress Epistemologies of the South: Critical Perspectives II, held at the Federal University for Latin American Integration (UNILA) in 2017. I thank Angela Souza, Marcos de Jesus Oliveira, and Waldemir Rosa, colleagues and anthropologists from UNILA, for the invitation and kind interaction during that occasion. The third section of this chapter summarizes data and reflections previously published elsewhere (Pinho, 2015, 2016), as well as reflections and presentations made on various occasions: at "Queering Paradigms V" in Quito, Ecuador, in February 2014; at "FRONTERAS 2014: Interdisciplinary

Meeting on Gender and Sexuality Research", in Bogotá in August 2014; at "Quebrando Tudo II: Pagode and Discourses Around Peripheral Cultural Production" in July 2015 in Cachoeira; at the Black Consciousness Debate Seminar—Epistemologies of Resistance in November 2015 in Brasília; as well as at the "Brown Bag Series" of the African and African Diaspora Department Studies at the University of Texas in February 2014 in Austin, and finally at the "Brincadeira de Negão 2.0 Seminar" held in August 2014 at UFRB in Cachoeira. I also thank Franklin Gil Hernandez, Luz Gabriela Arango (in memoriam), and Ana Flauzina for the invitations to the meetings in Bogotá and Brasília, and João H. Costa Vargas, Dora Santana, Gustavo Mello, Agatha Oliveira, Luciane Rocha, Daniela Gomes, and Maria Andrea dos Santos Soares for their discussions and all their support in Austin. This chapter primarily reflects the work of the Negão Play Project [Projeto Brincadeira de Negão—BN], which slightly predates the concerns that gave rise to this book. In reality, BN and the project of this book were developing in relatively parallel ways, and discussions about masculinity and antiblackness were shaped through dialogue, particularly during my stay in the United States in 2014. This is reflected in the presentations I made during this period, as well as in the general perspective that informs the ethnographic discussion in this chapter. Therefore, the space constructed within the BN project and the interaction with the students, who were part of the team, were fundamental for developing many ideas present here. I would like to thank all those who were part of this team at various times: Paulo Roberto dos Santos, Gimerson Roque, Valdir Alves, Jefferson Parreira, Amanda Dias, Maiana Brito, Lucas Santana, Beatriz Giugliani, Thais Gomes Machado, Julio Cesar Cerqueira Araujo, and Israel Cerqueira.

Chapter 3 was originally conceived as a commentary for the exhibition "Corpos em Luta" [Struggling Bodies], part of the CachoeiraDoc festival, which has been held annually in the city of Cachoeira, organized by Amaranta Cesar and Ana Rosa Marques, professors of the undergraduate course in cinema and audiovisual, and my colleagues at UFRB in Cachoeira. Amaranta was one of the Corpos em Luta exhibition curators, and I am grateful for her invitation to discuss the selected film program. I also thank Aline Nzinga, from the Reaja ou Será Morta, Reaja ou Será Morto! campaign, who shared the commentary session with me on September 9, 2017. These comments were later converted into an essay and published in a slightly different version as a chapter in the anthology Desaguar em Cinema: Documentário, Memória e Ação com o CachoeiraDoc, edited by Amaranta Cesar, Ana Rosa Marques, Fernanda Pimenta, and Leonardo

Costa, and published by Edufba. I am grateful to the editors for kindly authorizing the republication here.

Chapter 4 is being published here for the first time and was also prepared as a paper for presentation at the Tepoztlán Institute in 2019. I thank David Kazanjian, once again the dominatrix of the session where I presented, as well as Ana Pohlenz de Tavir and Christen Mucher, who were discussants. Paulo Ramos, Julio Cesar Cerqueira Araujo, Christen Smith, and Anderson da Mata contributed to the discussion with suggestions and critiques, for which I am very grateful. A shorter version of this work, excluding the discussion of Ayrson Heráclito's work, was presented at the workshop Future Africa—Visions in Time, organized by the Graduate Program in Ethnic and African Studies at UFBA and the Bayreuth Academy for Advanced African Studies in Salvador da Bahia, also in 2019. Luis Felipe Ortega read and commented on one of the versions of this chapter from the perspective of visual arts, and I appreciate his insights and suggestions.

Chapter 5 was originally written for this book and has been unpublished until now. In addition to the people and institutions mentioned above, I would like to thank the Coordination for the Improvement of Higher Education Personnel (CAPES) for granting me a Senior Postdoctoral Scholarship in 2013, which enabled my travel and stay in Austin—fundamental to the development of my work and the flourishing of the ideas gathered here. Between 2014 and 2019, the National Council for Scientific and Technological Development (CNPq) and the Bahia State Research Support Foundation (FAPESB) provided scholarships for undergraduate, master's, and doctoral students associated with the Negão Play Project (BN). These scholarships enabled the students to effectively pursue their activities, facilitating the completion of several undergraduate theses, master's theses, and doctoral dissertations within the framework of the project. Part of the discussion in Chapter 4 formed the basis of a project I submitted in 2019 for the Richard E. Greenleaf Library Fellowships at the Latin American Library of Tulane University in New Orleans. Receiving this scholarship not only allowed me to delve deeper into research on visual representations of Blackness in colonial Brazil but also provided a brief yet impactful encounter with the Mardi Gras Indians and relevant literature on this performative tradition, which informs the discussion in the final section of Chapter 5. At Tulane, where I stayed during the first couple of months in 2020, I received institutional support from the Latin American Library. I am deeply grateful to Hortensia Calvo, its director, and the wonderful library staff: Rachel Stein, Penelope Ojeda, Verónica Sanchez, and Christine Hernandez. Their availability, kindness, and extreme competence were decisive in making the most of my time at Tulane. I extend my heartfelt gratitude to Christopher Dunn, Marc Perry, and Kim Butler, who served as constant and generous interlocutors during my time in New Orleans. They introduced me to various facets of the history and cultural life of the Black community in The Big Easy, enriching my experience with their warm hospitality. Lastly, I would like to express my deep appreciation for Eder Boaventura, my partner, friend, accomplice, and confidant, whose patience, joy, and love have been invaluable.

In today's context, where standpoint is of paramount importance, I find it fitting to conclude by sharing my own standpoint at this moment. Djamila Ribeiro's contributions to the discourse are well-documented and draw from the Black feminist thought of Patricia Hill Collins and Lélia Gonzalez. She underscores the significance of recognizing the social *locus* of the subject to comprehend how social hierarchies translate into epistemic privileges—privileges that are often activated by the very invisibility of the connection between a position of power—rooted in lived experiences and defined by historical social structures—and the prerogative of enunciation. For instance, the overrepresentation of white men in positions of power in society led to a situation where the canon of Brazilian academic thought on Blackness was produced by individuals who viewed Black people as the Other in their daily lives. Thus, the issue is not that white people cannot talk about Black people but rather that Black individuals cannot be reduced to mute objects, described and explained in the third person. In other words, the issue lies in the white privilege that allows white voices to dominate discussions on Blackness, thereby shaping the nature of the knowledge produced. When Nina Rodrigues asserted that individuals of African descent were intrinsically incapable of social advancement or moral autonomy, he conflated his subjective, prejudice-laden perspective, supported by a racialized social order, with scientific objectivity. As Frantz Fanon observed, "For the colonized subject, objectivity is always directed against him" (1961, p. 69). For the colonized subject, this constructed objectivity within the colonial framework becomes an apparatus of oppression, violence, and dehumanization, establishing a space of death wherein the Humanity of the racialized "native" is continually sacrificed.

In Djamila's analysis, as well as in much of Brazilian and African American Black feminism, identity plays a pivotal role. It highlights the connection between an individual's social position, being part of a historically constructed group labeled as the Other, and the subjective experiences of oppression and silencing. For instance, the poverty that quilombola women frequently endure, the oppressive conditions in both work and domestic spheres, and the denial of their intellectual capability, beauty, and self-worth can be understood from the perspective of a specific individual, a tangible woman who has a name and address. She comes to recognize the sources of her suffering not as a result of some supposed innate inferiority tied to her identity as a woman and a Black person, as society has conditioned her to believe, but rather as stemming from an unjust and unequal social structure with a history as extensive as the national society itself. Thus, the significance of self-esteem, self-care, Black beauty, and other categories that politicize experience becomes apparent. However, an unintended consequence of this discourse is sometimes a tendency toward an inflation of subjectivity. While this is understandable given the historical negation of Black personhood, it cannot, however, justify an uncritical acceptance of models of subjectivity and understanding that merely mimic critical engagement. This inflation is not precisely about one's standpoint but rather about the individual's location and experience, taken as intrinsic and autonomous in relation to their social position. Why is it so important to speak about oneself? Why is it more important to talk about oneself than to listen to the other? Why are my pain and suffering so significant? Why do these pains and sufferings not pertain exclusively to me? The individual, as we commonly know it, is a socio-historical ideological construct. A device of biopower. Full in its self-referentiality, the individual claims to find the foundations of their own subjectivity and the categories to describe it in the alignment between the world and how they experience it, overlooking thick layers of historicity and the maze-like structure of categories and epistemological configurations that enable someone to say, "I am". This approach only recognizes an emancipatory project when it emancipates the individual themselves, as someone finds their "true self". Once, many years ago, I asked a friend, a Black man like me: "Why are you against racism?" His answer still makes me think to this day, because he replied, "Because racism affects me". Sometimes, where we imagine finding an emancipatory project, we instead encounter the affirmation of the old bourgeois, individualistic project, not merely in opposition to collectivism, but in the sense that it sees the individual—taken as a singular, original, indivisible, and ahistorical entity—as the alpha and omega of social life, the standard and paradigm for issuing judgments or a platform for political claims.

I mention all of this to convey a particular discomfort I feel when talking about myself or placing too much emphasis on my personal experiences as a parameter for judgment. This does not imply that I am unaware of my own standpoint—how could I be? —nor do I downplay the personal circumstances that define my identity, such as being born in one city and not another, being the child of specific parents rather than others, or living in a specific historical context, instead of another. It suggests that my experiences and personal history hold less importance, except to the extent that they can inform a standpoint or serve as a foundation for critical intellectual inquiry. It's not that I lack my own narratives of mourning and exclusion, nor that I haven't shed tears alone in dark streets, burdened by racism and haunted by homophobia. I am no stranger to the bitterness of blood in my mouth from insults and humiliation, feeling denied and rendered invisible, treated like an exotic creature or a pet demon. However, how relevant can my individual struggles be when confronted with the vast oceans of desolation and brutality faced by my ancestors? At times, I envy some people, generally younger ones. Certainties come easily, the enemy is unmistakable and unified. With a glamorous blonde woman by their side, dressed in a suit and tie, wearing an imported watch, the pursuit of individual success and the ostentation of material progress bring no shame or remorse. The celebration of one's individuality, along with unwavering revolutionary faith in oneself, often leads individuals to see themselves as champions of truth and justice, standing in opposition to those who do not share their exact views. This perspective creates a simplified world for these individuals, one devoid of contradictions between truth and justice, power and knowledge, as well as the self and their desires, where distinctions between gods and men, and history and personal experience, become blurred.

I, however, intractable, find no rest in leaving my own "self" unexamined. Under the sign of negation, rather than identity, I recognize or am pushed toward constructing a positionality that is rooted in denial. Every denial and each "no" that defines me marks my location, which is certainly more privileged than that of most Black men in the diaspora but not privileged enough to save me from bondage. Everything that I am not and cannot become defines the condition for creating a space for a standpoint and a subject position. I am not heterosexual. I am not dark-skinned. I am not a practitioner of candomblé. I do not identify as a communist. I did not grow up in a favela. I am not an artist. I do not drive a new car. I am not associated with any political party or organization. I am not a man in the way that others may be. Yet, in essence, I am just as much a man as any other. Perhaps, in truth, I resemble you only slightly or reflect the lineage of all my unnamed ancestors.

Yet, everything we are, everything I am, seems fragile, weakened, filled with futile ambitions in a world falling apart. Everything we imagine ourselves to be or to live for seems destined for impersonal dissolution, like the voice of a ghost amidst the whirlwind, at a deserted crossroads at midnight.

CHAPTER 1
THE PERSON OF THE SLAVE:[17] SOCIAL DEATH AND POLITICAL IMAGINARIES OF THE AFRICAN DIASPORA IN BRAZIL

"Now is the time of our death
We will die in the aesthetics of this conventional angiography
We will die in this poet finally transplanted
We will die in this poem
Lesser and mortal
My cruel continental assassin."
— **Nelson Maca, "Tell the Pigs I Stay," 2015**

AFRICA AND DEATH

In 1977, during the Black fortnight organized at the University of São Paulo by sociologist and activist Eduardo de Oliveira e Oliveira (Trapp, 2015), the historian and pioneering Brazilian Black intellectual Beatriz Nascimento remarked:

> During those four centuries of slavery, we see the Brazilian Black individual acting as a participant in society, even though sometimes denying their own racial origin. When I arrived at the university, something that shocked me was the perpetual study of the slave, as if we had only existed in the nation as slave labor, for farming and mining (ORI, 1989).

---

[17] The title of this chapter tries to echo Beatriz Nascimento's affirmation about "the person of the Black man" discussed further in this book.

In another moment of this historical gathering, recorded in the film "Ori—Head and Black Consciousness" (1989), Hamilton Cardoso, a Black activist and socialist, a key figure in reshaping political rhetoric and positionality for Black Brazilians during the 1970s, pondered:

> So, to the extent that Black people seek to preserve their own culture, they have every right to identify with all of African culture. Whether this is the right path to solving the Black problem is a question that only makes sense when discussed within the Afro-Brazilian community, given that the Afro-Brazilian community remains completely marginalized from the national development process. But now I ask, who speaks about Africa in Brazil? (ORI, 1989).

Thus, we see how a political choice toward Africa was proposed. Both statements converge to define a moment of discursive inflection in the language used to articulate (a new?) political identity for Black Brazilians. The context was the peak of the Brazilian military regime, initiated by a coup in 1964 with the support of broad sectors of the press, economic elites, and a conservative middle class, attached at that moment, as unfortunately to the moment we live now, to values associated with family, God, and country. All of this was, of course, shaped as an ideal of the nation (Andrews, 1992; Figueiredo & Cheibub, 1986–1987; Skidmore, 1985, 1998; Pires, 2018). Influential figures from earlier periods of Black political mobilization, like Abdias do Nascimento, were in exile. Others, like José Correia Leite, who emerged from the Black mobilization of the first half of the century, contributed to this moment of reimagining (Andrews, 1992; Félix, 1996; Fontaine, 1985). However, there was something new. Among other factors already highlighted, there was the influence of institutionalized left-wing groups, like the Socialist Convergence, of Trotskyist inspiration, in which Hamilton participated. Consequently, there was the impact of anti-capitalist rhetoric, reinforced by the effects of African decolonization and the influence of the Black Panther Party (Cardoso, 1984; Hanchard, 1994; Nascimento & Nascimento, 2000; Gonzalez, 1982; Pinto, 1990). Also new at the time, though to a different extent now, was the tentative presence of Black people at the university, proposing the Black man and woman as subjects of knowledge and architects of their own history. Indeed, it was precisely at this moment, and this is the center of my interest here, that Brazilian Black activism rejected, or would reject, identification with the enslaved past and the figure of the slave as the central theme for reconstructing a political subjectivity. Consequently, it made sense to say that these new Black intellectuals repositioned themselves and sought to reposition our sensibility and emancipatory agenda by forging a new connection toward the denial of slavery and an affirmation of Africa and Africanity. This movement was, and remains, largely possible due to the strong presence of cultural traditions of African origin or perceived as such. This diffuse legacy within the fabric of social experience, objectified as formal structures like music and arts, and institutions like African religious houses or Black religious sisterhoods/brotherhoods, clearly indicated that Black people in Brazil, even while enslaved, were always more or less African or had concrete contact with Africa, as we will see. Thus, within the horizon of forming my own political sensibility and racialized subjectivity, as well as that of millions of Black Brazilians, the reference to Africa and Africanity has always been a constant. And all of this involved rejecting the slave—at times referred to as enslaved—precisely as a measure of this denial of the ultimate negation, of human personhood, of that subject whom history had positioned as merchandise for four hundred years.

However, from my recent contact with literature associated with Afro-pessimism in the United States, as well as with the emergence and consolidation of anti-Black genocide as a central political category for racial emancipation politics in Brazil, the centrality of Africanity seemed, and seems, no longer to cover the entire possible map for insurgent and critical Black sensibilities. We have a sociological backdrop for this, beyond the revisions in the field of critical and interpretative paradigms of Black social thought (Vargas, 2010b, 2012; Sexton, 2011; Wilderson, 2010; 2010). Thus, the concept of "social death" and its connections with multi-dimensional anti-Black genocide, along with the impact of the concept of necropolitics on the emphasis on dispossession structures rather than the celebration of traditions and identities based on African culture (declined under various conceptual modalities), seems to outline a conceptual and political transit or passage that has implications for understanding who we are, how we got here, and what we seek for the future.

This chapter represents an initial endeavor within a larger project aimed at mapping and critically examining the intertwining sociological, subjective, and aesthetic elements that inform our understanding of historical and contemporary experiences. Through this exploration, I aim to provide a framework that elucidates our historical trajectory while offering a guiding perspective for the present. Central to this inquiry is the nuanced transition between Africa and the institution of slavery, which emerges as a pivotal discursive and interpretive structure. This paradigm situates/enhances various facets of Black life and struggles in Brazil, inviting a deeper understanding of these complex dimensions.

Eduardo de Oliveira e Oliveira died in 1980, according to Rafael Trapp (2017), "hounded by racism and homophobia" (p. 2). However, in the circles of Brazilian Black activism, it is said that he either committed suicide or allowed himself to die, succumbing to severe depression. Hamilton Cardoso, after being run over "on May 1, 1988, after a party at the Peruche Samba School, where he had watched a performance by [the Afro-Bahian group] Olodum with friends"[18] (Pereira, 2009), never fully recovered. He suffered from severe pain, paranoia, and depression, eventually taking his own life on November 5, 1999. Beatriz Nascimento was murdered in Rio de Janeiro on January 28, 1995, when she was trying to defend a friend being attacked by her violent partner. Three prominent Black intellectuals and activists, central to the reinvention of Black political imagination, were struck down at the height of their intellectual productivity and maturity. What forces could have targeted them? A woman, a gay man, and a socialist—each different, yet united by the same tragic and violent fate— (a fate, notably, shared by thousands of other Black men and women in Brazil). Does the shadow of death and despair illuminate the (re)invention of the self as a political strategy for subjective survival?

In the following pages, as I previously mentioned, I will partially introduce themes that will be more fully developed later. This is how I begin to address the conditional status of the enslaved as a "person", in the anthropological sense, within the framework of the colonial death zone. Next, I explore the political significance of the Africa-sign as a catalyst for the reconversion or transfiguration of racial terror. Finally, I aim to more precisely define the dynamics of this transition or oscillation between Africanity and slavery as a form of social death.

The Person of the Slave in the Space of Death

Slavery, defined by total dispossession and the radical alienation of the subject from themselves, or the suppression of autonomy and dignity in its most extreme forms, has been described by Orlando Patterson as a form

---

[18] In "Hamilton Cardoso" by Dulce Maria Pereira, posted on the Geledes Blog on 05/21/2009. See: https://www.geledes.org.br/hamilton-cardoso/e last accessed August 5, 2025, at 2:34 pm EST.

of social parasitism or, more precisely, total social domination. From the perspective of the enslaved person, slavery can be synthesized as a condition of social death. This notion is rooted in the original act of violence that reduced a man or woman to enslavement—a process stemming from war, in its idealized terms, but also from deception and plunder. This act was justified, in an idealized framework, as a historical and individually concrete alternative to death. "Archetypically, slavery was a substitute for death in war" (Patterson, 2008, p. 24). However, this substitution did not imply forgiveness or absolution but rather a "conditional exchange". This exchange exacted a price: the loss of personal dignity and, ultimately, the erasure of social existence as a "person" with no recognition of social being outside the domain of the master. Stripped from the social relationships that define personhood, the slave became socially uprooted—lacking familial or statutory ties, civil rights, or ritual obligations. Severed from the web of social relations that integrate individuals into society (Patterson, 2008; Meillassoux, 1995), the enslaved individual was left without ancestors or descendants, existing only as "no one without inheritance or legacy. In the words of the poet Derek Walcott: "Now each man was a nation/In himself, without mother, father, brother" (Walcott, 1990, p. 153).

This disconnection stripped the enslaved of any claim to personal honor or dignity. By definition, slaves were dishonored in a general sense, with this dishonor becoming hereditary, typically transmitted through the maternal line, encapsulated in the Latin dictum partus sequitur ventrem. Patterson's characterization of slavery, as part of a broader historical-sociological conceptualization, applies equally to the modern enslavement of Africans in the Americas. It reveals "what slavery really meant: the direct and insidious violence, the namelessness and invisibility, the endless personal violation, and the chronic inalienable dishonor" (Patterson, 2008, p. 33).

The "original act of violence" holds particular relevance here, as it constitutes the foundational event in the establishment of societies, or, at the very least, colonial societies. This act reflects what Nelson Maldonado-Torres (2008) defines as the "paradigm of war", a civilizational ethos that institutionalizes violence, brutality, and terror as modes of governance and subject formation. This ethos underpins the normalization of war as the suspension of all ethics and politics in favor of a "death ethic that renders massacre and different forms of genocide as natural" (Maldonado-Torres, 2008, p. 11). Here, however, we are reminded of Cesaire's critical insight.

The colonial massacre, tolerated in places such as Congo or Haiti, becomes intolerable when it targets the white man on European soil:

> What he (the Christian bourgeois) cannot forgive Hitler for is not the crime in itself, the crime against man, it is not the humiliation of man as such, it is the crime against the White man, the humiliation of the White man, and the fact that he applied to Europe colonialist procedures which until then had been reserved exclusively for the Arabs of Algeria, the coolies of India, and the niggers of Africa. (Césaire, 2000, p. 36)

Even an author often accused of insensitivity to the trauma of colonialism and slavery, such as Marx, explicitly acknowledges the central—and I would argue the structural—role of violence and radical dispossession as core mechanisms of colonialism and its associated system of slavery. Although Marx recognized the historical significance of Britain's invasion of India as a brutal phase in Humanity's evolution, he did not shy away from exposing the cowardice, brutality, and hypocrisy of the British. More importantly, he underscored the fundamental fact that without violence and terror, colonization would not have been possible: "[...] the universal existence of torture as a financial institution of British India is thus officially admitted" (Marx & Engels, 1964, p. 183).

For Maldonado-Torres, the original and boundless violence of the war paradigm is a necessary stage in the colonial process. I would further argue that it is structural, embodying the prevalence of the war model as a paradigmatic element in the formation of colonial societies built on genocide and slavery. In this sense, "the decolonial turn includes the definitive entry of enslaved and colonized subjectivities into the realm of thought at institutional levels previously unknown" (Maldonado-Torres, 2008, p. 8).

Thus, terror and brutal violence, as historical experiences, should also be processed as analytical and political categories in Black and anti-colonial thought. Michael Taussig's (1993) concept of the "space of death" is particularly useful for establishing critical categories to analyze forms of subjectivity shaped by the destruction of the person.

Taussig reflects on accounts of colonial violence in the Putumayo region of Colombia during the early 20th century as a way to interrogate the "social being of truth", rather than the truth of social being. This can be understood as the centralization of violence in defining the social being of the colonized body, manifesting as an ontology of terror. Such violence produces consequences that are ontological in nature, shaping subjectivities that are violated and dispossessed in a manner so comprehensive and overwhelming that it plunges both the world and the individual into an almost hallucinatory dimension. Taussig is explicit in this regard: "[...] the space of death is crucial to the creation of meaning and consciousness, nowhere more so than in societies where torture is endemic and where the culture of terror flourishes" (Taussig, 1993, p. 26). In this context, the hyper sensory proliferation of violence, spectacularized sadism, and public torture establishes a historical space for the imposition of devastating hegemony over bodies and consciousness. At the same time, it generates a regime of meanings that shapes narratives of social life and the production of subjectivities. As Orlando Patterson (2008) observes, "[...] there is no known slaveholding society where the whip was not considered an indispensable instrument" (p. 23). In this way, the social pedagogy of violence and terror constitutes the foundation for the establishment of a new order, one materialized, as Bourdieu might argue, in both the "brains" and the social space, including institutions, as a way of materializing a social order that seems objective precisely because it is embedded within categories and structures (Bourdieu, 1999).

This historical link between colonizers and their ethics of war and the colonized/enslaved as non-persons is mirrored in the structural connection between physical violence and forms of signification (or non-signification). The colonial space of death serves as the mechanism of transition that establishes the enslaved person as a categorical construct of colonialism.

> And by this, I mean us to think-through-terror, which as well as being a physiological state is also a social one whose special features allow it to serve as the mediator par excellence of colonial hegemony. The space of death is one of the crucial spaces where Indian, African, and white gave birth to the New World. (Taussig, 1993, p. 27)

In the North American academic environment, the critical thrust of what is known as "afropessimism" rests on the incorporation of Patterson's robust definition of slavery as "social death". Extrapolating from its historical contexts, Frank Wilderson III and other scholars (Wilderson, 2010) insist on equating Blackness in modernity with slavery, along with all its political and subjective consequences and corollaries. Wilderson (2018) "theorizes the structural relation between Blackness and Humanity as an irreconcilable encounter, an antagonism. One cannot know Blackness as distinct from slavery, for there is no Black temporality which is antecedent to the temporality of the Black slave" (p. 27). Extreme and gratuitous violence defines Blackness, framing the Black body as shaped and defined by foundational violence, inalienable indignity and dishonor, and uprootedness. Wilderson seeks to draw what he describes as ontological consequences from this condition, which are also understood as having profound and distinctive implications for political agency, as further elaborated by João H. Costa Vargas (2012, 2017). According to this perspective, Black people lack the conditions for political articulation within the sphere traditionally known as "civil society", in Gramscian terms. Additionally, there is no comparable measure of Black "suffering" relative to other subjugated groups, including colonial subjects such as Indigenous peoples and Arabs. This implies that the possibilities for political coalitions are limited, contrasting sharply with other Afro-American political paradigms, such as that of the Black Panther Party, which leaned toward coalitions based on a shared perspective defined precisely by colonial conditions and the Third-Worldist rhetoric inaugurated by the spirit of Bandung (Wright, 2008; Diawara, 1998). In contrast, by not engaging with the economic dimension—more specifically, the political economy—or even the broader geopolitical colonial framework, Wilderson emphasizes the antagonistic (irreconcilable) dimension of Black experience. This experience is defined far beyond material constraints and is shaped by a "libidinal economy" that perversely intertwines desire and meaning, creating a field that cannot be fully captured by class analysis. In fact, the enslaved condition that defines Blackness establishes the Black subject not merely as a non-person but as non-human, a distinction that Patterson explores at length. The enslaved condition does not merely serve an economic function; rather, it fulfills distinct needs rooted in parasitism, entailing complex negotiations of Humanity/Inhumanity, desire/terror, honor /dishonor, freedom/bondage.

In my engagement with Afropessimist literature, two aspects stood out prominently. First, its focus on ontology—a debate I had considered either resolved or irrelevant, owing to my engagement with poststructuralist (post metaphysical)[19] thought. Second, the perceived erasure of historical and semiotic conditions for the (re)construction of Black subjectivity and its forms of political identity beyond slavery, death, and "nothingness" (Gordon, 1999; 2018; Sexton, 2018; Moten, 2013).

The void that emerges in this framework, largely indebted to Fanon, defines not only the contours of Black subjectivity but also its anti-representational ontology. As Lewis Gordon puts it, "the Black therefore does not symbolize crime and licentious sexuality in an anti-black world. The black is crime and licentious sexuality, bestiality and all the arrays of social pathologies" (Gordon, 1999, p. 79). Authors not explicitly aligned with Afropessimism, such as Stefano Harney and Fred Moten (2013), take this concept further: "Blackness is the site where absolute nothingness and the world of things converge" (p. 95). Similarly, Jared Sexton (2011, 2018) elaborates at length and with nuance on the paradoxes of "nothingness" in the experience of Blackness.

However, as a Black Brazilian man, and particularly as a Bahian, my sociocultural experience—as well as that of millions of other Afro-Brazilians and Afro-Latin Americans or Caribbeans—is saturated with references to Africa and elements of Africanity. There is no void. Where such a void might otherwise be imagined lies the supplement of the Africa-Sign, as I will explore further in subsequent discussions. Historical connections, links, and reinterpretations have left palpable traces—in language, institutional forms, symbolic categories, devotion to the orishas, and the embodied celebration of various modes of Black and/or African music, as will become evident in the chapters ahead. This stands in contrast to the relative void or scorched earth often depicted in the Black experience in the United States, as poetically rendered in Claude McKay's (1995) "The Desolate City".

> My spirit is a pestilential city,
> With misery triumphant everywhere,
> Glutted with baffled hopes and lost to pity;

---

[19] In Derrida's (1995) framework, the sign always indicates or returns to an unattainable origin, an absence that is continuously reconstituted and a signifier that invariably refers to another signifier. This perspective deconstructs the "metaphysics of presence", which conceives being as a state of being-there. The very idea of representation as signification— where an indicator stands in for something "elsewhere" represented by the signifier—no longer withstands critique. Within this context, the separation between content and its representation arises as an ideological effect of the "metaphysics of presence". This framework presupposes, as an (ideo)logical necessity, the existence of an ultimate, concrete foundation of objective content to be uncovered at the end of the chain of signifiers.

Strange agonies make quiet lodgment there.
Its bursting sewers ooze up from below,
And spread their loathsome substance through its lanes,
Flooding all areas with their evil flow,
And blocking all the motion of its veins.
Its life is sealed to love or hope or pity;
My spirit is a pestilential city.
(p. 294)

Thus, Africanity (or ancestrality), at the very least alongside slavery, forms the foundation for a Black ontology or subjectivity. As Beatriz Nascimento critiques, and as numerous agents of the Black movement have broadly defined, the politically subjectivized form of identification for Black Brazilians is grounded in the relationship with Africa rather than with slavery and its foundational violation. This perspective carries culturalist contradictions, which I will explore further.

In this regard, the thought of Afro-Brazilian activist and researcher Lélia Gonzalez offers a valuable counterpoint, particularly through her concept of "Améfricanity" [Améfricanidade] (Gonzalez, 1988). Gonzalez mobilizes this concept to provide an alternative to the notion that Latin America is fundamentally "Latin", that is, deriving its identity and rich sociocultural life exclusively from European sources or matrices. More significantly, it counters the idea that "the formations of the unconscious in Latin America are exclusively European" (Gonzalez, 1988, p. 69). For Gonzalez, the African and Amerindian presence forms the true substratum and fabric of the culture and subjectivity of Latin American countries. An additional critical opposition she made relates to what she identifies as the imperialist positioning of the United States, particularly regarding African Americans. This imperialism is evident in terminologies such as Afro-American or African American, which implies an exclusivity, as though other Black people on the continent are not also American—or, more precisely in this context, Améfrican.

As I am anticipating, interpretations and categories that emphasize the African connection inevitably suffer from a degree of culturalism. This leads, surprisingly, to Lélia Gonzalez's argument (1988), which is similar to Gilberto Freyre's argument, particularly when she highlights the "Moorish" past of the Spanish and Portuguese as a precursor for the "articulation of racial relations", precisely the argument Freyre makes in "Casa Grande &

Senzala" (Freyre, 1995). Similarly, Lélia's focus on discussing national formations or the constitution of "Brazilian culture" introduces a paradox or tension within her hemispheric perspective.

To navigate these challenges, Lélia proposes the concept of "Améfricanity" [*améfricanidade*], which serves three purposes: (1) it decentralizes the dominance of U.S. frameworks, fostering connections among Black populations across different Latin American national societies; (2) it links our historical experiences to Africa while charting distinct pathways for Africa and the Diaspora; which methodologically offers an advantage, as it could (3)

> recover a specific unity historically forged within different societies in a particular region of the world. Therefore, Améfrica, as an ethnogeographic system of reference, is a creation of our own and of our ancestors on the continent where we live, inspired by African models. (Gonzalez, 1988, p. 77)

At the beginning of this chapter, I recalled how Beatriz Nascimento critiques the obsession with studying the enslaved. Her objection fundamentally centers on rejecting the objectification and dehumanization identified as central to the Black experience by scholars such as Wilderson and others aligned with approaches that position the foundational violence of slavery as a central political and analytical category. It is in this same sense that Beatriz Nascimento reflects on what she terms "the person of the Black man". She insightfully observes: "the economic question is not the greatest drama, you see. Despite being a significant drama, it is not the greatest drama. The greatest drama is precisely the recognition of the person of the Black man, which has never been acknowledged in Brazil" (Ori, 1989).

Thus, we see that the objectification inherent in slavery and the dehumanization of racism operate to prohibit the recognition of personhood in Beatriz Nascimento's thought. This prohibition, the impossibility of the Black man being recognized as a person, is precisely what the enslaved individual—as a fungible and complete commodity—could not achieve. Yet, we must ask: how can we define a "person"? The theoretical tradition of social anthropology has established the interpretive canon on this subject through the classic essay by Marcel Mauss (2003), with whom I will conclude this section.

A key contributor to the journal *L'Année Sociologique* (1898), founded by Émile Durkheim, the putative founder of sociology and social anthropology, Marcel Mauss produced several essays that are now considered foundational texts. Unlike the later functionalist-empiricist tradition, Mauss approached conceptual problems through a universalizing and comparative perspective (which, in some respects, engaged with anthropological evolutionism, a method he explicitly termed the "comparative method").

This perspective can be seen in his "Outline of a General Theory of Magic" (1904); his seminal and central "The Gift: Forms and Functions of Exchange in Archaic Societies" (1925); "Techniques of the Body" (1934); and, relevant here, "A Category of the Human Mind: The Notion of Person, the Notion of 'Self'" (1938), which I will briefly address" (Mauss, 2003; Lévi-Strauss, 2003)).

In this essay, traversing a wide ethnographic and historical spectrum, Mauss seeks to interrogate, from a standpoint that we might recognize as a genealogical perspective, what he considers to be a "category of the human mind", the formal preconditions for understanding which, blinded by ethnocentrism or oblivious to the historicity of forms of thought (or of thinking about thought), we often assume to be innate. However, these ideas are far from innate. Faithful to Durkheim's principle of the primacy of the social, Mauss challenges and interrogates the universality of the word "I" [or "self"]. Converging into a single inquiry, Mauss investigates the socio-historical genesis of the ideas of "subject", "self", and "person", recognizing their overlapping characteristics within the balance of universality and particularity.

Among the Pueblo Indigenous peoples of North America, for example, we observe a concept of personhood in which the individual is indistinguishable from their clan. Ritual functions are enacted as ceremonial performances, imbued with the significance of masks, titles, positions, and the social roles of officiants. In this sense, clan-based ritual performance defines the individual through their ritual position, which Mauss interprets as an original form of personification. Similarly, among the Kwakiutl, studied by Franz Boas in the Northwestern United States, we find the same clan-based reality, where classes, clans, and human individuals interact and are produced through ritualistic means. In this context, "all actors are all men[20]", collectively performing a drama that is simultaneously aesthetic, cosmic, mythological, social, and personal. This drama is deeply engaged with the positive existence of ancestors and the perpetuation of things

---

[20] E.N. Please note that we could not verify the original source of this quote, which was uncited in the original text, but decided to leave this in the text as it is in the original.

and their spirits. The ritual ensemble finds its ultimate expression in the "Potlatch", the infamous agonistic theatricalization of political opposition between chiefs. Here, too, the "person" remains a character in cosmological dramas.

Indigenous societies in North America provide a model for the social construction of the person. However, to follow Mauss's genealogical exploration of the person, we must shift to the evolutionary trajectory identified with Western societies. First, in Roman society, we encounter the Latin term *persona*, which initially refers to a social category of understanding, still closely tied to the tragic and ritual mask—indeed, this is the root meaning of the word persona, which later evolves into *person*. However, it is in Rome that, for the first time, the human person emerges as a complete (independent) entity. Thus, the person becomes more than a mask (a place in the social order)—it also becomes a fundamental juridical fact embedded within the state's legal framework. In this context, Roman citizenship translates into the status of civil persona, and the "juridical" person emerges as the individual's true nature. More specifically, this applies to the free man (that is, someone who is neither enslaved nor a woman), who possesses ownership of his own body. "Moreover, the right to the persona had been established. Only the slave is excluded from it. Servus non habet personam. He has no personality. He does not own his body, nor has he ancestors, name, cognomen, or personal belongings" (Mauss, 2003, p. 189).

Under the influence of Stoicism, the notion of person acquires a moral connotation, associated with "consciousness". As Dionysius of Halicarnassus suggests—according to Mauss—self-consciousness became the hallmark of the moral person. With the subsequent Christianization of the empire, the moral person becomes a metaphysical entity rooted in the unity (substance and mode/body and soul) of the human person.

In modernity, as both a corollary and a prerequisite for its emergence, we witness the transformation of metaphysical, moral consciousness into psychological consciousness. It is based on this psychological anthropocentrism that Descartes establishes a new epistemology, positioning man as the subject—not of ritual or morality, but of knowledge. This forms the foundation of Cartesian deductive thought: cogito ergo sum ["I think, therefore I am"]. Ultimately, Mauss concludes, this trajectory culminates in the political definition of the person as a subject of universal rights. Each individual is entitled to their "own self", and these "selves" are bearers of inalienable rights, as articulated in the Universal Declaration of Human

Rights (2018): "Everyone has the right to life, liberty, and personal security", p. 03).

It is easy to discern traces of evolutionism in this genealogical perspective, even though it is tempered by relativism and Mauss's characteristic humanism (Brumana, 1983). However, it is crucial to focus on how, in the Western tradition, the dominant and the dominated are articulated through what Maldonado-Torres (2008) identifies as the ethos of war. This ethos encompasses ritualistic, juridical, psychological, moral, epistemological, and political dimensions, which, in this context, converge to define the notion of person. These overlapping dimensions, when operating politically within the colonial context, constrain the boundaries of the definition of the person. As Beatriz Nascimento notes, this denial of person is embedded in the figure of the enslaved, the one who must, in theory, be negated to affirm the "self" of the master. For Mauss's evolutionary genealogy to make sense, with its sequential linkages, the enslaved would need to remain excluded. However, even while keeping Mauss in mind, we can observe that overturning this denial cannot be reduced to an act of mere will. This is due to the objective reality of historical categories such as "person" or "slave". As Orlando Patterson—a scholar acutely attuned to the symbolic dimension of social life—argues, these categories cannot be easily dismissed. This is particularly true because they are essential to affirming the Humanity of the master while simultaneously negating, parasitizing, or objectifying the Humanity, or personhood, of the enslaved.

THE AFRICA-SIGN

The modern Black movement, which emerged in Brazil during the decline of the military regime in the 1970s, is associated with a broader movement for the reorganization of social movements and the politicization of society and daily life during that period (Figueiredo & Cheibub, 1986–87; Fontaine, 1985; Gonzalez, 1982). In Bahia, which I have been able to observe more closely, this resurgence of the national Black movement—evidenced by significant results such as the implementation of racial quota policies in universities and the emergence of numerous collectives of young Black students—is closely linked to a broader local movement of re-Africanization (Pinho, 2001 2003; Risério, 1981). This incorporation endowed the Bahian movement with unique characteristics tied to re-Africanizing transformations while also transmitting these traits to the broader national Black movement. Among these characteristics are the centrality of "Black culture" and the affirmation of Africanity, or what I have termed the

Africa-Sign, as a discursive device of subjectivation (Cunha, 1998; Pinho, 1990). For instance, while in São Paulo's Quinzena do Negro at USP we observe certain developments involving the rejection of the enslaved identity, in Bahia, we see the proliferation of Africanized cultural forms and representational structures. These elements supplement, in a poststructural sense, the presumed historical void left by the devastating legacy of colonial slavery (Bhabha, 1998).

The Quilombo of Palmares and the generic form of the "quilombo" have been significantly redefined through this reorganization of the Black movement in the 1970s. With this reinterpretation, the quilombo increasingly represents an alternative model of societal organization that challenged colonial powers and reimagined an African world based on free labor, communal land ownership, holistic traditional values, and more (Nascimento, 2007; Nascimento, 2002). With the "rehabilitation of the quilombo", the Afro-descendant utopia incorporates a historical model as a reference from the past to envision possibilities for the future. On this topic, Beatriz Nascimento, in "O conceito de Quilombo e a Resistência Cultural" [The Concept of Quilombo and Black Cultural Resistance], states the following:

> It was in the late 19th century that the quilombo came to be understood as an ideological instrument against forms of oppression. Its mystique began to fuel the dream of freedom for thousands of enslaved individuals working on the plantations of São Paulo, often through abolitionist rhetoric. This transition from a concrete institution to a symbol redefined the quilombo. (Nascimento, 2007, p. 122)

Abdias do Nascimento is another early proponent of this reappropriation of the quilombo, presenting a model of "Afro-Brazilian praxis" that he terms *quilombismo*. This praxis, rooted in a history of resistance expressed on multiple levels, also serves as a political program for transformative action, encapsulated in the "ABC of Quilombismo" (Nascimento, 1982, 2002, 1980).

It is evident that the narrative of the Black autonomous organization forms part of a broader strategy to redefine the interpretative foundations of the present. This redefinition provides a perspective on the national past and the place of Black people within it, fundamentally framing them as insurgent agents capable of critiquing and overcoming oppression and inequality. Central to this perspective is the consistent reference to Africa, which serves as an essential element in this disposition. It operates as an effective strategy to reject the bondage that denied Black persons their recognition, that is, a negation of the negation.

Recent historiography has highlighted the prevalence and extent of quilombos throughout enslavement, as well as the correlations between quilombos in Brazil and Africa, particularly Angola. This research has increasingly provided a robust foundation for constructing a counter-narrative to the history of slavery. In this counter-narrative, the enslaved and African individuals are not merely passive cogs within the system but active agents of their own liberation (Cardoso, 1986; MNU, 1988; Nascimento, 1982; Reis & Gomes, 1996). Similarly, the historiography of slave or Black revolts, including those with significant participation by mixed-race[21] individuals or freed slaves, such as the Malê Revolt in 1835 and, earlier, the Revolt of the Búzios or the Tailors' Revolt in 1798, provide a historical backdrop for understanding both enslaved resistance and the organized efforts for the liberation of Black Brazilians (Reis, 1988; Reis & Gomes, 1996; Reis & Silva, 1993, 1989; Freudenthal, 1997; Andrews, 1992, among others).

As articulated in a document from the Unified Black Movement:

> The scribes of official historiography, aligned with the interests of the ruling elites, claim that African Black people were docile and servile, passively submitting to slavery. On the contrary, the history of Black Brazilians reveals a series of movements, insurrections, revolutions, and rebellions—evidence of the struggle of African Black people against the system of bondage in Brazil. (...) The history of Black people in Brazil is a history of resistance. It spans nearly 500 years of struggle against slavery, racism, oppression, and exploitation. (MNU, 1988, p. 54)

---

[21] T.N.: The author uses the term *pardos* to reflect the sociocultural context. In Brazil, *pardos* refers to individuals of mixed racial or ethnic ancestry, often encompassing a combination of European, Indigenous, and African heritage. The term has historical roots and is one of the categories in Brazil's official racial classification system, which includes *brancos* (white), *negros* (Black), *amarelos* (Asian), *indígenas* (Indigenous), and *pardos* (mixed-race). Created by the Brazilian Institute of Geography and Statistics (IBGE), it is a sociocultural construct rather than a strict biological or genetic classification.

Long before the Quinzena do Negro at USP, in 1944, Abdias do Nascimento, alongside other intellectuals, founded the Black Experimental Theater [Teatro Experimental do Negro — TEN]. Unlike earlier movements, the TEN "demanded the recognition of the civilizational value of African heritage and Afro-Brazilian identity" (Nascimento & Nascimento, 2000, p. 207). The TEN played a pivotal role in shaping a counter-ideological interpretation of Brazil's racial politics. It brought together artists and intellectuals, as well as poor Black individuals, illiterate people, and domestic workers. In addition to producing plays, it was instrumental in cultivating intellectual and artistic leaders and organizing the National Convention of Black Brazilians in 1945. This event was a direct response to the Afro-Brazilian Congresses of the Northeast, organized by Gilberto Freyre and Edson Carneiro, which were harshly criticized for exoticizing Black people and treating them as mere objects of study (Nascimento & Nascimento, 2000, p. 211).

As the main leader of TEN, Abdias do Nascimento is undoubtedly the key figure in the transition and consolidation of a new perspective—one that reinterpreted the history of Black organization prior to 1945 and influenced the development of Afro-descendant political representation after that period. Through quilombismo and other strategic intellectual interventions, Abdias introduced discussions of identity and political struggle centered on the representation and formation of a Black political subject. This construction is profoundly shaped by what I call the Africa-Sign.

On June 18, 1978, approximately one year after the Quinzena do Negro in São Paulo and 34 years after the founding of the Black Experimental Theater [TEN], the Unified Movement Against Racial Discrimination [Movimento Unificado contra a Discriminação Racial — MUCDR] was established. Shortly after, on July 7, the organization held a public demonstration on the steps of the Municipal Theater in São Paulo. On July 23, the MUCDR was renamed the Unified Black Movement Against Racial Discrimination [Movimento Negro Unificado contra a Discriminação Racial — MNUCDR]. During its first congress, held in December 1979 in Rio de Janeiro, it was renamed again to the Unified Black Movement [Movimento Negro Unificado — MNU], the name it retains to this day (Nascimento & Nascimento, 2000; Cardoso, 2002; Félix, 1996; Hanchard, 1994).

The July 7 act was organized as a protest against the death of a young Black man, Robson Luís. The newspaper *Versus* detailed the case of Robson Luís and the protest that marked the public emergence of Brazil's new Black movement. Robson Luís, a 21-year-old married resident of Vila

Popular, died on April 28, 1978, at the Hospital de Clínicas in São Paulo. His face was disfigured, and his scrotum had been mutilated while in custody at the 44th Police Precinct in São Paulo. According to *Versus*, the police officer responsible for the beating reportedly said, "Black people must die beaten up" (Cardoso, 1978).

In Bahia, the early development of the MNU can be traced to the group NEGO —Estudos sobre a Problemática do Negro Brasileiro [Studies on the Problems of Black Brazilians]. On July 5, 1978, this group became aware of the July 7 protest and expressed their solidarity. Soon after, the group became the Bahian branch of the MNU. Members included Lino de Almeida, Gilberto Roque, and Luiz Alberto, a union leader, co-founder of the Workers' Party (Partido dos Trabalhadores — PT), and later a parliamentarian (Silva, 1988). The activities leading to the establishment of the Bahian MNU were deeply intertwined with cultural elements that characterized the Re-Africanization movement. The Afro bloco Ilê Aiyê had been founded in 1974, and although the Black Soul movement that served as a backdrop for racial politicization in Rio and São Paulo was less influential in Bahia, it was complemented by the "afro soul" wave represented by Ilê Aiyê and other cultural organizations and trends (Risério, 1981).

The question of identity, a central theme in the rhetoric of this modern Black movement, thus found in Bahia a privileged platform within the broader history of Black organization.

Image 1 — Campaign flyer for Luiz Alberto's candidacy to the Constituent Assembly.
Source: Author's personal archive, 1987.

If identity was a crucial issue for other social movements in Brazil and worldwide, it also played a central role in the process of constructing a racialized political alternative in Salvador. A colonial city with a long history of slavery, a Black majority, and rich, multifaceted African cultural traditions, Salvador became a fertile ground for the Re-Africanization movement. This environment was deeply infused with "cultural" references, drawn from both Afro-Brazilian academic or quasi-academic studies and the Afro-descendant discursive traditions manifested in Carnival. In this sense, the creative torrent of symbolic flow and racial-cultural performance galvanized by the Re-Africanization of Carnival provided the identity elements necessary for shaping the movement and forging a new subject: the Black person as the "new man" (Flor, 1992; Silva, 1988; Rodrigues, 1996).

This "new man", or the young Black subject on the stage of political struggles and subjectivity politics, emerged in direct relation to Africa and Africanity. This contrasts with other contexts, such as the North American Black radical movements, where Africanity did not hold as central a position. While Africa undeniably played a role in the invention of Afro-American identity, it is difficult to argue that its influence was as central, comprehensive, and complex as it is in Brazil and possibly in other Latin American and Caribbean countries with significant Black populations, such as Cuba or Colombia (Fraginals, 1977).

The Black movement in Bahia arose amidst significant tensions. The first of these involved the "cultural" origins of part of the activist agenda, which clashed with the more overtly political, Marxist-inspired project of another faction. This tension divided the nascent movement into two groups: "political" and "culturalist" activists. Furthermore, some activists of this period were involved as actors and educators, and this middle-class or university-level engagement became another source of contradiction within the group. They struggled to articulate a truly popular language that could engage and resonate with the consciousness of the "negro massa" [the Black masses].

At the heart of this institutionalized Black political movement lay the Black subject, but who is the Black person? How can we define them as an active agent in history who preserves memory and political continuity? The response from Black activists of this period centered on the concept of Black identity as a symbolic-cultural construct. In modern Bahia, this identity was primarily a re-Africanized Blackness, derived from cultural traditions—objectified in institutions and discourses—of Black or African origin. This definition of the political subject as a cultural subject permeated the Black movement and generated significant developments, operating within the tension between political and culturalist factions. It was this dynamic interplay that shaped the movement, forging a space where culture and politics intertwined in the construction of Black identity and agency.

It is in Carnival that the cultural aspect of the movement gains space and legitimacy, intertwining with forms of reinventing subjectivity and enabling a diffuse reconnection of ordinary Afro-descendants (those who are not activists or intellectuals) with the sources of their everyday identity—now questioned and contested by conflicting discourses of political identity (Bacelar, 1989). These tensions, however, are not confined to Bahia, as Hanchard has shown, but are integral to the formation of Black political consciousness in modern Brazil (Bairros, 1996; Fry, 1995; Hanchard, 1994;1996a.; 1996b).

The issues of culture and identity thus became the contested core of a demand for recognition and the driving force behind mobilization for economic and social equality. Lélia Gonzalez eloquently underscores the central role of culture as the foundation of our political identity:

> Mass cultural entities have been of great importance insofar as, by engaging with cultural matters, they simultaneously enabled the practice of a political agenda, paving the way for the emergence of ideologically driven Black movements. (Gonzalez, 1982, p. 22)

The cosmology of candomblé and the music of Afro carnival groups soon came to represent, for Black people across Brazil, a source of "roots" or identity, providing a sense of comfort in the face of a cultural hegemony that denied both specificity and value to Black cultural achievements. At the same time, this very Black "culture" has served as a unifying link, enabling discussions of a Brazilian Black identity deeply connected to long-standing popular traditions such as batuques, candomblé, capoeira, and others (Hanchard, 1998). When shaped as a political ideology, this cultural identity embodies a utopian promise of self-realization as Black and of history as the emancipation of Black people, manifesting as the fulfillment of promises inherent in tradition. This enables us to speak of counter-hegemony or, using an emic term, "resistance" (Pinho, 2015).

As I have argued, this reconstitution is rooted in a long-standing tradition, with the modernizing rupture of the Re-Africanization movement in the 1970s representing a break within the tradition itself. Since at least the 19th century, various records document how enslaved Africans and "criolos", Black Brazilian-borns, created social forms of association and aesthetic and cultural structures during the experience of enslavement, dispossession, and total violence. In the 20th century, after abolition, particularly in Bahia but also in other contexts, the centrality of African references remained strong.

Black music, as an African presence in the form of samba and chulas, permeated the entirety of social life throughout the century, extending beyond Carnival. Jocélio Teles dos Santos (1998) offers numerous examples of these "thunderous entertainments", which spread through the city, reterritorializing spaces through conscious, meaningful practices: "The batuques, officially defined as dances or gatherings of Black Africans or their descendants, took place in the streets, squares, houses, and yards of Salvador since the 18th century" (p. 17).

I believe that it is possible to identify a continuously reinvented appeal around what I call the Africa-Sign. The set of reverberations from this appeal, manifested in various moments documented by literature, fiction, or concrete practices, can be described as a counter-hegemonic discourse. This discourse functions as an instrument of ongoing political struggle, forming a consistent thread that constitutes a counter-discursive and critical tradition rooted in historical connections to Africa and the recognition of "African personality" or ancestrality.

This tradition has operated in history as a "supplement". As Derrida and other poststructuralist thinkers like Homi Bhabha have shown, supplementarity redefines the center or establishes significance by attempting to add to an absence or original lack that can never be fully resolved (Bhabha, 1992). The Africa-Sign, as I conceptualize it, fulfills precisely this structural function of supplementation. Through this process, critical and counter-hegemonic discourses can (and have been) constituted, as is evident in the process of Africanized subjectivation. On the other hand, Africa gains discursive and political functionality by occupying, in a sense, the role of what Claude Lévi-Strauss (2003), in his introduction to Marcel Mauss's work, called a floating signifier, understood as an excess of meaning that amplifies the complementary relationship between signifier and signified, enabling meaning to be supplemented.[22]

Throughout the 20th century, and with renewed emphasis after the military regime, we observe an intense connection with Africa through the elaboration of what I term the Africa-Sign, a symbolic, supplemental structure of political agency. Analogous to the transnational agency and self-inscription processes identified by Edmund Gordon and Mark Anderson (1999) for the African diaspora, this structure demonstrates a similar mechanism of Africanized political and self-subjective agency. This process presents various modes of connection and reconnection to the critical practice of Pan-Africanism, African nationalisms, and, most significantly, popular culture in Brazil. However, how can the recognition of

---

[22] "So, in man's efforts to understand the world, he always disposes of a surplus of signification (which he shares out among things in accordance with the laws of the symbolic thinking which it is the task of ethnologists and linguists to study). That distribution of a supplementary ration—if I can express myself thus—is absolutely necessary to ensure that, in total, the available signifier and the mapped-out signified may remain in the relationship of complementarity which is the very condition of the exercise of symbolic thinking." (Lévi-Strauss, 2003, p. 43).

these modes align with the centrality of violence, genocide, slavery, and social death as structuring categories for Black political subjectivity?

METAMORPHOSES

As previously noted, this chapter aims to establish initial conditions for interrogating a transition or transformation, rather than a binary duality, which frames the figures of the enslaved and the African as two supplementary alternatives. This effort entailed a preliminary mapping of critical theoretical reflections by intellectuals and the engaged thought of activists, as well as contrasting historically inscribed forms of Black identification with those emphasized by critical revisions of epistemology or even potential ontologies. The field of critical thought that emphasizes the centrality of slavery focuses on dispossession, violence, erasure, terror, and genocide as categories that allow us to engage critically with the anti-Black world. In this view, as Fanon (1983) asserts, we might envision "a program of complete disorder of the world". On the other hand, the field that centers Africanity, strongly connected to popular traditions in Latin America, emphasizes resistance, particularly cultural resistance and the recovery of African cultural and civilizational values. It views the Black people in the diaspora not as descendants of slaves, a condition imposed contingently and accidentally, but as descendants of powerful and vibrant African cultures and civilizations. The consequences and further developments of these articulations will be discussed in the following chapters. For now, however, it is crucial to highlight how this conceptual articulation reflects a historical transition, theorized as a transformation in the structuralist sense, in which each version of a myth is a transformation of another, with all versions being "true" (Lévi-Strauss, 1975). The passage from African to enslaved represents a transition from a relatively autonomous subjectivity—rooted in distinct cultural foundations—to total uprooting. In different historical-sociological contexts, these transitions unfolded as transformations of that original expropriation or violence, which serves as the basis for the possibilities of development within this relationship. Paul Gilroy emphasizes the middle passage, the critical moment of forced transposition aboard slave ships between Africa and the Americas, as a *locus* for theorizing the experience of newly enslaved subjects, subjected to the machinery of colonial terror. He underscores the instability and modernity of racial terror in this context (Gilroy, 2001). In a sense, the middle passage could be considered a historical rite of passage, with clear personal effects on the enslaved individuals buried in historical archives, as well as broader and more complex political and ontological effects observed in the structural transition that transformed Yoruba, Igbo, Fon, and other subjects into slaves. As in the classic structure of a rite of passage (separation – liminality – integration), this transformation involves dying (symbolically) and being born again with a new social status (Turner, 1974). Those who underwent this historical, metaphysical, mystical, concrete, and personal passage died on the shores of Africa and in the holds of slave ships. The question becomes: After this descent into the infernos of the anti-Black world, have we been capable of an effective rebirth?

CHAPTER 2
ARRASTÃO: DECOLONIZING GENDER AND SEXUALITY IN PAGODE BAIANO

"We have here the whole range from overall negation to singular and specific recognition. It is precisely this fragmented and bloody history that we must sketch on the level of cultural anthropology."
— **Frantz Fanon, Racism and Culture, 1956**

ARRASTÃO

In March 2020, at the onset of the COVID-19 pandemic, which abruptly imposed drastic changes on the daily lives of millions due to quarantine measures, São Paulo rapper Rincón Sapiência released the music video "Arrastão" in collaboration with the Bahian electronic/pagode group ÀTTOOXXA. Celebrating the joy and sensuality characteristic of Afro-Brazilian experience, particularly Bahian popular culture, the artists reinterpret the heterogenous *corpus* that informs this experience—what Raymond Williams terms a "structure of feeling" (Williams, 1979)—rooted in the peripheral realities of Bahia. At the same time, they emulate the rhythmic creativity of pagodão, which electronically updates a centuries-old trajectory of aesthetic inventiveness and cultural resistance. The tactile and multi-textural sensuality of Black skins, set against a backdrop of the "favela" or "quebrada", portrays a scene of racial and sexual rebellion within a controlled environment that metaphorically captures the countercultural Afro-Bahian insurgency.

The trope of the arrastão, akin to the rolezinho of the 2010s, theatricalizes central aspects of anti-Blackness in Brazil. This racialized panic is often coded as moral hysteria by the media and bourgeois public opinion, as demonstrated in the following examples.

For instance, on November 30, 2013, an open-air funk dance party at Enseada do Suá beach in Vitória, Espírito Santo, was dispersed by the military police using their customary methods. While some claimed the dispersal was due to fights or the presence of minors and drug trafficking, others argued it was merely local youth enjoying themselves and listening to funk, a genre demonized as the soundtrack of Brazilian favelas. A cellphone video circulated online shows a group of boys fleeing the police and seeking refuge at a nearby mall, Shopping Vitória. The police were called, and the youth were detained and forced to line up. Heavily armed officers made them sit shirtless on the floor of the mall's food court with their hands on their heads before escorting them out in single file, met with applause from onlookers[23] (Pinho, 2018; Belchior, 2013; Kreep, 2013a, 2013b; Miranda, 2013).

A few days later, on December 9, approximately 6,000 to 10,000 young people—according to media reports and Rádio CBN (Central Brasileira de Notícias)—gathered for an event organized via social media outside Shopping Itaquera in São Paulo. The city, a financial and industrial hub of Brazil, is notorious for its stark socio-spatial segregation. While news sites described the event as a "*funk* party", mainstream newspapers and TV outlets labeled it an "arrastão", "debandada", or "invasion". The police responded with even greater violence than in Vitória, deploying rubber bullets and tear gas (Kreep, 2013a, 2013b; CBN, 2013).

On a sunny Sunday in 2014, nearly a year after the emergence of the rolezinho phenomenon, the Rio de Janeiro Military Police launched "Operation Summer" on the beaches of the city's South Zone. This area, a major tourist destination and home to the local middle class, became the focus of a large mobilization involving 650 military police officers, supported by civil police and municipal guards. According to *O Globo*, a Brazilian newspaper, the first day of the operation coincided with several public disturbances, including beach thefts. The newspaper reported that groups of young people roamed the sand, robbing and frightening beachgoers. A street beer vendor told a Globo reporter that "the feeling was one of panic". At least 15 people, including eight minors, were arrested, and the police used tear gas and dogs to quell the alleged unrest (Leal & Menasce, 2014).

We can trace back to the 1990s when the beaches of Rio de Janeiro witnessed a phenomenon that set the stage for the hysterical media reaction to rolezinhos. This refers to the infamous arrastões (crowds of alleged

---

[23] See: www.youtube.com/watch?v=WoLa1Rw42b8 Last accessed August 6, 2025 at 1:37 pm.

looters). It all began in 1992, during the gubernatorial campaign of Benedita da Silva, the first Black woman to run for governor of Rio de Janeiro, who was leading in the polls at the time. On another sunny summer Sunday, reports of arrastões emerged and soon multiplied. A web of connections with deep historical significance resurfaced, crystallizing in the arrastões, which were primarily a media-driven phenomenon reflecting fear of racialized and "dangerous" urban crowds, a fear that has haunted Brazil's white public opinion throughout the postabolition era. The arrastão thus became a central trope in the production of moral panic in contemporary urban Brazil, articulating the bodies of young Blacks with crime, favelas, and, of course, funk music (or its Bahian counterpart, pagodão). These young Black boys would occupy the beach in much the same way as they "invaded" shopping malls, singing funk as they went (Amar, 2013; Cunha, 2001).

This chapter focuses on pagode baiano as a central object of interest, treating it as an indicator of social structures and experiences objectified as racialized and gendered categories embedded in public social life and historical records of both aesthetic and political invention. The objectification of these categories, which will be described and analyzed, occurs through essentially performative modalities, transfigured into specific "scenes" in which the "resistance of the object" (Moten, 2003) can be articulated. As I will elaborate in the final chapter, the "scene" can be defined within a performative, experiential, and productive register, whether as ritual or as the coordination of repertoires. It establishes a context for symbolic action that is not necessarily representational, defining subjects and resources for resisting or reconfiguring social death, genocide, or structural anti-Blackness. This "scene" is located within a specific context, as Raquel Souza (2017) observes: "In Salvador, Bahia, the police's deadly violence inscribes race into space, and, in doing so, produces the city's outskirts as a land in which the state's right to kill is given" (p. 34). State violence inscribes race—and, I would add, gender—through its violent practices, creating a scene in which subjects are sustained through practices grounded in repertoires, as Christen Smith (2016) also suggests. Against the "site-specific" dimension of the scene, understood as a coordination of vernacular repertoires (Kwon, 1997), the state, the market, or other institutions establish a "setting" that is codified and regulated, subordinated to the logic of representation rather than lived experience.

As I propose, pagode baiano serves as a scene of racialized and gendered subjective rebellion, offering a critical, vernacular counterpoint to the monumentalization and codification of African and Afro-Brazilian traditions within an ideologized setting. In this setting, "miscegenation", as both a political category and a central trope of national/colonial culture, can be interrogated. In this sense, in the first section, I aim to define the articulations of race and gender that produce miscegenation as an operative concept within the colonial setting. In the second section, drawing on the research and intervention experience of the project "Brincadeira de Negão: Subjetividade e Identidade de Jovens Homens Negros no Recôncavo da Bahia" [Black Man's Play: Subjectivity and Identity of Young Black Men in the Recôncavo of Bahia], I will ethnographically outline the architecture of the scene of rebellion—of race, gender, and sexuality—within pagode baiano.

An important remark: Our project has developed as one focused on racialized masculinities, a field in which I have personally been engaged in recent years. This means that a masculine perspective would necessarily receive more visibility here. However, this subjective position, or emphasis on Black masculinity, should not be mistaken for an attempt to universalize or erase the voices and experiences of women. On the contrary, it seeks precisely to reframe the man within his contingent, structured, and local precarities. The masculine voice that occasionally speaks here speaks solely for itself and fully acknowledges, I acknowledge, with no negotiation, the central role of Black women in telling their own stories.

THE COLONIAL CONTEXT OF MISCEGENATION

"The history of Blackness is testament to the fact that objects can and do resist", Fred Moten tells us (2003, p. 1). In a certain sense, Blackness as a critical formation within the framework of "Black reason" entails a tense equilibrium between two foundational sources for the Black subject in modernity (Mbembe, 2014). These archetypal images, subjective representations, and conceptual figures contribute to a structure of meanings, which can also be understood as a colonial political economy. These figures might be described as the "slave" or, alternatively, the "African". Each of these vectors of political and subjective articulation carries its own potentials and contradictions. In Brazil and Latin America, Africanity has been the central element in critical and emancipatory discourses and practices, both vernacular and scholarly. However, in anglophone contexts, the figure of the slave, slavery, and social death have gained increasing prominence (Wilderson, 2018, p. 1).

The perspective of Africanity, and even the African one, is undoubtedly of enormous relevance, embedding itself in a long and fruitful tradition of political, social, and artistic thought. Recently, African critiques of Western categories and their application in African contexts have gained significant attention, exemplified by the work of Oyèrónkẹ Oyěwùmí (1997). However, even Oyěwùmí's work has been criticized for being essentially "nativist" or "authenticist" (Bakare-Yusuf, 2003).

In this chapter, I adopt a perspective that seeks to explore the critical potentialities of the concept of social death to interrogate the possibilities and constraints for a decolonial critique of gender and sexuality. This approach aims to recognize a Black, Afro-Brazilian, or diasporic perspective, defined by the historical formation of Blackness under the weight of patriarchal, colonial, and fundamentally anti-Black power structures, as a definitive stage in decolonial critique. To pursue this, it is essential to consider the backdrop of the discursive formation of miscegenation in its structural connection to the racialization of gender and sexuality.

As is well known, in the New World, what we might anthropologically refer to as Afro-descendant "kinship" has long been subject to surveillance, admonishment, pathologization, and even criminalization by the state. From an anthropological standpoint, kinship theory—particularly within British structural-functionalism—is, broadly speaking, a theory of practice that reveals how societies self-institute over time, maintaining relative stability through structural positions that incorporate and neutralize social change (Radcliffe-Brown, 1989). In the Americas, however, such control historically relates to sexual interdictions, Jim Crow laws, the criminalization of Black men, the erasure of Black families, and the ideology of "purity of blood" (Stolke, 2006; Cohen, 1999; Wynter, 2003). Slavery, in turn, is the haunting presence within the machinery of kinship, as explored in "Is Kinship Always Already Heterosexual?" (Butler, 2003).

The enslaved body, reduced to "flesh", is simultaneously much more and much less than the empirical support for the structural reproduction of society. To treat the body as natural—or as merely secondary to meaning, as if a physical, unquestioned infrastructure serves as the foundation upon which meaning is inscribed—is to enact a kind of "forgetting". It ignores how the material body has become a trope, a produced, contested, conquered, and plundered territory of the colonial enterprise. This omission obscures how the body, in its variations and characteristic positions, is discursively and politically constructed (perhaps most profoundly by the state), making it historical and contingent (Butler, 2003). This contingency is defined by the suppression of meaning imposed upon the enslaved, situating the Black body at what Hortense Spillers (1987) describes as the "zero degree of social conceptualization that does not escape concealment under the brush of discourse or the reflections of iconography" (p. 67). In the context of slavery-based colonialism and the anti-Black world, the Black body must struggle, resist, and object within a predefined arena to be recognized as aligned with a coherent and legible subjectivity.

However, within the discursive formation of miscegenation, the Black body is totemized, representing the nation as fundamentally mestizo. Yet this essentialization operates as a grand phantasmagoria, structured around the same racial categories of the 19th century, exposing the deeply colonial character of Brazil's racial ideology. The contradictions of the racialized social structure inevitably weigh upon the constitution of a fractured, violated, and deterritorialized subjectivity, which aligns with the objectification of Black people in the national discourse. This objectification denies their existence as subjects and citizens, as persons and as "human".

The preparation of the body for labor and for the exploitation of others is a political-economic process that transforms the body into a symbolic repository of domination. As Aníbal Quijano (2007) notes, "corporeality is the decisive level of power relations" (p. 124). The control of the body and the condemnation of subaltern groups to a "geography of skin and race" (Cardoso, 1986), embodied in their subjugated, expropriated, stripped, and abused bodies, lies at the core of the configuration that theoretical critique must confront. This confrontation enables us to envision the colonial body as the axis of a centuries-long political struggle.

If it is indeed true that the sexual cultures of Brazil, as well as those of other Latin American countries, allow room for ambiguity and fluidity in social relationships and identities, this ambiguity has often been interpreted as a certain permissiveness of social boundaries. Such permissiveness unfolds either as an inventive, playful characteristic or as an association between sexual ambiguity and broader racial or ethnic ambiguity—without, however, challenging the boundaries themselves.

The construction of the nation, particularly through the lens of the gendered Black subject, is thus deeply entangled in the strategies of the discourse of miscegenation, as highlighted by Sexton. This is particularly significant in the Brazilian context, given the centrality of the mestizo (mixed-race) narrative as an interpretive paradigm (Sexton, 2008; Pinho, 2004). Sexton rightly argues that miscegenation has never impeded the full operation of white supremacy in the United States, the Caribbean, or other regions.[24] Celebrating miscegenation and emphasizing syncretic,

---

[24] Notably, despite the ideological emphasis on *mestiçagem* (racial mixing), at least half of the Brazilian population identifies as "white" according to the Brazilian Institute of Geography and Statistics (IBGE). More specifically, 47.7% of the population self-reported as white in the 2010 demographic census (http:// censo2010.ibge.gov.br/sobre-censo).

mestizo, or hybrid characteristics, whether to define the phenomenological or ontological nature of colonial subjects, inevitably implies the logical recognition of an original moment of purity or the existence of a stock of "pure" races, for in order for miscegenation to be meaningful. As Sexton also observes, the ultimate foundation of the praise for mestiçagem lies in the denial of Blackness and the deliberate effort to suppress and silence it (Pinho, 2004; Sexton, 2008). Or, as Mariza Corrêa (1996) aptly stated, it represents the negation of the "negra preta".

In Gilberto Freyre's work, the figure of the Brazilian mulatto occupies a particularly significant role, as is well known. The mulatto, through their presence in the urban-historical scene and in the discursive landscape of an entire constellation that Freyre helped to construct, serves as both an agent and a product of the process of accommodating antagonistic classes—whites and Blacks, in Freyre's terminology. Moreover, the mulatto bacharel (mulatto Bachelor of Law) embodies the transitional, modernizing phase of Brazilian society, moving from a colonial "Eastern" structure toward urban modernization. Ultimately, the mulatto becomes the typical representation of the new "technical" element essential to the transformation of Brazilian society, as it moved away from rigid, estate-based structures toward a supposedly open, class-based societal model, in opposition to the caste system (Freyre, 1995, p. 2000).

While not neglecting their physical attributes or the "pure prestige of this beauty", Freyre voyeuristically frames the mulatto's tanned, mestiço, and national body—adorned with French or English ideas and a gallant aptitude for charm or flattery—as a means of climbing the steep ascent of social mobility. In this sense, the mulatto represents the embodiment of social mobility, integration across social divides, and the construction of a national body, dark-skinned yet wearing a white mask. However, the national body of the mulatto appears to signify much more than a mere accommodation of antagonisms or an eroticized synthesis of racial contradictions. The insertion of this significant corporeality into the historical and cultural narrative establishes a space of unresolved tension, a terrain for a subjectivity defined by and habituated to crisis.

This crisis reflects the indecisiveness or inconclusiveness between diverse, often self-contradictory discursive and political systems that find personification in the figure of the mulatto. Around this constitutive crisis, the formation of Black, dark-skinned, or parda [mixed-race] subjectivity in modern Brazil is shaped, a process warranting further emphasis on specific dimensions of this ongoing dynamic.

The articulation of mestiçagem [racial mixing] as the creation of an external boundary to racial purity exists as a myth that necessitates impurity, as a fantasy or a fixation on subverting the very boundaries that establish and define a cohesive identity for whiteness. This interaction (of miscegenation) operates within the framework of heteronormativity, seamlessly aligning with the discourse of racial difference production. At the core of this residual logic, which positions Blackness as the waste or remainder of the destabilization (or re-stabilization) of stable identities and subjectivities, lies the mestiço offspring as the living border of purified whiteness (Moutinho, 2004).

Miscegenation, as a secular heteropatriarchal act, thus underpins (or merges) the integrity of race and the identity of the nation. This mobilization, however, appears as a "structured installation at the nexus of sexuality and violence" (Sexton, 2008, p. 232), as euphemized by the historical and mythical narratives of colonial miscegenation (Carneiro, 2011). For instance, this can be seen in the foundational myth of Bahia, which centers on the union between the Indigenous woman Catarina Paraguaçu and the Portuguese castaway Diogo Álvares de Souza, known as Caramuru (Polito, 2005; Santos, 2013).

> Spouse (the beautiful one says), I ignore your name;
> Yet your heart I know, for in my chest
> Since the moment I saw you, I have adored you:
> I do not know if it was already love or respect;
> But of what I saw then, and what I now examine,
> I am certain that from two hearts, only one was made.
> I desire your baptism, I desire your church,
> Let my people be yours, and your God, mine.
> (Durão, 2005, p. 80)

It is not, on the other hand, by chance that popular thought is steeped in the belief that sexuality is dangerous and must, if not suppressed, at least be controlled and confined within the narrow limits of its social function, namely, reproduction. However, sex, as a social relation, is itself produced and serves as a point of articulation for the construction of sexually distinct and separate bodies (Rubin, 1975). Nevertheless, or perhaps because of this, the sexual system is not monolithic but is permeated by ongoing battles and conflicts over values, methods, arrangements, privileges, and legitimacies. Thus, in many cases, the struggle to regulate sexual life becomes a struggle to differentiate "acceptable" bodies and sexualities from those deemed unacceptable or unassimilable. These marginalized bodies and sexualities are frequently relegated to ghettoized, peripheral, or marginalized forms of social existence.

The dissolution of sexual binaries and the critique of the discursive and political foundations of the social representation of sexual dimorphism should, therefore, not be seen merely as an intellectual postmodern whim. Instead, it should be recognized as a critical tool for dismantling oppressive structures of race, class, and nation that depend on these oppositions to sustain their practices and discourses. The foundations of such transformations, or their inspiration, should be sought in practical and vernacular modes of social life and sexuality, notably in those situated at the borders, the peripheries, and "contact zones", sexual ghettos in the urban centers of large cities, marginalized yet inventive experiences of bodily reinvention that occur under conditions of poverty, segregation, and violations of rights. This approach must also consider how the processes of colonization and racialization have historically constituted a project of gendering, introducing gender categories into the colonial space of death as a tool of domination, operationalized through continuous and extensive sexual violence (Terrefe, 2020).

What perplexes me is the fervor with which young Black voices, often male, advocate for fidelity to the dichotomous complementarity between Black men and women as the civilizational political foundation of the "Black family". This advocacy conveniently overlooks the fact that the nuclear, monogamous, patriarchal family is a Western invention, a tool for the subjugation of women, the "perverse", and racialized, hyper-sexualized subjects.

The consideration of such issues allowed political scientist Cathy Cohen (2004) to develop a "Black" critique of queer studies, which primarily focus on the reproduction of the essentialized dichotomy between heterosexuality and homosexuality. As Cohen argues, challenging heteronormativity requires openness to understanding how intersectional variables shape queer subjects in diverse ways. Moreover, an intersectional approach should highlight how other social subjects are persecuted and degraded due to sexual behaviors intersecting with race and class. It should also demonstrate how oppression, injustice, and violence connect to the subjective experiences of certain social actors, without necessarily presupposing stable subjects or identities defined as bearers of essentialized and autonomous sexualities.

To address the issues raised by queer theory in the Latin American context, I would consider the Brazilian and broader Latin American settings and the local forms of inequality reproduction. These contexts are fundamentally marked by the coloniality of power, which establishes the frameworks and structures for defining racialized bodies and for controlling, surveilling, and disciplining sexualities (Quijano, 2007). As Carlos Figari (2007) points out, "the discourses and silences" surrounding sexuality have been, and continue to be, sources of injustice, violence, and deprivation of rights in Latin America. They occupy a central place in structures of domination and stigmatization of the poor masses, who, for example, are often viewed as promiscuous and non-modern. Their ways of life, largely shaped by the specific trajectories of modernity in the region, are typically framed as backward, hierarchical, and obscurantist, or as passive victims of the past and tradition.

The differentiation and colonial hierarchization of bodies demand their regulation, particularly through mechanisms of racialization and sexualization. These processes serve to distinguish between the "savage" (Black, Indigenous, and mixed-race individuals) and the "civilized", which Figari (2020) describes as the "constitutive metaphor of the Latin American colonial system" (p. 1).

In this context, the colonizer, portrayed as white and heterosexual, like Caramuru, occupied the discursive position of the sexually active, penetrating, and civilizing male, a producer of history and culture. Meanwhile, Black people, Indigenous people, women, and sexual "perverts" were relegated to a passive position as objects of domination and discipline, associated with the abject realm of untamable and dangerous sexuality. This enthronement of the white male was, in fact, fundamentally a process of legitimizing the economic expropriation of goods, bodies, territories, and labor. Thus, slavery, the "ghost in the machine", retains its structural character, simultaneously influencing both sexualities and races (Figari, 2006).

In modern times, authoritarian states and regimes, such as the Brazilian government of 2021, have paid considerable attention to sexuality, viewing it as a territory to be conquered, mapped, and controlled by masculinist powers in militarized states (Amar, 2013). However, within the colonial struggles that produced racialized bodies and subjects, counter-hegemonic forms of resistance also emerged. These forms are popular, vernacular, dispersed, hybrid, and often ironic, exemplified by cultural expressions such as funk and pagode. Alternative models of sexuality and body, masculinity and femininity, and identity have provided the foundation for a modern epistemic otherness rooted in colonial bodies and peoples.

These alternative epistemologies and corporalities have been excluded from national, symbolic, and political agreements, relegated to the status of residues, curiosities, or evidence of backwardness. Alternatively, they have been incorporated and cannibalized by near-white or criollo elites in modernist efforts to appropriate popular cultural expressions. When Black or Indigenous cultures are anthropophagized in this manner, they become totems used to exorcise the physical presence of Black and Indigenous people themselves, rather than their cultures (Latin American Subaltern Studies Group, 1995; Nunes, 1994).

This colonial or racializing aspect of Latin American structures of domination has been described as a specific coloniality of power. The structural and ideological effects of colonialism did not end with the national emancipations of the 19th century. On the contrary, these emancipations often represented a new form of subjugation, mediated by internal colonialism, and transmuted into analogous forms. These forms were embedded in racial mysticism, sexual hierarchies, colonial patriarchy, and its various mutating manifestations (Maldonado-Torres, 2007; Quijano, 2007).

These structures are also forms of subjectivation. As bell hooks (2004) argues, Black men, in their struggle for recognition, adopted the Western patriarchal model—rooted in modern capitalist slavery—as their framework for power. Hooks refers to this as "plantation patriarchy", a model against which Humanity itself was measured. Similarly, Maria Lugones (2007) asserts that "the white colonizer constructed a powerful inside force as colonized men were co-opted into patriarchal roles" (p. 200).

Teresa Caldeira (2000, 2006) describes as "disjunctive" the contradictory nature of democratization processes in Brazil and Latin America. This disjuncture is evident in the militarization of societies and the criminalization of the poor, legacies of authoritarian regimes. Under the guise of combating drug trafficking and crime, repressive policies perpetuate violence and the criminalization of subaltern masculinities (Amar, 2013). Thus, individuals positioned outside the "national pact", urban outcasts, racialized and sexualized, are subjected to what the state deems appropriate treatment. The modernization of Latin American societies has advanced in tandem with the reproduction of colonial forms of domination, characterized by persistent inequality and "modern" authoritarianism. The criminalization of the poor, particularly racialized poor men, is intrinsic to this political economy of the body, in which phenomena such as the "arrastão", the "rolezinho", funk, and pagode set the stage.

The concrete acts of lethal violence represent perhaps the most dramatic aspect of this disjunction, manifested as the broader complex of anti-Black genocide. This phenomenon was initially described in its multidimensionality by Abdias do Nascimento and has recently been revisited by Ana Flauzina, João Costa Vargas, Jayme Amparo Alves, and others (Flauzina, 2008; Alves, 2013; Nascimento, 1978; Vargas, 2010a). The anti-Black genocide and the lethal actions of the racialized colonial state in Brazil can be interpreted as transformations or metamorphoses of social death.

In "Slavery and Social Death", Orlando Patterson (2008[1982]) argues: "Enslavement, slavery and manumission are not merely related events; they are one and the same process in different phases" (p. 412). Thus, the enslaved condition, defined by natal alienation, essential indignity, or, in a phrase, social death, does not end with manumission or abolition. Instead, it persists over time, solidifies in history, and is reflected in cultural representations (Sexton, 2011).

In the colonial world, or one marked by the coloniality of power, slavery did not truly end. It remains a shadow shaping the contours of subjectivation, social life, participation in culture, and citizenship. This framework also informs the racialized formation of masculinities, which are defined through a specular and perverse relationship with the White Man. These dynamics underscore the political centrality of sexuality in the invention of (post)colonial pornotropic power, as well as in the invention of Blackness itself and its inherent contradictions (Gordon, 1999; McClintock, 2010).

The condition of social death is intrinsically linked to the structural position of Blackness, which is defined not only as the negation of whiteness but also of Humanity itself. This framework renders Black subjects killable, Black bodies violable, and Black culture expropriated, reduced to the ghostly emanation of a dancing corpse that entertains, as on the plantation (or in modern Bahia), its masters (Sexton, 2011; Hartman, 1997).

The political work of decolonization, therefore, must necessarily involve bodily decolonization as a form of political emancipation. This entails recognizing the historical mechanisms of inequality production embedded in settings, trajectories, identities, and bodily performances. It also requires understanding the specific ways in which these dynamics interact structurally and dynamically with the constitution, representation, and circulation of bodies. The colonial political economy of the body appears intrinsically tied to a libidinal political economy of sexual abuse. As Maldonado-Torres (2007) states, "Once defeated in war, they are seen as perpetual servants or slaves, and their bodies become part of an economy of sexual abuse, exploitation, and control" (p. 139).

We return to Gilberto Freyre, the authoritative founder of the primary discursive matrix in this constellation, which outlines the foundational structure of the colonial racialization of gender and sexuality, directly tied to our objectification as slaves. The coloniality of power, a defining feature of systems of representation and classification and racial/sexual regimes of truth, thus imposed, under the pressure of violence and depersonalization, the prevalence of the slaveholding sadism that Freyre himself describes.

Much like Gayle Rubin (1993), who, in her analysis of psychoanalysis and structuralism, acknowledges the utility of their diagnoses but critiques their politically skewed interpretations, I also see in Freyre a compelling diagnosis that articulates domination and eroticization. Within the familial structure of colonial patriarchy, the subjugation of Black men and women to labor inherently contained, as is not difficult to imagine, elements of despotic eroticization imposed upon the body of the other (Aidoo, 2018). As even Freyre (1995) himself admitted, "There is no slavery without sexual depravity" (p. 316).

The sexual education of young masters often climbed the soft ladder of Black bodies: first, by sexually subjecting the "moleques", young Black boys who were play companions for the young masters, and later, the housemaids and mulatto women who were readily available as slaves.

> The furor femineus of the Portuguese was often exercised upon victims who did not always reciprocate in pleasure. However, there are accounts of instances where the sadism of the white conqueror was met with the masochism of Indigenous or Black women. This applies to the sadism directed from men toward women—frequently preceded by the dynamic of master toward the moleque. Through the submission of the moleque, the young master's play companion, often referred to as a punching bag, the white master was frequently initiated into physical love. (Freyre, 1995, p. 50)

As Robert Young further develops, the production of sexualized and racialized subjects under colonial regimes cannot be disentangled from the material and economic production processes of the colonial world and its hierarchies. In this sense, slavery and the plantation functioned as both a setting and a laboratory for the racialization of sexuality.

It is clear that the forms of sexual exchange brought about by colonialism were themselves both mirrors and consequences of the modes of economic exchange constituted the basis of colonial relations. (Young, 2002, p. 181)

As Luiz Mott illustrates, perhaps inadvertently, the anthropologist is the author of a significant and highly original body of work on colonial sexuality, contributing to the emergence of insights into past moralities and powers. Mott cites, for example, Captain Cardonega, who in 1681 penned the following scandalous lines about Angola: "Among the gentiles of Angola, there is much sodomy, with them engaging in their impurities and filth with one another, dressing as women. They are called quimbanda in the local language, and in the districts or lands where they exist, they interact with one another." (1992)

Mott's work also brought attention to figures such as Xica Manicongo, an enslaved person—who we would today describe as transgender—and a sorceress accused by the inquisition of sodomy and dressing as a woman. Through Mott's authoritative voice, we hear the story of this quimbanda sorceress, reinscribing the immense bodily, sexual, and political otherness (that was forged under the terror of slavery) within Freyre's framework of the "synthesis of antagonisms". In another instance, Mott describes the case of Pero Garcia, a married 42-year-old sugar mill owner in Peroaçu, who was brought before the inquisition in 1618. He was accused of committing the sin of sodomy with two freed mulattos, who were "residents in his household", and two slaves, one of whom was between six and seven years old at the time. Confronted with such sources, Mott (1988) cautiously reflects: "In this case, it is impossible to determine whether there was physical violence or moral coercion on the part of the master toward his subordinates" (p. 30).

Sexuality, desire, and the eroticization of racialized bodies thus emerge, despite mestizo interpretations, as one of the primary languages of (colonial) power and (racial) domination in Brazil. This is because it is precisely through the articulation of pleasure and power that the racialized historicity of colonialism becomes incarnated in bodies, constituting them as sites of representation and production. This articulation links the self/ body/ society, defining subjects as either dispossessed or dominant within the erotic games that stage both pleasure and violation. These dynamics, as we shall see, underline the theatrical interplay between desire and domination in the colonial context.

THE SCENE OF REBELLION IN BAHIAN *PAGODE*

On a hot and humid night, I find myself standing in front of one of the many bars lining Porto's bustling and vibrant waterfront, in the city of Cachoeira. Just a few meters away is the square 25 de Junho, a polyphonic center of a "fractal" re-territorialization of Black diasporic culture, interwoven with colonial memory and the fugitive[25] discursivities of the Black experience, a transatlantic process of revaluing all values (Gilroy, 2001).

From within the masonry structure housing an inner courtyard, the deafening sound of a "paredão de pagode"—at the time, I didn't fully understand what it was—hits me like a massive wave of vibration and sensuality. At the entrance, a group of young Black men in caps and baggy clothes form a sort of barrier. Some secure their oversized caps with colorful girl's barrettes. Dancing and chatting, they create a kind of waiting room, a prelude to the main interior space. When I decide to step inside, a narrow corridor leads me toward the main hall. Suddenly, a loud bang electrifies the air. Smoke and the acrid smell of gunpowder overwhelm the senses. A gunshot has been fired. Panic erupts, with people running and screaming amidst the haze and the overwhelming blast of percussive music pounding: "You want it? Take it! Want it? Take it! Want it? Take it! Want it?"

It was only years later that I began to understand the performative structure underlying this precariously witnessed scene. After attending several paredões and engaging more consistently with the Brincadeira de Negão Project, the contours of meaning and invention within these collective gatherings of low-income youth—almost all of them Black—became clearer. They would assemble around the electronic sound system, mounted on a wooden stand and attached to a car like a trailer, easily moved and transported.

The Paredão de Som, or more specifically, the Paredão de Pagode, is a culturally driven and sociologically situated invention. Its origins date back to the 1970s, rooted in the ancestral *sound system* culture that, from the Caribbean to New York, transformed Western music through the invention of hip-hop and the reinvention of public engagement with the body and the streets. Within the broader politics of representation in the African

---

[25] The term *fugitive* is employed in the sense developed by Harney and Moten (2013): "We're in trance that's under and around us. We move through it, and it moves with us, out beyond the settlements, out beyond the redevelopment, where black night is falling where we hate to be alone, back inside to sleep till morning, drink till morning, plan till morning, as the common embrace, right inside, and around, the surround." (Harney & Moten, 2013, p. 19)

diaspora, *sound systems*, paredões, or the "aparelhagem" from Brazil's North and Northeast regions reflect a self-conscious and reflective engagement with the socio-historical contradictions and the racialized Black body in the modern global class society.

Image 2 — Paredão de Pagode in Cachoeira
Source: Author's collection, 2010.

In Cachoeira, along the Feira do Porto waterfront, as in many other contexts, the music of pagode baiano or pagodão, often performed through what I have recently learned is called "automotive sound" or "paredões", becomes an occasion for the ritualized celebration of specific values and formal structures. These are framed in this context as the ritualized performance of socio-historical and structural contradictions. Such values and structures bear no connection to the bourgeois repertoire of respectability and decorum (Gordon, 1997). On the contrary, they evoke an atmosphere of debauchery and hypersexualization, featuring the choreographic evolution of unassimilable and "abject" subjects, such as travestis[26] and other gender non-conformists and sexual dissidents. They also include young men from the peripheries, embodying the *vida loka* aesthetic with caps,

[26] T. N.: *Travesti* is a specific gender identity and cultural category in Brazil that has specific social and political significance. Travestis do not align perfectly with Western understandings of gender as they embrace a fluid identity that challenges binary norms.

tattoos, and batidão [a big golden necklace] (Pinho & Rocha, 2011); and women and girls adopting a dangerous or "thug" style, who shake their asses to the ground and "rub their pussies on the asphalt", thus mocking decency and morality.

These "unworthy" or "abject" subjects are often aggressively associated with pagodão as a *locus* of this "abjection"—a space marked as dirty, dangerous, and a territory of anti-civilizational "low behavior" (Pinho, 2014).[27]

Historically and structurally, the fundamental indignity, indeed, the dehumanization of racialized subjects has been tied to their sexualization. Race as sexuality underpins both the recurrent condemnations of Black impropriety and their musical expressions, as well as the efforts of those attempting to convince the white world that Black people could be just as respectable as any other race, honest women, upright men (Gordon, 1997). However, in pagode, as in other contexts, it emerges as the collective performance of subjective dissidence. Here, we can observe a dizzying parade of marginalized subjects moving through deteriorated settings: the "whore", the "thief", the "fag".

The sexualization of race and the racialization of sexuality rely on moral boundaries that remain fundamentally colonial. These boundaries define bodily epistemologies designed to produce or attempt to produce docile bodies, a newly "assimilated" habitus that exists in permanent contradiction with the fundamental, epidermal, phobogenic reality of Blackness, as Harney and Moten (2013) argue.

Lewis Gordon insists on the articulation of gender to the "ontological precariousness"—nothingness—that defines Blackness in the anti-Black or colonial world. As many scholars have emphasized, the racialization of sexuality and the sexualization of race are fundamental mechanisms of postcolonial biopolitics. From this perspective, Blackness, as a structural condition shaped by a framework of inherently violated subjective dispositions, is fundamentally an absence or void, defined by an ontological precariousness rooted in a phenomenology of racism as lived through the body. This precariousness reflects "the lived experience of the Black man", as an emptying, self-abandonment, and a yearning for recognition through the gaze of whiteness, the only gaze that could, albeit inadequately, offer Black Men the certainty of their own "being" (Gordon, 1999; Fanon, 1983).

---

[27] It is worth noting that the rebellious and fugitive aspects of pagode carry many contradictions, which can sometimes be difficult for the communities where these events take place to endure. These include, notably, the degradation of public spaces and living conditions, as well as the opportunities that the paredões sometimes create for the eruption of violence. On the other hand, such contradictions or side effects are an integral part of the rebellious scene being perpetrated.

Historically, Black communities have sought to escape this dilemma by embracing so-called politics of respectability. Adopting, often to our own detriment, the same Eurocentric, bourgeois, patriarchal values that oppress us. Across the spectrum of sexual preferences, there emerges a shared anxiety to conform, often through negation, to the moral expectations of dominant culture. As Mara Viveros-Vigoya (2015) and others have shown, in Latin America's postcolonial societies, morality functions as a colonial boundary, defining "us" and "others". In this context, Black communities often respond with hyper-moralization and the demonization of women with autonomous sexual behavior or men engaging in homoerotic practices. Here, what I want to emphasize is the political significance of Black sexual insubordination, as it destabilizes integration policies that uphold bourgeois morality, patriarchy, and heterosexual norms as paradigms.

The inseparability of Blackness from the commodity form—*absolute nothingness and the world of things*—is historically and structurally established as a general racial antagonism. This defines a structural condition of fungibility, as described by Saxton and Hartman, marking a death-in-life ontology that persists as a paradigmatic model for racialized subject formation. In this view, the experience of the hold (of the slave ship) to this paradigmatic *corpus* represents an experience of vertigo and fantasy—hallucination—amid the terror of oppression and the incessant struggle against one's own body. As Frank Wilderson (2011) states: "Black subjectivity is a crossroads where vertigoes meet, the intersection of performative and structural violence" (p. 1). Similarly, Manthia Diawara (1996) notes that the Black imaginary is far from being a fixed space, much less a repository of colonial stereotypes, yet it cannot avoid engaging with them. But it is, conversely, a space in transformation and self-production in dialogue with unrecognized forms, stereotypes, and/or traditions, which is implicated in continuously reinventing it. The intersection of sexuality and licentiousness in Black culture or the diaspora's imagination can either be channels of expression or starting points for critical deconstruction and reinvention. This remains an open subject, framed by the "war of positions" over the legitimacy of representations of the Black body, its "respectability", or its potential for integration. Suppressing behaviors deemed sexually inappropriate or incompatible with "civilization" often plays a central role in these debates.

Edmund Gordon employs the concept of "cultural repertoires" to illuminate pragmatic identity politics shaping male subjectivities within African American communities (Gordon, 1997). This "repertoire" includes respectability, rooted in patriarchal reinterpretations of African traditions and Christian ideals of decency and responsibility. As Cathy Cohen (2004) notes, it largely aims to achieve social integration and mitigate racism's effects through behavioral discipline and control over women's sexuality and bodies.

The paredão de pagode, this mobile and portable sound system structure, with its technological setup for high-powered sound amplification, operates as a *site-specific* (Kwon, 1997) device that creates its own ambiance, rejecting respectability. Often associated with "automotive sound systems", it amplifies and spectacularizes the experience or essence—of "baixaria" in pagode music through mobility. These performances unfold on beaches, at gas stations, or, as I have often witnessed, along at the shores of Ribeira, in Salvador. There, hundreds of young people, predominantly Black teens from surrounding areas, gather to dance, drink, and enjoy music blasting from parked cars in double-file lines. These "fugitive" parties are abruptly paused whenever police intervene, only to resume once they depart (Harney & Moten, 2013; Pinho, 2014). This performative event in Ribeira mirrors similar gatherings across Salvador's peripheral neighborhoods, connecting the transgressive use of public space with the articulation of popular sexuality enacted as the "baixaria" described by Ledson Chagas (2015). This makes a dispositif [apparatus], which is created like a set of practices, enunciations, symbols, and technological implements.

At least three meanings for the term "dispositif" are available and interrelated within the re-conceptualization effort I propose here. The first meaning is connected to theoretical debates on contemporary art, as discussed by Carvalho (2008). In this case, the apparatus acts as an "experience activator", reconfiguring the traditionally contemplative position of Western art to prioritize the body and lived experience. Here, technology functions as an intensifier of non-linear or "molar" perceptions of the aesthetic and subjective experience of (post)modern individuals. In this context, "the body becomes the privileged site of these experiments" (Carvalho, 2008, p. 43). Second, in Michel Foucault's framework, summarized by Agamben, dispositif is: (1) a thoroughly heterogeneous ensemble consisting of discourses, practices and institutions; (2) a strategic network within power relations; and (3) a means of validating statements. The dispositif of sexuality exemplifies these dimensions: it unifies diverse elements, incites discourse, and wields power to construct the modern subject (Agamben, 2005; Foucault, 2003). Agamben introduces a third dimension, defining dispositifs as mechanisms that have the capacity "to capture, orient, determine, intercept, model, control, or secure the gestures, behaviours, opinions, or discourses of living beings" (Agamben, 2005, p. 14). Thus, essentially functioning as a "machine of subjectification".

Modern capitalism saturates the environment with such devices, producing and dismantling subjectivities in processes Agamben (2005) compares to a "lifeless body" crossed by colossal processes of desubjectification. These three interpretations are not mutually exclusive but operate within a network of perspectives linking "subject" and "power" through the intensification of the "body", object of an "intensification", a platform for subjectification or an artifact of the dispositif of sexuality. The paredão de pagode embodies this framework, intensifying connections between subjectivity, technology, and cultural history—forming a "repertoire", as Diana Taylor (2003) describes, of fragmentations and experiences in an electrifying element of invention, shaping and controlling subjectification processes amidst the contradictions that render it volatile. This "staged" objectification, simultaneously a *locus* of subjection and resistance, highlights the regulatory discourses, sensibilities, and structures of feeling that it disrupts.

Paul Gilroy frames the hybrid transvaluation of the formal elements of the socio-historical experience of slavery, such as ineffable terror, sublimated into what he terms the counterculture of modernity. Fred Moten repositions this dynamic as the insurgency of the object—the commodity—a fungible, tortured embodiment of the fundamental aporia of an economic system that socially produces life while intertwining with death. This system simultaneously presupposes and negates the human being as a commodity (Gilroy, 2001; Moten, 2003). As Gilroy (2001) asserts, "Thinking about music—a non-representational, non-conceptual form—raises aspects of embodied subjectivity that are not reducible to the cognitive and the ethical" (p. 163). It is unsurprising, then, that sexuality and style assume such prominence in these collective, ritualized, and performative assemblages, unsettling the West by recentering the Black body. Sexuality, with its "conflicted representation", emerges as a point of contact between the disciplinary power of modern Western society and the body, a sensorial matter, a phenomenological anchor of the self. It functions as a mask, imposed through fire and iron, mediating the contradictory objectification inherent in the scene of enslaved subjection. Fundamentally, it reflects a sexual perversion integral to a political economy (Hartman, 1997). In this context, sexuality, embodied as "baixaria", becomes both the instrument and the epitome of the essential indignity of an object that dares to represent itself, and must, therefore, be silenced. The kidnapping of the African voice, qua Black, occurred and is repeated in its structural form of dispossession and abuse and implies the dystopian production of a subjugated sexuality that either rebels or becomes domesticated as mestizo respectability. The hypersexual and violent scene of the paredão de pagode is thus a scene of rebellion.

Musical genres associated with Black, African, or "favelada" culture carry a long history of being portrayed in police records and crime journalism as markers of disorder, violence, immorality, and the "debasement" of Western—which we could read as white—values in Brazil. The semantic nexus, sustained by discursive practices, linking "popular", "Black", "African", or "favelada" culture is neither obvious nor automatic but has been historically reconstituted as the site of an underlying ambiguity or ambivalence that shapes the nation as a space of political and discursive negotiation between the descendants of colonizers and the Others of the nation.

The so-called "pagode baiano", which draws massive crowds to public events, dominates contemporary Bahia's soundscapes alongside genres like "arrocha" and "funk", and garners millions of views on online platforms, is, much like "*funk* carioca", frequently associated in media and police records with violence, degradation of the public sphere, and criminality, as we observed before when I described the arrastão (Pinho, 2016). Produced as an abjection, this Black, popular subject who lives in the favela is simultaneously positioned as the foundation of the nation's political pact and yet rejected when making autonomous cultural choices, which are demonized as dark symbols of savagery and "ancestral atavisms".

On June 24, 2014, in São Francisco do Conde, a city near Cachoeira in Bahia's Recôncavo region, ten people were injured, and one person was killed in a shootout during the passage of a sound truck featuring a prominent figure in pagode baiano, singer Igor Kannário, popularly known as "The Prince of the Ghetto".

The crime was attributed to a rivalry between gangs from the nearby city of Santo Amaro, the birthplace of Tropicália icons Caetano Veloso and Maria Bethânia. On the *Correio da Bahia* newspaper website, a reader named Peter Luna expressed, with indignant fury, a common opinion about the singer in question, pagode baiano more broadly, and its fans:

> Many people may not agree with my opinion expressed here. (...). They hire a band that, let's be honest, only plays garbage, incites violence, with immoral songs and pounding beats that make people, already high on drugs, even crazier. That's the truth! Another thing, the ones who like

and follow this stuff are mostly people from the periphery, the majority being illiterate, uncultured, drug addicts, criminals, traffickers, prostitutes—people who have nothing to lose in life! Just look at the images, it's clear. The women, if you can even call them that, are all-in, taking part in the depravation, just like the men. So, what else could you expect to happen? My apologies to this guy who calls himself the prince of the ghetto. You are not a prince at all, man. (*Correio da Bahia*, June 24, 2014)

Young people interviewed in the cities of Cachoeira and São Felix as part of Brincadeira de Negão Project expressed divergent opinions about "Kannário" compared to the one above. For one interviewee, a singer of *funk melody* and openly romantic in his style, Kannário not only incites violence but also promotes the use of illicit drugs. In contrast, another interviewee, who is an Ogan[28] in his candomblé temple, and a former Muay Thai practitioner, described Kannário as almost a leader, the voice of the favela.

There are some people who listen to Kannário and say: "Oh, this guy has no lyrics, he can't sing"; he doesn't seem to have lyrics because you don't know how to listen to the music or the message he's delivering. It's like reggae: some people say reggae is for crazy people or drug users. Reggae isn't about drugs. Reggae is a message—a message the singer is sending to those who enjoy reggae and understand its meaning. Igor Kannário does the same, but not with reggae, with pagode... He delivers a message; he is the voice of the favela. He speaks loudly for everyone to hear what many people in the favela try to say but no one listens to. That's why, in any favela in Brazil, Igor Kannário is embraced; he knows how to voice what the favela wants to express. (Interview, São Felix, 2013)

Thus, for many young people in Cachoeira and São Felix, as well as across Bahia, pagodão artists like Edcity (former member of the band "Fantasmão") or Kannário are valued because they speak the "truth" of the

---

[28] T.N.: In Candomblé, an Ogan is a male initiate chosen by the orishas to play the sacred drums and sing during rituals and ceremonies.

favela or the ghetto. This truth is fundamentally defined by violence. As one of our interlocutors in São Felix explains:

> So that people all across Bahia know what's happening in that place, you know? That's why he [Igor Kannário] is criticized, because the government nowadays only cares about money, money, while the favela is completely torn apart, full of dealers and killers. (Interview, São Felix, 2013)

One of the recurring categories or tropes in the discourse of the subjects within this context, appearing in song lyrics and media representations, is the concept of the "favela". In the context of pagode baiano, this trope is typically contrasted with the "shore". This contrast arises from the geographical and socio-economic layout of Salvador, a city situated at the entrance of the Bay of All Saints. The northern face of the city, oriented toward the Atlantic shoreline, is more valued and hosts predominantly middle-class or white neighborhoods. Conversely, the southern face, facing the Bay of All Saints, is home to the city's popular and historic neighborhoods. Between these two areas lies the so-called "city core marked by extreme urban poverty. This area includes neighborhoods such as Cabula, Cajazeiras, Fazenda Grande, and Pau da Lima, where the majority of Salvador's poor and Black population reside. Thus, the dichotomy of "favela" versus "Orla" [shore] carries not only a geographical meaning but also, and perhaps more importantly, a socio-symbolic significance, allowing for the interchangeability of "favela" with "periferia." In this way, pagoda baiano reflects and reinforces categories rooted in everyday lived experiences, giving tangible shape to social identifications and coalescing subjectivities and categories. This establishes the favelada [favela-based] structures of feeling in opposition to those of the orla.

Another significant category emerging from ethnographic dialogue in the Recôncavo region, which functions as a "structure of feeling" and embodies a specific performance of masculinity, is the concept of "botar a base". This embodiment is both literal and symbolic, as masculinity is condensed into a culturally regulated pose, representing a possible expression of what it means to be a man. "Botar a base" means adopting a physical stance, assuming a combative position. For instance, Catchamer, one of the key interlocutors in the project, illustrates this in a Facebook photo where he poses with boxing gloves. This pose conveys a clear metaphorical meaning, asserting one's masculinity while simultaneously challenging that of the interlocutor. There is, of course, a "theatrical" or performative element to it. It is an enactment in which fearlessness is displayed as a fundamental attribute of manhood. The simulation of violence, its theatricalization, frequent threats of aggression, and even physical confrontations are constant elements in the cultural universe of these subjects, reflecting the broader social landscape.

Within the anthropological tradition, performance studies can be closely linked to the work of Victor Turner (1982). Turner helped define the notion of social drama as the structured enactment of social contradictions, which can become visible and manipulable—that is, objective—through stereotyped behavior. Social dramas are laden with emotional and symbolic intensity, often admitting a cathartic dimension and compelling social antagonisms to align in an agonistic format. As a methodological tool for ethnographic practice, Turner (1982) recommends paying close attention to moments of heightened dramatic intensity, which are structurally defined by elaborated stages. Religious rituals, theatrical dramatizations, and children's games, for example, can be seen as symbolic texts that reveal key aspects of the culture under study, particularly its contradictions and tensions. Turner's model allows almost any form of standardized collective behavior to be interpreted as a ritual expression, whether religious or secular, offering insights into the central structures of the culture in question.

Richard Schechner (2013) has also recently reminded us of the heuristic potential of performance studies. Central to this approach is the incorporation of performance as a mode of establishing, transmitting, and questioning knowledge. This is a point Diana Taylor (2003, 2006) also emphasizes. Taylor is particularly concerned with how performance, defined as expressive behavior, can store and convey knowledge, especially in non-Western or "non-literate" contexts. Socially regulated performances, such as rituals or historical-dramatic enactments—like the ones Taylor analyzes in Tepoztlán, Mexico—can thus be considered embodied modes of knowledge transmission. Similarly, this applies to the Nego Fugido of Acupe, which will be examined in Chapter 5.

Taking performance seriously requires redirecting attention away from discursive or text-based modalities and instead considering the dimensions of bodily presence and the stage/scene—a duality that, in my reading, corresponds to the archive/repertoire distinction, as will be discussed in Chapter 5. This perspective aligns with Smith's discussion in "Scenarios of Racial Contact: Police Violence and the Politics of Performance and Racial Formation in Brazil":

The dialogue between social actors, roles, physical locations, social scripts, gestures, behaviors and attitudes creates racial subjectivities informed by hegemonic epistemologies of race. All of these emerge from tense meetings that are filled with uneven power distributions and informed by historical legacies, social identities and spatial landscapes. (Smith, 2008, p. 3)

The literate modalities of historical and cultural knowledge are associated with what Taylor calls the "archive". In contrast, the "repertoire" encompasses "embodied" modalities, which rely on presence. While embodied modalities are characteristic of non-literate societies, they are by no means exclusive to them. Even within the "literate" world, these modalities continue to produce, register, and transmit knowledge. In the context of a class-based, racialized society, it is evident that social distinctions and power dynamics interact creatively with both modalities. This interaction is particularly visible in practices like "botando a base", where an ideology of gender and race is embodied (Taylor, 2003, 2006).

As expressed in a song by the now extinct pagode group "Fantasmão", which was very popular, "botar a base" represents a masculine attribute tied to confronting contradictions and assuming the role of a "man" within the context of the favela. This is described in the song "Não Vá Que é Barril":

> Ô tiradinho a miserável não bota a base atrás do trio
> Não vá que é barril, não vá que é barril...
> Se um estuprador, pedófilo, na depressão caiu
> Não vá que é barril, não vá que é barril...
> Ô carnaval, Alto das Pombas, Nordeste, Boca do Rio
> Não vá que é barril, não vá que é barril, não vá que é barril, não vá que é barril. Troca tiro com a Rondesp, dá de testa com a Civil
> Não vá que é barril, não vá que é barril, não vá que é barril, não vá que é barril, Não vá que é barril, não vá que é barril, não vá que é barril, não vá que é barril. (Fantasmão, 2009)

> Hey u reckless wannabe don't put the base behind the trio

Don't go it's a trap, don't go it's a trap...
If a rapist, a pedophile has fallen into depression
Don't go it's a trap, don't go it's a trap...
Oh carnival, Alto das Pombas, Nordeste, Boca do Rio
Don't go it's a trap, don't go it's a trap, don't go it's a trap,
don't go it's a trap,
Shooting at Rondesp and confronting the Civil Police
Don't go it's a trap, don't go it's a trap, don't go it's a trap,
don't go it's a trap,
Don't go it's a trap, don't go it's a trap, don't go it's a trap,
don't go it's a trap.

When I recognize the political significance of this posture, I am not referring to any institutional framework or programmatic intentionality, but rather to the practical expression of a contradiction mediated by contested symbolic structures in a society fractured by social inequality and racism. This mediation is also embodied, as the body, being a vessel of meaning, is symbolically laden with these very contradictions that constitute subjects (Hartman, 1997).

Thus, I would argue that "botar a base" manifests as: (1) a performance of everyday life, enacted within interpersonal interactions; (2) a stylization of this performance, adapted as a mode of dancing during the pagode "agitation"; (3) as a synthesis—a structure of feeling—of a masculine posture, one that is corporeal, fearless, and linked to the favela and its unique cultural codes, where the alcaguete (informant) has no place and "dar testa" (to confront) the police is "barril" (tense, dangerous). In the circulation between these different cultural registers—each interpreting the other— the meaning of this posture materializes in a performative scene that transfigures social death and structural antiblackness.

PAGODE, SOCIAL DEATH, AND SUBJECTIVITY

Social death is the ontological condition of the Black subject in an "anti-Black" world, essentially, the (post)colonial modernity or "Babylon" (Sexton, 2011; Wilderson, 2011). Building on the phenomenological readings of Frantz Fanon, Lewis Gordon and others emphasize the (overdetermined, I would say) impossibility of Black existence as truly human (Gordon, 1999, Fanon, 1983). This impossibility extends beyond the essential Inhumanity attributed to Blackness—defined by the slave condition, which has been aptly described as "social death", with its fundamental corollaries of natal alienation, generalized dishonor, gratuitous violence, congenital indignity, and fungibility.[29] All these factors collectively signify that reconciliation with the institutions of Western modernity is not possible. The public sphere, the realm of the State, and the traditional mechanisms of political engagement within the framework of white-dominated institutions are fundamentally incompatible with Black existence under these conditions.

> That black life is not social life in the universe formed by the codes of state and civil society, of citizen and subject, of nation and culture, of people and place, of history and heritage, of all the things that colonial society has in common with the colonized, of all that capital has in common with labor—the modern world system. Black life is not lived in the world that the world lives in, but it is lived underground, in outer space. (Sexton, 2011, p. 28)

Inhabiting the zone of death (or the "non-being"),[30] the "underground" or "outer space", Black individuals—like the "colonized"—living the Black life under social death, view the promises of modernity, such as "social inclusion" or institutional participation, with irony. This perspective, articulated by Fanon (2005) in "The Wretched of the Earth", reflects a deep skepticism toward the institutions and ideals of modernity.

As João Vargas and others point out, life in the "ghetto", or under material conditions marked by segregation, dispossession, precarious access to services, social marginalization, and hyper-surveillance, represents a stage in a cyclical continuum between freedom and incarceration (Vargas, 2010a, 2010b;). This is not merely a statistical probability but also a structural vector of experience and meaning. The sensibility of imprisonment "leaks" from the state institution into the favela through the real or symbolic presence of armed groups who control, or try to control, the drug trade, perpetuating a constant state of war with the police. This context fosters the social production of a sensibility, or "structure of feeling" shaped by

---

[29] *Fungibility* can be understood as a property of the commodity, shared by the condition of enslavement: "the fungibility of the slave—that is, the joy made possible by the virtue of the replaceability and interchangeability endemic to commodity." Moreover, it is emphasized that "the fungibility of the commodity makes the captive body an abstract and empty vessel, vulnerable to the projection of others' feelings, ideas, desires, and values." (Hartman, 1997, p. 21)

[30] Grosfoguel (2012), following Fanon, defines the zone of non-being as that region of social life where non-humans are relegated.

modes of subjectification and aesthetic forms marked by genocide/social death, and the persistent threats of violence, incarceration, and death.

The criminalization of an entire population segment, young Black men from the favela, amounting to millions in Brazil, underscores the expansive nature of the processes of "criminal subjection". This sinister equation defines "social death" in Brazilian society. If every favelado is deemed a criminal—or complicit in crime—and if "the only good criminal is a dead criminal", the members of "Fantasmão" ironically assert their identity by proclaiming themselves as ghosts: "Eu sou negão, eu sou do gueto / e você quem é? Sou Fantasmão, eu sou do gueto / e você quem é?" [I am a Black man, I come from the ghetto/ and who are you? I am Fantasmão; I'm from the ghetto/ and who are you?]

Unsurprisingly, alongside this "criminal subjection" (Misse, 2011; Mattos, 2012, which transforms the entire favela population, especially racialized men, into "criminals" and potential enemies of the State, the culture, language, symbols, categories, and even ethics forged in the harsh environment of prisons permeate the symbolic social expressions of the ghetto or favela. This dynamic is formally represented in pagode baiano.

A form of imprisoned subjectivity defined by confinement and feral resistance to the State. This subjectivity emerges within an ambiguous and contradictory relationship, using pure violence—torture, intimidation, and death—as a language to delineate a social space—the zone of death—which becomes a scene for subjectification. An example of this dynamic can be seen in a Facebook page titled "Polícia Baiana", which, like many similar platforms, incessantly shares news and images from the criminal world. One such post features a video, seemingly recorded by the individuals involved, from a prison in Feira de Santana, Bahia.[31] In the video, an inmate leads a group of prisoners in singing a medley of funk and pagode songs, exalting the criminal faction to which they demonstrate loyalty. The young man leading the chant, tattooed and wearing a cap, directs threats at the "alemão" (rivals). Singing a well-known pagode song,[32] the inmates affirm their allegiance to "Caveira" [skull], which, according to media reports, is a local ally of the São Paulo-based PCC—Primeiro Comando da Capital (First Capital Command), a mortal rival of CP—Comando da Paz (Peace Command).

Pagode, whether in "the void" or the "hold", presents a performative structure and can only be fully understood in this way. It is not merely a market-oriented musical genre, as such a perspective would reduce

---

[31] https://www.facebook.com/1481366395470431/videos/1609921072614962/?fref=nf
[32] https://www.youtube.com/watch?v=S537pS6Y1CU

its critical potential of mobilization of meaning to a market-oriented format—a "logistics", in the words of Harney and Moten (2013)—that seeks to obscure the contradictory and explosive roots of Black subject positions, defined through the connection between pagode and social death.

Access to this deeper structure, a line of flight, a fugitive ritualization of an aesthetic of radical dehumanization, finds its form in performative modalities. In this sense, I argue that "pagode" baiano, as a historical expressive form, which connects subjects to the formal/structural resources for their agency, can only be adequately understood through an approach grounded in performance theory. What is commonly referred to as "pagode" is doubly represented within the relevant cultural horizon. It encompasses both the musical genre and its associated market universe—record labels, bands, managers, websites, and songs commodified for trade—and the event or "performance" of pagode. These two dimensions are closely connected, of course, but their connection is rooted in tension and alienation on one hand, and resistance and reinvention on the other, a reinvention processed within a historical structural form that employs the body, memory, art, and history within the circle of indignity, death, and dispossession, in the "hold" or "underground". From this perspective—which might also be called "gnoseological" (Lukács, 2010)—pagode can articulate a contradiction between the commodity form and Blackness, the subject who exchanges itself with the Other. Or the "object" that resists by positioning itself outside the national mestizo pact.

CHAPTER 3
BLACK BORDER: BODY AND STRUGGLE IN THE BLACK AUDIOVISUAL SCENE

"We wanted a revolutionary art, not just skin flicks. We were Malcom's Children, and we wanted a Malcom Art! One that was in itself an example of Malcom X's call for Black Self-Determination, Self-Respect and Self-Defense plus W. E. B. DuBois's true Self-Consciousness."
— **Amiri Baraka, Emory Douglas: A "Good Brother," a "Bad Artist," 2007**

A DEVASTATING SCENARIO

According to Renato Sergio de Lima, director of the Brazilian Public Security Forum, in an interview with the British newspaper *The Guardian*, the increase in homicides in Brazil constitutes a "devastating scenario", with 63,880 people murdered in 2017 alone. The responsibility for these deaths is directly or indirectly attributed to State actions (Phillips, 2018).

Shockingly, between 1980 and 2014, approximately one million people were killed by gunfire in Brazil. In the last ten years, homicides have been the leading cause of death among young people aged 15 to 29, especially Black men living on the outskirts of major urban centers. Furthermore, data from the Mapa da Violência [Violence Mapping] indicates that of the 42,000 homicide victims in 2014, 29,000 were Black youth, 94% of whom were male (Waiselfisz, 2014).

This scenario is undeniably devastating and the devastation it encompasses forms the reference point for the experience of Blackness within the colonial and anti-Black world we inhabit. Devastation, dispossession, and death are attributes of a "structure of antagonisms" that defines the conditions of possibility for the formal articulation of meanings and subjectivities.

From a phenomenological perspective, the embodied consciousness of racialized vulnerability creates an alignment of meanings and sensibilities under the impact of what I have previously called the "shootout"[33] (Pinho, 2015), the daily coexistence with death and violence. The "Black body fallen to the ground" (Flauzina, 2008) becomes an element of the subjective landscape and the pedagogy of terror that defines the zone of death, the intimate enemy of Brazil's favelas and urban peripheries. This geography of death, topography of violence, and the "shootout" of fear, pain, and confusion form the living matter of the experience of social death in our context (Idem; Alves, 2013).

What appears represented or performed in instances of everyday popular life, or expressive cultural forms such as hip-hop or even pagode, can be elaborated as an experience by the subject and represented as an expressive form capable of objectifying, and in this sense, translating, the constant fear and helplessness inherent in this language of violence and terror? This question could also be characterized, both historically and structurally, within a broader theoretical framework. Such a framework is found, for instance, in Afropessimism as articulated in the works of Frank Wilderson (2010), or in readings informed by the concept of "antiblackness", such as those by João Costa Vargas (2017), as I have sought to discuss here.

The theatricalized violence of every day, as discussed by Christen Smith, and the definition of structures of feeling, forms of violence subjectivation as transient attributes of the subject, can thus be reflected upon, or more aptly framed, if considered within broader historical and formal terms (Smith, 2016). Alternatively, as Ricardo Aleixo eloquently argues regarding the poetic voice of Alex Simões, the challenge lies in navigating, within necropolitical times, between the subject and poetry, or between the subject and poiesis, as I would phrase it (Aleixo, 2018).

In "Red, White & Black — Cinema and the Structures of U.S. Antagonisms", Frank Wilderson (2010) is clear on this point. Social death, defined by Orlando Patterson (2008) as a central element of the universal condition of slavery, is redefined as a core element in the definition of Blackness within the U.S. context. This condition of slavery is characterized by social death—a political, semiotic, subjective, and fundamentally ontological transcription—as the central nature of its positionality (Wilderson, 2010). The gratuitous nature of violence, the inalienable natal dishonor, the uprootedness, and the liminal condition—human being and

---

[33] Reference to the song by the pagode artist Edicity: "The shootout is about to start, it's about to start/Clack, Clack Boom/Clack, Clack, Boom" (2013).

peça-da-guiné—constitute a modality of circumscription and production of the enslaved person that fundamentally denies their Humanity. This denial serves to grant legitimacy—and perhaps more crucially, legibility—to the anti-colonial white world in a way that is fundamentally irreconcilable. The opposition, structured within the experiences and categories of intelligibility and sentiment—such as the "shootout" and "baixaria"—between Blackness and the Western world cannot be described merely as a contradiction resolvable through dialectics, but rather as an antagonism whose resolution necessitates the obliteration of one of the positions. As Spivak, addressing the condition of the colonial woman, observes in a related context, there are no mechanisms of compromise or transcendence for the incommunicability and the essentially non-human status projected onto the (Black) body, subsumed into the ontological condition of the enslaved, socially dead (Silva, 2019; Spivak, 2014). In this sense, such a subject is not of the world and cannot be conveniently represented, a point highly relevant to our discussion. Thus, as Wilderson (2010) concludes:

> The knowledge that the black position is indeed a position, not an identity, and that its constituent elements are coterminous with and inextricably bound to the constituent elements of social death—which is to say that for Blackness there is no narrative moment prior to slavery. (p. 27)

Social death, as a lived category of the structural articulation between the anti-Black world and Blackness as an irreconcilable and really existing impossibility; anti-Blackness, as a descriptive category of the historical nature of a central structural antagonism, which empirically denies the coexistence between the Black person and the world, or between Blackness and civil and political action in the public sphere; find a third complementary expression in the concrete manifestation of many deaths and a scenarization of death as structural objectification, which Abdias do Nascimento in the past, and a growing number of black activists and intellectuals in the present have called genocide. (Bourdieu, 1999; Nascimento, 1978). As Ana Flauzina (2014) develops:

> It is essential to recognize that genocide is not a category confined exclusively to the narrow domain of legal discourse. In fact, the seemingly solid foundation established

by the 1948 Convention represents a space of intense political contestation, where the very concept of genocide
and the issues associated with the criminalization of this
practice are actively debated. (p. 122)

As a contested concept, the genocide of Black people has been increasingly framed as a political category that transcends the boundaries of legal
and demographic frameworks. It operates by incorporating the intractable
categories of social death and anti-Blackness, covering a broad conceptual
and symbolic spectrum. This conceptualization serves as a heuristic tool
for political intervention and as a gnosiological device embedded in the
experiences of diverse social actors: housewives and intellectuals, artists
and workers.

Anti-Blackness (1), social death (2), and the genocide of Black people
(3) together help to describe the formation of this devastated landscape.
This landscape is understood in its complete objectivity, both as a formal
structure of meaning and as a historical horizon of significance, codified
in legible forms through the State and the market, and in opposition to
spaces of resistance, as I explore in other chapters of this book. As an
analytical framework, this triad allows me to pose a set of theoretical, political, and aesthetic questions. This, to some extent, is the challenge I un-
dertake in this chapter: to revisit my experience and engagement with the
Corpos em Luta exhibition at the CachoeiraDoc 2017 festival. Under the
curation of Amaranta Cesar, this program confronted all who attended its
screenings, taking place on yet another warm evening in the beautiful Cine
Theatro Cachoeirano in the Bahian city of Cachoeira, framed by the ruins
of colonialism.

The striking yet devastated city of Cachoeira serves as an apt backdrop for the issues I aim to address here. I intend to analyze the films
exhibited—"Alma no Olho", "Now!", "Notícias de uma Guerra Racial
Subnotificada", and "Experimentando o Dilúvio em Vermelho"[34]—as a
form of critical intervention from the zone of non-being. This analysis
seeks to explore the possibilities and potentialities of interpellation for the
Black body, which is not merely in struggle but represents the objectified
confluence of these unaddressed massacres (Grosfoguel, 2012).

---

[34] In addition to these, "Now Again" and "Monangambeee" were also screened but will not
be discussed here.

BLACK BORDER

In a somewhat dated yet nonetheless classic essay, Susan Sontag (1987b) critiques "interpretation" in a call for an "erotic of art" as opposed to a hermeneutics of the aesthetic fact. The function of criticism, she dramatically insists, should never be to show "what something means" (Sontag, 1987, p. 23). Sontag's objection is grounded in a critique of the Aristotelian mimetic theory of art as representation. Adopting a sensualist stance, she ultimately calls for the recovery of the "senses" (Sontag, 1987).

What is relevant to recover from Sontag's argument here is her distinction between the model, or artistic form, and its capacity to represent content. Or, as she frames it, a question about the "value of art"—whether as formal acuity or, more importantly, the imperative for art to justify itself within the Aristotelian framework of mimesis. Art, understood as representation, may be adequate or inconsistent, with the tools for its evaluation thus situated outside of the artwork itself.

> Our time is a time in which the project of interpretation is largely reactionary and stifling. Just as the exhaust gases from automobiles and heavy industry pollute the atmosphere of cities, the profusion of art interpretations today poisons our sensibility. (Idem, p. 16)

Such is the interpretative excess characteristic of "post-mythological" Western epistemologies, which, as Susan Sontag herself argues, separate representation from the world. This separation produces the foundational rupture of meaning as an ideological element tied to the power of the State, the law, and writing (the code of codes). Doesn't Pierre Clastres (1990) suggest that when he speaks of "primitive societies", societies without a State, or better saying, against the State (p. 130)? We see a similar perspective in the representational ethics of Mesoamerican and pre-Hispanic traditions, exemplified in their extraordinary deer-skin codices. These books, written on the skin of the sacred animal, symbolize themselves. The deer, a ritualistic creature offered in sacrifice to the hunter—who, in turn, ritually identifies with the victim—embodies this unity. The deer-skin books are the deer itself. Concept and medium, image and what it represents, are one and the same.

> There is substantial evidence suggesting that, unlike what we know from monotheistic religions, these gods hardly exist independently of their images, which could be found in codices, sculptures, or even personified in rituals and dances. This is why the images are not re-presentations; they are the gods. (Neurath, 2013, p. 51)

The Black body, under the regime of Western representation, deferred by the distinction between formalized representation and its objectified content, nevertheless remains within the specular abyss that resists being captured by the machinations of the symbolic. Perhaps for this very reason, it is better approached as "flesh", as Hortense Spillers (1987) suggests: "Before the body there is the flesh, that zero degree of social conceptualization" (p. 67).

Lewis Gordon and other scholars, in critical engagement with the work of Frantz Fanon, have developed a critical repertoire for understanding Blackness as embodied through two main elements. First, the Black body—which is, in essence, the Black person—is denounced as "a thing among other things". Second, the Black individual, with their ghostly yet objective body, is conceived as "pure absence", thereby resisting symbolization (Gordon, 1999). Where reason resides, or where the anti-Black world asserts its rationality, the Black person cannot be. Conversely, where the Black person is, or "when" the Black person exists, this anti-Black world cannot materialize. The insoluble antagonism between Blackness and the world, as articulated in Fanon's work, serves as an interpretive paradigm for a categorical ontological void—Blackness is, in sum, absolute negativity—but also as a site for political interpellation. In this framework, being "nothing" and being "something" converge in a peculiar coincidence within a relational universe where one term signifies pure absence—the Black—and the other pure presence—the white (Idem). Gordon further asserts that in an anti-Black world, the Black person inhabits the absent form of human presence. This absence is defined far beyond the realm of political economy—considered in the production of social forms under the intervention of the category of labor, as I discuss in Chapter 5—but more fundamentally by a libidinal economy. In Wilderson's (2011) terms: "The libidinal economy of modernity and its attendant cartography [...] achieves its structure of unconscious exchange in a way of a thanatology in which Blackness overdetermines the embodiment of impossibility, incoherence and incapacity" (p. 44).

Under the overdetermination of this libidinal economy, Gordon argues, Black consciousness is saturated in the flesh, embodying the quality of being a thing, a form of existence overlapping is merely an object. To exist fully in total objectivity, without division or separation as the foundation of meaning, implies inhabiting a presignified world or being imprisoned within it as "a thing among other things". This condition becomes a significant obstacle to representation and interpretation, particularly because it presupposes a content that, in the case of the Black "person", is the negation of objectified self-consciousness (Silva, 2019). Prohibited or obliterated by the phobogenic and anxiety-inducing condition observed by Fanon, the reflexive self-consciousness of Blackness (true self-consciousness) becomes a projection into absence—a lack of self and any stable ontological contours. This places it outside dialectics, or beyond a dialectical process that could allow for the emergence of intersubjectivity and, ultimately, the subject itself. As Afropessimists insist, this negation of Humanity and recognition renders the Black/slave an irreconcilable being in relation to the "world". For Gordon, this phobogenic, epidermal, and material condition—inscribed as a chilling code upon burning flesh, epitomized by the exclamation—Look, a Negro!—implies that Black people do not inhabit a symbolic realm because: "It is locked in the serious, material values of the real" (Gordon, 1999, p. 79).

Black people are our own bodies, and our bodies are pre- or non-symbolic. Thus, Black people and our bodies cannot be represented or interpreted, nor trapped within the vile materiality of flesh, defined by fungibility imposed through gratuitous, brutal, and repeated violations in History—slavery—and across all layers of social structure and symbolization in an anti-Black world. In this context, an "erotic of art", as Sontag (1987) describes, is negated by the "irresistible sensuality" of the Black body, as Spillers (1987) puts it. This is because Black personhood is defined by the absence of subjectivity (Sontag, 1987; Spillers, 1987). Gordon (1999) advances this argument politically, emphasizing Wilderson's assertion of the irreconcilable antagonism between Blackness and civil society: "It should be clear that political theories that separate Society into public political and private civil societies offer no resource for blacks" (p. 82). Excluded from representation and barred from action in civil society, the Black individual, while an entity of the world, is not in the world, in "our world". How could Black individuals, whose negation or obliteration sustains the stability of this society, be partners or political agents within it?

Given the structural prohibition of Blackness from signification or representation—understood as a mode of existence defined by the absence in the world—we might question how in practice and lived reality, the Black subject, confined and in contradiction with their own body, can produce meaning or act as an agent of stable and codifiable significations. As explored in Chapters 4 and 5, the grammar of Afropessimist signification insists on Black opacity to meaning-making, ultimately framing such inquiries as questions of the impossible. This impossibility arises because the semiotics of racialized meanings is grounded in Western epistemological traditions that oppose sign and signifier or content and representation. More fundamentally, as Denise Ferreira da Silva (2019) argues, Western thought and its post-Enlightenment onto-epistemological pillars, articulated through the category of "Negridade", produce the racial subject as "destined for obliteration" (p. 133). In this framework, the Black individual cannot be represented because they exist as pure immanence. Both nothing and a thing. Or an object that incorporates—rather than represents—the structural void necessary for the coherence of the anti-Black world.

An alternative way to address this difficulty—can the Black individual as subjectified self-consciousness be represented?—is found in the interpretative concept of the "Black border". Paula Von Gleich (2017) questions herself if Afropessimism is correct and Black existence in the Western world is defined by non-existence, social death, and exclusion from public action and signification, how do we explain the persistence (and flourishing) of Black traditions, people, and culture, both "popular" and "erudite"? Two pathways may help answer this question. First, the concept of the "contact zone" developed by Mary Louise Pratt (1991). Second, Stefano Harney and Fred Moten's (2013) notion of "fugitivity", as explored in "The Undercommons". Let us start with the latter.

In "The Undercommons: Fugitive Planning & Black Study", Harney and Moten (2013) critique colonial imagery in cinema. For example, in the 1987 film "Shaka Zulu", the colonizer is surrounded by barbaric natives. While the stereotype is offensive, the encirclement is strategic. "Our task is the self-defense of the surround in the face of repeated, targeted dispossessions through the settler's armed incursions" (Harney & Moten, 2013, p. 17). In 21st-century Brazil, these armed incursions are far from metaphorical. The "death-in-life" of Black existence remains the condition for branquidade [whiteness] in the so-called "mixed" nation, as discussed in Chapter 2. The narrative of the Brazilian nation is, fundamentally, the settler's narrative, which is fortified by the war against Indigenous peoples, the massacres of quilombos, and monumental symbols like the Bandeirantes Monument in São Paulo's Ibirapuera Park, etc. Yet, the nation, the national State and the "national culture", are "surrounded" by countless quilombos, by the scenes of objection, the rebellion in pagode, and the ancestral practices like Nego Fugido, as we will see further. Stefano Harney and Fred Moten also discuss about "study" and "fugitive planning" as well as working "with and for" the undercommons—who build ruptures and escape plans, living here and now in a way that prefigures futures beyond compromise, as fissures in the space–time of Western epistemological cartography. Blackness, in this framework, while not strictly afropessimist, like this radical refusal of the "world" and its incompatibility with whiteness, projects a fugitive horizon—like the paredão de pagode at the beach in Ribeira. A horizon where us, who were "shipped", alienated since the moment we are born (from an ontological perspective), inhabit both here and elsewhere, and nowhere else. The Quilombo. Or, as Beatriz Nascimento suggests in the movie "Ori", a transatlantic journey reconciling body and territory, ancestrality, and the head, the Ori . Navigating the "space of death" or colonial "contact zone", this framework allows for an interrogation of Blackness as vertiginous paroxysm and self-defense, in a less "pessimistic" way. By reinventing informal practices of escape through "study" and "planning". These acts are, as Harney and Moten put it, the "futurial presence of forms of life" that make escape possible.

Mary Louise Pratt (1991), in turn, argues against the idea of community as a unified or unifying foundation for "language, communication, and culture" within social groups. She develops the influential notion of the "contact zone". Using as her starting point heterogenous texts written at the historical and cultural interfaces between colonizers and the colonized— most notably the hybrid text written in 1623 by Felipe Guáman Poma de Ayala in both Quechua and Spanish—Pratt describes a mode of meaning production that is not defined by unity or coherence among a population, a language, a culture, or a socio-historical experience. Instead, it operates as a model or imperfect translation that transcends "speech communities". More specifically, Pratt (1991) defines the contact zone as:

> Spaces where cultures meet, clash, and grapple with each other, often in contexts of highly asymmetrical relations of power such as colonialism, slavery, or their aftermaths as they are lived in many parts of the world today. (p. 2)

In these conflict-ridden regions, across various combinations of time and space—from colonial Peru to cosmopolitan New York, new forms of narrating the "encounter" have been developed, particularly in the form of what Mary Louise Pratt calls autoethnography. These are narrative modalities that deviate from national or interpretative communities, presenting texts in which individuals describe themselves, their culture, and their values in ways that engage in dialogue with how others represent them, particularly as "Others". Autoethnographic representations are constructed as responses—collapsing the boundaries between genres and languages—offered by the hetero-represented Others as acts of self-representation. In this context, at least temporarily, the self-conscious Black subject may achieve self-representation as a form of self-recognition. It suggests the possibility of suspending the formal division between subject/object that governs both representation and, inevitably, self-representation. However, as Pratt explicitly warns, these representational forms are neither "pure" nor regressive; they are intensely produced as outcomes of violent and asymmetric encounters. Often addressed to dual or multiple audiences, autoethnographies—like Latin American testimonies[35]—represent these narratives "merged or infiltrated to varying degrees with indigenous idioms to create self-representations intended to intervene in metropolitan modes of understanding" (Pratt, 1991, p. 3). In this sense, as with the slave narratives discussed in Chapter 5, the question of the audience and the metropolitan model of consciousness become crucial.

What happens if we consider the "contact zone" as defined and structured by what Michael Taussig (1993) calls the "space of death", as discussed in Chapter 1? As a historical link between colonizers and their ethics of war, and the colonized/enslaved as non-persons, as well as the structural connection between carnal violence and forms of signification (or non-signification), the colonial space of death operates as the mechanism of transition that establishes the slave as a colonial category, one that is impossible to adequately represent, as Taussig argues.

What Gleich proposes, then, as a way to incorporate the radical critique of afropessimism while allowing for the possibility of signification and agency, even within the framework of social death, is precisely a revision of the concept of the contact zone. This revision shifts toward recognizing the fugitive dimension of Black cultural invention under the impact of the zone of death and the crushing objectivity of anti-Blackness (Gleich, 2017). In this sense, the idea of "border", as margin, frontier, or limit, is invoked. "Fugitiveness entails borders", she says—borders that must be crossed or have their limits overcome, so that, through such crossings, new thresholds can be established as horizons for deferred signification within history and the history of representations. Afropessimism, by proposing

---

[35] On testimonies, see Yúdice (1992).

a structurally immeasurable divide between Blackness and the anti-Black world—between inclusion and exclusion from civil society and regimes of signification—implies the presence of an epistemological border or edge. This border, or crossing, is akin to a passage, such as the Middle Passage of the transatlantic slave trade, which empties the Black "person" of any ontological content external to the process of natal alienation itself. Yet, it allows for the emergence of strategies beyond representation, such as performance.

There are, of course, problems with Pratt's theorization. The materialization of antagonism, or the structure of anti-Black antagonism, resists being adequately conceptualized as a postcolonial translation of contact zones. Conversely, the notions of fortification and settler frameworks found in Wilderson and Moten appear more fruitful. These emphasize the notion of interiority vs. exteriority—not only in the colonial/spatial sense but also in a semiotic/ontological one, akin to the framework of Deleuze and Guattari (1986, 1996) and Viveiros de Castro (2014).

Pratt's definition of the relationships between colonizers and the colonized (including the enslaved) as relationships of subalternization does not align with Wilderson's conceptual framework. Subalternization presupposes the construction of hegemony and counter-hegemonies as forms of domination based on the production of symbolic/ideological consensus, implying some degree of recognition. In the case of the slave, however, domination appears as a "natural" expression—relevant here is Viveiros de Castro's (2014) definition of "natural" as that which must be negated for Culture or Society to be instituted—of gratuitous, extreme violence, without appeal or remorse. Pratt's idea of the border still presupposes some form of "contact", which is ontologically interdicted for Black people situated in an anti-Black world. From this perspective, it becomes difficult to explain, as noted earlier, the forms of invention and resistance among Black people. Here, the concept of fugitiveness becomes useful. "We may imagine fugitivity as conceptualizing the lived experience of blackness as constant practice of refusal to accept and to remain within the ostracized position of social death" (Gleich, 2017, p. 6). Conceived in this way, guerrilla fugitiveness challenges and crosses borders, attacking them and evading them, without necessarily achieving a complete overcoming. "In this way, fugitivity might be understood as running up against the absolute and impermeable border between social death and civil society that nonetheless remains intact" (Idem, p. 8).

In summary, the concept of the Black border can be understood here as a methodological category pointing to the impossibility of consolidating a position of representation coinciding with the reflexive self-conscious-ness of a subject who cannot find solid ontological foundations for their establishment outside the contact zone as a zone of death. The Black/slave's condition of "thingness" implies an opacity to the symbolic, a resistance to signification, in the scene of objection. This imposes theoretical limits and incompatibilities with notions of culture based on meaning or interpretation.

In this sense, "Black culture" could be approached not in semiotic or representational terms, as I will further discuss in Chapter 4, but in per-formative terms. It operates fugitively amidst scenarios of violence and racialization to produce knowledge and beauty in ways not tied to a symbolic epistemology, but rather grounded in the body/flesh that emerges from the colonial zone of death as the immanent material of an intervention, or ob-jection, directed toward the "outside" of the onto-epistemological frame-work of Western thought and aesthetics.

In the following two sections, we will see how these premises might help produce a fugitive reading of the films presented at Cachoeira in 2017, during the Corpos em Luta exhibition.

ALMA NO OLHO, NOW!

With materials leftover from another production, Zózimo Bulbul created the short film Alma no Olho [Soul in the Eye] in 1973, which is widely re-garded as one of the most accomplished and significant audiovisual exper-iments produced from a Black perspective in Brazil. Critics highlight the formal concerns of the filmmaker and his avant-garde approach, which, without relying on spoken words, encapsulates in just over eleven minutes the journey of the Black man—from the idyllic savannas of Africa to bond-age in a predominantly white world, and ultimately, to liberation (Ferreira, 2016; De Tal, 2014).

In this film, the body serves as the center of gravity, where the promises of freedom can either be stretched to their limits or become a source of resentment. As I have argued, the materiality of Blackness, represented through the Black body, is juxtaposed against a white background. "Cinema is a weapon; we Black people have an AR-15 and we certainly know how to shoot", Zózimo is said to have remarked. In Alma no Olho, with con-sciousness in the flesh and soul in the eye, the Black body becomes the weapon, the projectile, and the target of a narrative that advances toward immanence as an aesthetic strategy of semiotic displacement. It represents a process of reclaiming and reapproaching the body itself.

Through theatrical gestures and familiar symbols, the film narrates a story of self-recognition, alienation, and liberation, supposedly bypassing the mediations allowed by the deferred structures of formal signification. This functions as a meta-commentary operating at the intersection between the structural (syntactic) and the symbolic (semantic), or between code and text, as Azzan (1993) discusses concerning the anthropological frameworks of Lévi-Strauss (structural/syntactic) and Clifford Geertz (hermeneutic/semantic). Or, to borrow Ricoeur's terms, it exists between "language" (without subject or history) and "discourse" (intersubjective and historical).

> While the signs of language refer only to other signs within the same system, rendering language devoid of a world, time, or subjectivity, discourse is always about something: it refers to a world it seeks to describe, express, or represent. (Ricoeur, 1990, p. 46)

The opening scenes reveal a focus on detailing bodily parts—perhaps a coincidence between body and narrative, or an ironic commentary on colonial fetishization (Mercer, 1994; Bhabha, 1998). The tongue, ear, teeth, armpits, and a bead of sweat are presented as indices of the inescapable materiality of the body. These elements underscore, paradoxically, the impossibility of the full integration of the Black man, who is condemned to symbolize only through his dissection. Or, perhaps, through his disintegration into the objecthood of flesh, what might be termed "flesh" or "that zero degree" for intersubjectively mediated meaning. Where the body is magnified, as in this case, the person disappears. The mise-en-scène evokes the lost Africanity where body, man, nature, and divinity were said to be integrated, as imagined in the mythopoetic and quilombista utopias of Abdias do Nascimento (2002). The actor's broad smile and luminous joy, as he simulates running, align the physicality of the scene with the essential integrity of a character still unmarked by contradictions. Wearing African attire, singing, and dancing to the music of John Coltrane, Zózimo's Black body references an era of embodied plenitude, albeit one that remains generic and allegorical. The actor's self-aware beauty, so effectively utilized by Antunes Filho in "Compasso de Espera" (1973), heightens the ontological density of a body reconciled with itself. Then comes slavery and the Middle Passage, dramatized through strikingly plastic white chains clamped on the actor's Black wrists. Desperation and agony are expressed through acrobatic contortions. The narrative moves through the dehumanizing labor, sport, and art that mark transformations of the enslaved condition, still chained to the white world, diagrammatically represented as a vast Cartesian white square—an infinite horizon—as the backdrop. Wearing glasses and a suit, the actor eventually assumes the white masks. Holding a book, he smiles like a domesticated animal. Finally, he sheds his garments piece by piece, breaking free of the chains, and fills the screen with his newly liberated Black body. The body, in its reclaimed form, occupies the full surface of the frame, asserting its freedom.

Figure 3 — "Alma no Olho", still, 1973.
Source: https://www.youtube.com/watch?v=RTQlaxiokBA[36].

The Cuban filmmaker Santiago Álvarez, with his short film "Now!" (1965), formally challenges political conventions and codified visibilities, employing elements that justify themselves within the syntactic field but demand interpretation in a historical-hermeneutic sense. This film, often considered the precursor to music videos, exemplifies this approach. The structural formalism hinders interpretations of a semantic nature, akin to the anthropological formalism of Lévi-Strauss, where myth, for example, is "a form in search of content" (Lévi-Strauss, 1975). Similar to "Alma no Olho", here too, music serves as the narrative thread of the film. In "Alma no Olho", the chosen artist was John Coltrane, while in Álvarez's work, the featured artist is Lena Horne. In both cases, the tension between editing

---

[36] E.N. This video is no longer available at this link on YouTube. But now can be found here: https://www.youtube.com/watch?v=IbCa5ufiV3s

(syntax) and narrative (semantics) heightens the aesthetic disturbance that captivates the viewer's attention. As Kobena Mercer (2016) states regarding art in general and Black art in particular:

> If every signifier had an invariant relationship to a signified, formal innovation would be impossible. This is to say that when art takes us out of the ordinary by interrupting our Horizon of expectations, what we are exposed to is a glimpse of the invisible rules that ordinarily work to fix the polysemic surplus which gives art the potential to introduce something different and new into the world. (p. 10)

Produced in support of the civil rights movement in the United States, "Now!" introduces something distinct and innovative to the world. Set to the song that carries the same name, performed by the American singer Lena Horne, the film draws upon Horne as a heroine of the struggle for racial emancipation. Her powerful performance breathes life into the song, which unequivocally calls for direct action:

> If those historic gentlemen came back today
> Jefferson, Washington and Lincoln
> And Walter Cronkite put them on channel 2
>
> To find out what they were thinkin'
> I'm sure they'd say
> Thanks for quoting us so much
> But we don't want to take a bow
>
> Enough with the quoting
> Put those words into action
> And we mean action now
>
> Now is the moment
> Now is the moment
> Come on, we've put it off long enough
>
> (...)
> Now is the time
> Now is the time.

According to Sérgio Henrique Carvalho Vilaça (2013), Santiago Álvarez was the foremost cinematic chronicler of the Cuban Revolution, personally chosen by Fidel Castro to document and disseminate revolutionary ideals and achievements starting in 1959. Remarkably prolific, Álvarez also gained recognition for his formal innovations, exemplified in "Now!", where the narrative rhythm is shaped by dynamic, "music video-like" editing. This approach employs ironic and acerbic juxtapositions to expose racial discrimination and violence against Black people in the United States.

Writing about "zapping" in the early 1990s, Arlindo Machado (1993) observes:

> A new narrative begins to take shape from the fragments of genres, the remnants of other narratives, never fully achieving completion. Despite its exotic and disconcerting appearance, this may be the only syntagmatic form capable of withstanding the relentless fragmentation caused by zapping. This boundary-pushing narrative form finds its fullest expression in music videos. (p. 161)

The "boundary-pushing" iconography of police repression gains a suggestive reassembly in "Now!", transforming every fall or confrontation, every water jet or snarling dog, into an embodied performance of resistance. More importantly, each scene or frame takes on meaning through its relationships, within the sequence as a whole or along the axis of contiguity, forming a series akin to how Etienne Samain (1995) interprets the classical images created by functionalist anthropologist Bronislaw Malinowski in Melanesia.

The opening scene, featuring the iconic photograph of a meeting between Martin Luther King's group and President Lyndon B. Johnson, evokes James Baldwin's sharp critiques in "A Report from Occupied Territory".

> There was a game played for some time between certain highly placed people in Washington and myself before the administration changed and the Great Society reached the planning stage. The game went something like this around April or May, that is as the weather began to be warmer, my phone would ring. I would pick it up and find that Washington was on the line.

Washington: What are you doing for lunch—oh, say, to-morrow, Jim?

Jim: Oh—why—I guess I'm free

Washington: Why don't you take the shuttle down? We'll send a car to the airport. One o'clock all right?

Jim: Sure. I'll be there.

Washington: Good. Be glad to see you.

So there I would be the next day, like a good little soldier, seated (along with other good little soldiers) around a luncheon table in Washington. The first move was not mine to make, but I knew very well why I had been asked to be there. Finally, someone would say—we would probably have arrived at the salad—"say, Jim, what's going to happen this summer?" (Baldwin, 2016 [1966])[37]

And in the following summer, the rituals of repression and consequent police violence would repeat once more. Similarly, the "riots" would occur again, echoing those of 1943 in Detroit and 1965 in Los Angeles.

In Álvarez's film, one scene after another unfolds: Children and women are interrupted by silver-toned jets of water striking Black bodies that collapse to the ground, snarling dogs, and "law enforcement officers" leaping onto young Black men fighting to save themselves while engaging in revolutionary struggle. Hands raised in chains, college students rebel. A young Black woman writhes as if performing in a theatrical revue, dragged by countless hands of white police officers. Numerous images of young protesters being grabbed, tossed about, and assaulted, pushed by armed officers, cornered by sharp-toothed beasts, appear almost ecstatic, as though in unsuspected transcendence. Their heads tilt back, eyes closed, fainting into the arms of comrades, evoking religious or carnival-like trances, akin to those captured by Arthur Omar (1997) in "Anthropology of the Glorious Face". These moments emphasize the vulnerability of the human body, abandoned to the dual forces of State violence and revolutionary mysticism (Omar, 1997).

---

[37] T.N: See: https://www.thenation.com/article/culture/report-occupied-territory/

Figure 4 – "Now!", Still, 1965.
Source: https://www.youtube.com/watch?v=bd-IZvAUosc. Last accessed on August 6, 2025.

And, finally, the monstrous scenes of lynching. The burned body on the embers suggests that Blackness cannot be fully captured as representation within the register of the sign; it reaches its limit in the body/flesh that burns under the racial holocaust.

The political significance of flesh is also discussed, through an anthropological lens, in "Society Against" the State, where Pierre Clastres (1990) interrogates how and why certain social formations resist the centralization of the state, as well as the political and ontological consequences of such resistance. The regime of signification appears intrinsically co-determinative in this process. As discussed in the next chapter, denying the state implies inscribing the law onto the body itself, thus abolishing the separation between the codified representation of the law and its immanent experience. This imposition emerges on the "surface" of the tortured skin, as seen among the Guayaki and in Kafka's "In the Penal Colony", as cited by Clastres (1990). It seems to be precisely the abolition of distance between the represented and the presumed content—between the world and its forms of representation—that enables persistent resistance to political and semiotic unification and centralization. Viveiros de Castro observes that "primitive society" exists by "preventing the projection of a totalizing convention, a figure of the One that would incarnate and overcode it.

The heteronomous transcendence of the [mythical] origin then serves as a guarantee of immanence and the autonomy of social power" (Viveiros de Castro, 2004, p. 325).

In the modern anti-Black world, however, the Black body is marked by its epidermal condition, which resists symbolization, as we have seen. The tension between the irrepresentability of the Black body, and the Black person as their body, creates a boundary—a border. Between law and body. Between the State and meaning. Between immanence and transcendence. Between myth and History. Between civil society and social death. The persistence of the "inseparable law" among Latin American Indigenous peoples—a law not divorced from the world—requires us to acknowledge the ambiguities of the postmythological transition deeply. Gayatri Spivak (2014) has already highlighted these ambiguities in the politics of representation. The duality identified in the separation of the world from its "content", and between inert things and their deferred presence as meaning, resolves itself into the delegation of power necessary for political centralization. Ritual forms of rejecting the state, as Clastres argues, demand that the body serve as the surface of record. The immanence imposed on the Black body, in its phobogenic dimension, constitutes the perfect antagonism to link Blackness to civil society and the state-mediated public sphere. This negation, as Afro-pessimists assert, is foundational to the world, the public sphere, and the legitimacy of the State. As a pure body, the Black person has always existed outside the law. To represent them would be to return them to a regime of self-affirmation as pure negation or pure absence. Because what that body is does not belong to it (Derrida, 1995, p. 123). Is this Black border—between their body and meaning— not, ultimately, the border in which representations of Black culture and Blackness lose their sense of meaning? Their reason for being?

What is represented in "Alma no Olho"? The narrative is embodied and performed through the virtuosic use of the Black body against the white background. Each moment of the narrative, for instance, the boxing match, refers to something absent as a symbol. It strives to counteract the phobogenic stereotype through bodily pantomime, offering a derepresentation of brutality. The immanence of the body is not represented as "brutality" but is brutality itself (Gordon, 1999), fragmenting to resist signification. Between the brutal immanence of presignified social death and the fugitive inventiveness of Zózimo's pantomime, a border is established. Between a person, who can only be a type, and their body, almost a specimen responsible for an entire race, as Fanon definitively describes—and yet still seeking to represent themselves (Fanon, 1983). Such self-representation, however, is a negation. To "be", the Black person must negate the world; to represent the world, they must negate themselves. In "Alma no Olho", the mise-en-scène depends, of course, on the presymbolization of the Black body. A white artist, for instance, could not plausibly represent this role.

As Spivak (2014) argues, "the distinctions that shift between representation within the framework of the state and political economy, on the one hand, and the theory of the subject, on the other, should not be erased" (p. 41). The subjectivity of Afro-American or Afro-Brazilian peoples is not separated from the devastation wrought by the state and the violations of Black personhood that constitute Blackness itself. However, as Gleich (2017) emphasizes, within the contact zone—between the anti-Black world and forms of Black subjectivity—there exists fugitivity. This does not resolve the structural antagonism or emancipate Black people from their irrepresentable condition but instead signifies inventiveness, rupture, and objection. It embodies a bodily consciousness, and a historical insurgency of positivity defined through negation.

In the specific case of the films discussed in this section, it is important to retain the liminal tension between forms of syntactic signification—produced through contiguity, a sequence of images as code—and those of metaphorical or symbolic nature, which operate through substitution (Leach, 1978). On the syntactic plane, the body is flesh itself, the support of materialized alienation, the white mask in "Alma no Olho". On the metaphorical plane, the body is the person, the Black man, captured by slavery and social death. This formal limit—the Black border—seems to be the locus where Black art becomes conceptually possible.

EXPERIENCING RACIAL TRAGEDY

Poet Alex Simões emerges as an inspired transcriber of the struggles associated with Black and queer positionality in an anti-Black world, where the objectivity of aesthetic reality is cornered by the necropolitical forces shaping the social landscapes within which our subjectivities strive, amid fire and smoke, to interrogate themselves.

> I want to sing freely
> without having to be thankful for being alive
> or problematize why one fears feeling desire,
> boredom, or companionship
> where are my friends, my people,
> dead for countless reasons or

almost alive when faced with
which of the truths gives us relief?
not having answers might just be
the beginning of a certain indignation,
though disguised and in small doses
in the militant aesthetic of not
showing up neither to save the world
nor to bring to light what, in the deep. (Simões, 2018, p.
16)

In the deep, there is no stable ground for fixed meanings, no anchor, center, or base for significance. In the deep lies a fracture—or more aptly, a border or limit—that defines the totalizing opacity of social death. This ensures that Black individuals occupy a place outside the world and outside the law. However, being outside the law—in the border or contact zones, positions us simultaneously within and outside the settler-created world of meaning and power. In this sense, we can only signify in a "fugitive" way.

The boundary of the body, in its carnal and physiological sense, brings to mind, as it does for many critics, the exposure of corpses as a pornographic, obscene, and profane act. Notably, this is because such exposure defies signification, defined instead by the perishable, foul-smelling exile of the flesh. A stripped and bloodied body, disfigured by violence and humiliated by its nakedness, represents nothing—or more precisely, it represents the void, the absence, the vacuum. It is a non-person, a mere thing among other things. The two films I will now discuss highlight precisely this boundary, or closure, that compels the body to be itself while resisting interpretation in an almost obscene manner.

The first, "Notícias de uma Guerra Racial Subnotificada" [News From an Underreported Racial War], is described by its producers as "an anti-colonial documentary, a film of horror and racial terrorism, telling the stories of a people damned by the Brazilian state". The short film embodies both pain and strength; massacre and resistance; the fallen body and the defiant body; cries and roars of rage. Produced as part of the campaign "Reaja ou Será Morto, Reaja ou Será Morta" [React or You Will Be Killed], it is an element of what can be termed semiotic guerrilla warfare. It aims to shock, move, and provoke discomfort, compelling its audience to engage in the fight. The film centers on the event known as the Cabula Massacre, in which military police executed 12 young men in Salvador's Cabula neighborhood. It also addresses the case of Davi Fiuza, whose body was reportedly brutalized by 22 military police officers, including 19 cadets in training (Bahia Meio-Dia, 2018). The film is permeated by social death in its most egregious forms, and the outrage it provokes—the discomfort, repulsion, and nausea in the face of bloodied corpses—offers a disoriented synthesis of meanings struggling to represent the unbearable.

Davi's body was never found; instead, we hear the choked voice of his grandmother: "David was taken by 23 military police officers. It's like killing an animal, breaking its neck, breaking its arm, shooting it nine times. They claimed that my grandson confronted the RONDESP unit". She continues: "Nobody down here has the means to confront RONDESP".[38] The sad hypothesis offered by his mother seems, horrifically, more plausible:

> "This is what I think: among the nineteen who were in training... there's this thing they call a baptism. At that moment, they decided to carry out a holocaust on my son. David went through a holocaust, and after that, they were rewarded by being admitted into the Military Police of Bahia."

As I have previously pointed out elsewhere, there appears to be a sacrificial (holocaust-like) dimension to this case, almost totemic in the context of Black death and the accompanying spectacle of violence (Pinho, 2018). In this sense, the brutalized Black body becomes the "cursed share".

> The victim is a surplus extracted from the mass of useful wealth. It can only be removed to be consumed without profit, and consequently, destroyed forever. From the moment it is chosen, it becomes the accursed share, destined for violent consumption. (Bataille, 1975, p. 97–98)

The Black body, in its pornographic materiality, is meant to be consumed sacrificially, allowing global antiblackness to make sense and enabling the nation-state to consolidate its self-destructive contradictions into a negative objectification embodied in the Black body. This body serves as the vicarious object of the white power structure's phantasmatic projections. As exemplified in this case, social values are upheld precisely because the Black body has been shattered, its arm broken, its head severed, and its remains obliterated in the pyre of oblivion. As Dr. Andreia Beatriz, an

---

[38] RONDESP stands for "Rondas Especiais da Polícia Militar da Bahia", or Special Patrols of Bahia's Military Police

activist in the Reaja Campaign, reminds us in the film, all this destruction serves to remind us "what it means to be Black". A thing, like a corpse on the ground. Nothing, as the negation of the Black man's personhood.

David Marriott (2000a), in discussing photographs of racist lynchings in the South of the U.S. during segregation, poses a disturbing question: "What if the cultural traffic in images on the black men as phobic object—beaten, disfigured, lynched—is trauma enough?" (p. 13). Similarly, do the images of disfigured Black youth in "Notícias" contribute to further violence and dehumanization, perpetuating what Saidiya Hartman (1997) terms "the violence of the archive"? Do they complete the ritual work of exposing and humiliating the Black body? I confess that this was my immediate perception of the film. A profanation. If Black deaths serve a ritualistic function—to violently exorcise the nightmares of the antiblack world—doesn't the display of these deaths merely affirm this expiation? Does it perpetuate or oppose the work of violence that dissects the Black body and separates the Black individual from their physical form? As Marriott (2000b) further observes, "An image of White identity emerges from a spectacle of annihilation" (p. 6). Doesn't whiteness emerge strengthened from this miserable spectacle? While attempting to denounce, unsettle, and provoke empathy, the Reaja film inadvertently reinforces the objectification, obscenity, and sacrificial nature of Black deaths. What differentiates the display of blood on Cyclone-brand shorts in a narrow alley from the exhibition of massacred bodies in sensationalist, punitive journalism? Doesn't the fixation on the Black body—reduced to a corpse—simply reiterate the objectification of Black individuals? Doesn't it speak the same language? The body, resistant to signification or subjective agency, becomes merely a residue, a putrid burden of a ghost dissolved in (ir)reversible time.

This debate, of course, has its own intellectual tradition. Susan Sontag (1987), in "The Pornographic Imagination", warns us: "Pornography is ultimately not about sex but death" (p. 64). Through its extroversion and total depersonalization, represented in the stereotyping of emotions and a certain moral suspension, Sontag argues that "only in the absence of directly stated emotions can the reader of pornography find room for his own responses" (p. 59). More recently, Judith Butler revisited this theme in a way that aligns with our discussion here. They examine the dissemination of images from the torture at Abu Ghraib prison, where shocking photographs depicted American soldiers—both men and women—torturing and sexually humiliating prisoners. These images were widely considered obscene representations. Butler questions how pain is represented and how such representations affect us. What does it mean, then, to consider images as "structuring representations"? In the regime of representation under capitalism, or the "society of the spectacle" (Debord, 1998), images do not bring us closer to suffering. Instead, they distance us, through the voyeuristic operation of deriving pleasure from others' pain, thereby erasing any possibility of empathy. In this context, suffering does not humanize—it reduces us to "human animals".

> It is not, however, the practice of eroticized seeing that is the problem here, but the moral indifference of the photograph coupled with its investment in the continuation and reiteration of the scene as a visual icon. (Butler, 2015, p. 137)

This visual icon, then, is our dead body—the corpse on the ground—a chasm of meaning and the negation of any possible ontology in the face of this profaned object.

Musa Matiuzzi, in her performance "Experimentando o Dilúvio em Vermelho", approaches these issues differently, with a more reflective and self-aware engagement with the contradictions, antagonisms, and tensions inherent in representing the Black body within the framework of global antiblackness.

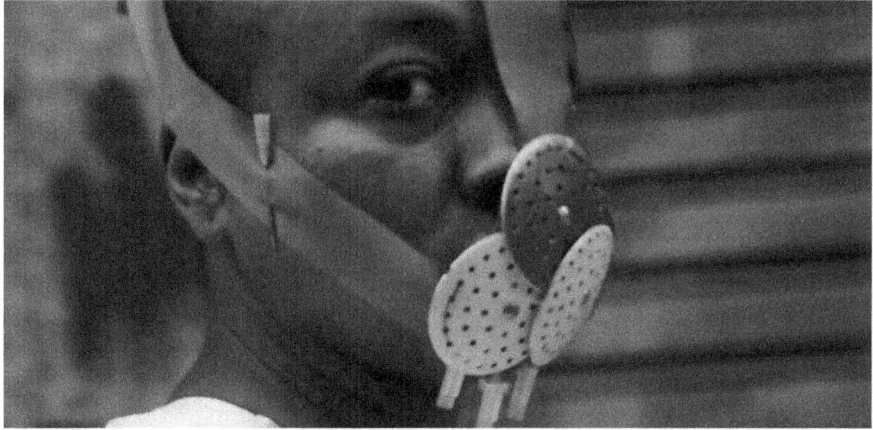

Figure 5 — Experimentando o Dilúvio em Vermelho, still from the trailer, 2019. Source: https://www.youtube.com/watch?v=VNSbWM4aCDg. Accessed in November 2024

The performance is presented as "a mechanism for creating counter-narratives (...) of people and invisibilities in space" (Luciana Ribeiro, 2017). In various public spaces, the artist pierces sensitive parts of her body with needles, releasing an abundance of blood. A red deluge of Black blood. As she explains: "I live under the ruins of what they call civilization". Among these ruins and ancestral evocations, she claims the role of a priestess who sacrifices her own body. In this sense, the flesh seems to rise as both a subversive mechanism and an objection. It is the Black body in its immanence that is (un)made in the performance, spilling blood and sense upon the void or over the ruins of a civilization inherently antiblack. By using her own flesh as the material for rebellion, Matiuzzi seeks to humanize herself, revealing her personhood hidden within itself. If the denial of Black Humanity is rooted in the impossibility of treating the Black body as flesh—existing beyond signification—then Matiuzzi aims to signify precisely through her flesh, inscribing a self-explanatory commentary in blood. This commentary is simultaneously immanent in its materiality and transcendent in its meaning.

As Saidiya Hartman (1997) observes: "The significance of the performative lies not in the ability to overcome those conditions or provide remedy but in creating a context for the collective enunciation of the pain" (p. 52). In this regard, Matiuzzi's performance operates in an opposite way to Reaja's film.

The "soul in the eye" or the integrity of "being", retelling stories through a bodily narrative that asserts corporeality while rejecting the fake History. The formalized and agile montage of the movie "Now!" decodes the Black body and its struggle within the revolutionary ecstasy framed by its fight for liberation. The visual pamphlet of the Reaja campaign, however, remains trapped in the same aporias of representing the Black body as a mortal abyss for its Humanity; and the bloody red—corporeal matter reclaimed—not to transcend contradiction but to inhabit antagonism within its flesh. The formal elements mobilized to address and embody such antinomies are a leap into darkness: inconclusive, perpetual, suspended at a threshold, a border, or a limit. The objectified body in its flesh is not distinct from itself. The law of the state, as a "separate law", cannot make such an effort, intervening in the signification of the Black body as the *corpus* of a society yearning for meaning. In its flesh-made-object, standing at the borders of the state and civil society, performed Blackness recognizes that affirming itself requires rejecting the world and its imposed image.

In both Matiuzzi's performance and Reaja's film, the border is not merely formal or epistemological, code versus meaning, body or flesh, but also ethical and ontological.

In "Onticide", Calvin Warren (2015) offers a framework for understanding the ethical dilemmas of representation in an antiblack world. These dilemmas are defined by gratuitous violence, the violation of bodies, and the fungibility of Black flesh—structural measures shaped by systemic racial antagonism and the middle passage.

> Black suffering is illegible and incommunicable because it lacks a proper grammar of enunciation. Suffering belongs to the human; it is an inescapable feature of the "human condition". The "violation of the flesh," however, is a murderous practice without a "proper name" or any name that is recognizable within the Symbolic. (Warren, 2015, p. 10)

Unrepresentable because it eludes the semiotic regime of representations, Blackness is (de)ontologizable in the same way—or for that very reason. The boundary of meaning in Black culture ("Alma no Olho" and "Now!") becomes the ethical limit of the Black man's personhood ("Notícias" and "Dilúvio em Vermelho"), as suggested by the ambiguity of the term *represent* (Spivak, 2014). The Black frontier is a limit—the only place where the Black individual can "exist", imprisoned in phobogenic materiality while being ethically unrepresentable in the world. This suspension, or tension, from the perspective of the antiblack world, resembles a dead end, where we seek escape through fugitive practices that precariously balance on these dangerous borders between being a thing and being nothing. Alternatively, it can be found in the immanence of ancestrality, as we will explore in the next chapter.

CHAPTER 4
"ATLANTIC BLOOD": SOCIAL DEATH AND ANCESTRALITY IN ALBERT ECKHOUT AND AYRSON HERÁCLITO

"Can beauty provide an antidote to dishonor, and love a way to 'exhume buried cries' and reanimate the dead?"
— **Saidiya Hartman, "Venus in Two Acts," 2008**

ATLANTIC BLOOD

In this chapter, I return to the reflection on Black art to revisit epistemologies and discursive practices that are strained by the middle passage and its metamorphoses. These are configured as two moments or positions within the political forms of Black subjectivity and imagination: "ancestrality" and "social death". At the center, or midpoint, of this constellation lies a dual-entry problem that rests upon the red waters of the enslaving Atlantic. This problem concerns the (im)possibility of representation for Black individuals, as many authors, including Lewis Gordon (1999), have emphasized. Not only can the Black individual not be represented, being immersed in "thingness" and fundamentally in immanence—a "thing among other things"—but Blackness itself, from the perspective defined by social death, could not be represented either. How, then, can we even speak of Black art? The opposition between "slave" and "African", or "social death" and "Africanity", thus seems to project itself as the tension between representation and immanence. In this sense, I aim to trace these tensions by examining the works of two very different artists, who, from distinct historical periods and perspectives, engage with the connection between forced displacement and forms of representation, immanence, and Black positionality. These artists are Albert Eckhout and Ayrson Heráclito, and it is precisely the distance between their approaches that I seek to highlight here.

Lewis Gordon, as we have seen, considers the incorporation of Blackness through two primary elements. First, the Black individual and/ or their body is described as a "thing among other things". Second, as "pure absence", resisting symbolization (Gordon, 1999). In this sense, the Black individual is their body, and their body is pre- or non-symbolic. This implies that Blackness, which cannot be represented or interpreted, is trapped within the materiality of the flesh, as described by Spillers (1987) and discussed in the previous chapter. Such entrapment phenomenologically constitutes the antiblack world. The emergence of this antiblack world is stitched together by the middle passage and the forced transposition it entails—a deracination, annulment, and irrevocable rupture defined by the political economy of colonial mercantilism. This economy established the material and symbolic means to effectuate a transformation that imposed an essential ontological rupture. Defined by overwhelming violence, but above all by an irreversible plunge into a sea of death, a sea of blood, the African's personhood deteriorated, with any possibility of recognition systematically denied. The middle passage introduces a form of death that subjectively defines the enslaved condition into History. The sea of blood, the ultimate transcendence, can be read as structured by a ritual framework: separation, liminality, or death, and reintegration. Alternatively, it may be understood in sacrificial terms, as the cursed part that must be cast away to produce prestige, power, and beauty, as discussed in Chapter 3 (Bataille, 1975).

Image p. 143
Figure 6 — "Atlantic Blood", Samuca, 2018.
Source: Photo by the author, 2018.

Sacrificed and killed in the blood-soaked Atlantic, the African individual is reborn as the enslaved Black figure, emptied of their former identity. This delirious scenario is neither innocuous nor sterile; as both a trope and a historical landscape, it is represented or understood as a boundary of representation in its own materiality. This idea is poignantly captured in Samuca's engraving, which lends its title to this chapter. Samuca, a young graffiti artist from Salvador, Bahia (Falcon & Garcia, 2014), is known for inscribing faces and masks on the city's walls. In this work, he juxtaposes a deep blue sky against a blood-red sea, channeling all his creative energy into the symbolic emblem of the slave ship. Through the dramatic plasticity of his engraving, he portrays the violent whirlwind of an irreversible journey—one of destruction, rupture, or structural sacrifice—that sets the stage for an impossible subject. This figure, submerged in maritime annihilation, seeks to rediscover itself: in blood, through blood, and amidst the sea—a liquid death, as red as dendê oil, as seen in the works of Ayrson Heráclito.

This chapter will explore how these themes emerge in the works of both artists. First, it will examine the allegorical typology of Albert Eckhout, who, in the 16th century, inaugurated a visual grammar of race and colonialism. Second, it will investigate the materiality of symbolic elements in Ayrson Heráclito's art, which transmutes the experience of slavery and colonialism into visceral and transformative expressions.

"AFRICAN WARRIOR"

Arriving in Dutch Brazil in 1637, the Dutch painter Albert Eckhout remained in the newly conquered territory until 1644[39] as part of the entourage accompanying Count Johan Maurits of Nassau-Siegen, the governor of what was then the captaincy of Pernambuco. Known for his reputation as an enlightened humanist, Nassau also brought with him other artists and scholars, including Franz Post, who painted grand scenes and landscapes, and Eckhout, who was dedicated to "verist" depictions with a naturalistic and "ethnological" approach. In 1654, Nassau gifted King Frederick III of Denmark with 26 artworks, 23 of which were created by Eckhout. Among these is a life-size painting titled "African Warrior", a representation of one of the racial "types" of the colony. Dated 1641, this painting is currently housed in the Ethnographic Collection of the National Museum in

---

[39] It is worth noting that the domination of the Dutch West India Company in Brazil's northeastern region lasted from 1630 to 1654.

Copenhagen (Etnografisk Samling; Costa, 2011; Belluzzo, 1994; Brienen, 2004, 2006).

Image 7 — "African Warrior" – Alberto Eckhout, 1641.
Source: Brienen, 2006.

Much has already been said about the painting, both from the perspective of the history of colonial transpositions or "exchanges" observed within this horizon, and from the formal perspective of pictorial or compositional analysis, typical of art history. However, our inquiry addresses, as many others have done, the centrality of images in shaping the colonial imagination in Brazil. Image creation in this context is far removed from any notion of epistemological transparency. On the contrary, it reveals how paradigmatic conventions of representation generate political meanings and how social stereotypes forged a visual mechanism—a "machine", as I hypothesize—that constructs a grammar for interpreting/producing Black bodies within the (post)colonial Brazilian horizon.

From this perspective, Eckhout's painting serves as an instance or provisional model for discussing possible elements of this racialized and gendered colonial grammar. Central to this discussion is the way colonial imagination established the matrices of contemporary Brazilian culture as a discursive apparatus of power, along with its potential futures. This connects with our broader inquiry into the racialization of masculinity, developed in other fields (Pinho, 2006, 2015).

Slavery has been identified as a foundational marker for the structure of meanings and the conditions enabling subjectivity as a political positionality, as we see here (Wilderson, 2010; Sexton, 2011). My focus lies on interrogating the invention of the "Black" individual, who was expected to meet structural/subjective requirements to align a historical body with a symbolically structured social position. The material connection between the Black body and labor, as well as the symbolic connection between the Black body and a regime of representations or epistemology, form the core of my concern. In both cases, slavery—or the enslaved condition—is theoretically contorted to locate Africans within the colonial space of the New World.

In the case of *african-american*, the expansion of this argument—acknowledging slavery as the fundamental fact shaping Black experience in the Americas—is robustly established and intricately linked to representation and its devices. In "Scenes of Subjection", Saidiya Hartman (1997) discusses the formation of Black subjectivity through a primordial scene, narrated by Frederick Douglass, of the brutal whipping of his aunt Hester in 1845: "This terrible spectacle dramatizes the origin of the subject" (p. 3). This scene is considered primordial because it situates Black "flesh" at the intersection of representation and dispossession. This connection recurs in representations of Brazilian slavery. In Jean-Baptiste Debret's lithograph, derived from an 1828 watercolor, a man writhes on the ground, his features contorted by pain. Immobilized by a stick placed between his legs, he awaits the lash (Debret, 1989; Bandeira & Lago, 2009). This and similar scenes have been canonized within the iconography of enslaved suffering. The violence depicted in these scenes and their indexical dimension—though shaped by technical conventions and stylistic choices—testify to the artist's agenda and a sociocultural landscape where the enslaved could be reduced to their bare flesh, bloodied and dehumanized. At the same time, these images establish a motif, a trope, for representing suffering as such and as the negative counterpart of the human condition (Hartman, 1997).

Image 8 — "Overseer Punishing Slaves", Jean-Baptiste Debret, 1835.
Source: Pedrosa et al., 2018.

The violence and violation of the Black body, beyond or concurrent with its economic functions—as highlighted, for example, even by Karl Marx (Marx & Engels, 1964)—do not exhaust its political and semiological plasticity for the spectacle of public torture and degradation. As David Marriott (2000a) emphasizes in the context of racist lynchings in the American South, the spectacle of destruction and physical annihilation of Black people, along with their consequent moral and personal devastation, is essential for producing the stability of whiteness as a socio-historical construct. The reduction of the Black individual, their body and personhood, to something non-human or sub-human, serves to confirm white Humanity. This raises, as James Baldwin (2018) asks, whether there has ever been a moment when Black individuals were "present in their own lives" (p. 157). Alternatively, where can we locate Black agency within these colonial confrontations and games of power? This question points toward the indexical dimension of artistic representation. As Cunningham (1996) argues, "The African American as captive body, materially and metaphorically, is public and on the block; to be bid upon in a circuit of linguistic, discursive, and axiological exchange outside the control of its own agency" (p. 137).

From this perspective, our analysis must focus on representation and objectification, as this entanglement reveals the relationship between visual conventions, objective social facts, structures of mediation, and representations that circulate—or are "displaced" within the colonial space. This colonial framework links the racialized/gendered body to the landscape. Before offering further observations on Eckhout's "African Warrior", it is necessary to revisit how contemporary decolonial critique approaches questions of gender and sexuality. We know how, historically, the coloniality of power and scientific racism in Brazil converged to construct precolonial (sexual) worlds as pits of racial atavism and sexual perversion. Against this "barbaric" abjection, heterosexuality and its normalization emerged, oriented toward a heterosexualized whiteness. As Richard Miskolci (2012) has argued, this process helped shape a national ideal of heterosexualization and whitening. The invention of the nation as a "racial formation", articulating race and sexuality in a national project of power and subjectivity, was thus deeply intertwined. This is evident in Gilberto Freyre's work, particularly "Sobrados e Mocambos" (2000), where the modernization of society during the transition from the colonial period to the empire unfolds into the creation of a male character, the mulatto bachelor, embodying a synthesis of these shifts. Freyre's mulatto bachelor—Europeanized yet described as "half-breed" and feminized—represents a typical Freyrean operation in which sexuality, desire, and the body are central operators of racialization (Freyre, 1995; Pinho, 2004).

In his later work, "Modos de Homem & Modas de Mulher" (2009), Freyre applies his gender framework to interpret Brazil as a "meta-racial" society. However, it is through his discussion of fugitive slave advertisements in newspapers that Freyre most closely approaches our concerns. These advertisements, with their shocking descriptions, offer a glimpse into the construction of a gendered and racialized body marked by (extravagant) ways of dressing.

> In the same newspaper, in an issue dated May 1, 1848, a notice describes an escaped slave wearing a "madapollam shirt with gold-buttoned cuffs and an embroidered

purple silk vest..." In another advertisement from the same year—May 13—it mentions another escaped slave who "took blue-striped trousers and a shirt." On April 14, 1836, an advertisement stated that the slave man, José, had fled "wearing blue-striped trousers." Similarly, in 1838, an announcement dated January 12 described a fugitive slave carrying a "blue-striped jacket." Elias, according to an advertisement from September 13, 1838, paired his white trousers with a "purple chintz jacket." Blue and purple hues shining in the garments of slaves. (Freyre, 2009, p. 198)

This reference to slavery is relevant because, as we shall see, one of the contentious aspects of the "African Warrior" painting relates precisely to the enslaved—or not enslaved—status of the man represented.

As part of the Dutch occupation of Brazil's northeastern region, Eckhout was, as previously mentioned, tasked with portraying the natural and human diversity of this new colonial possession. As Ana Belluzzo (1994) and others point out, this work aligns with the imaginative fabulation of the exotic Other, dominated by exuberant and surprising nature.

The "Brazilian types", life-sized, allegorical figures, are often mischaracterized as ethnological. Yet, as previously discussed, they are fundamentally allegorical and typological, constructed as pictorial examples or testimonies of different stages of civilization. These include the Tapuia pair: a woman carrying human limbs and a nude man, embodying cannibalistic savagery; the acculturated Tupi couple, wearing loincloths and knives at their waists; sexually ambiguous mestizos; and finally, the Black pair. The latter comprises a woman holding a lighter-skinned child, insinuating miscegenation, and wearing an "Asian-style" hat; and the man, who is of particular interest here (Brienen, 2006; Buvelot, 2004).

Facing the observer head-on, the male figure is striking for his overwhelming physicality, an effect amplified by the image's monumental dimensions (273 cm x 167 cm). He wears a loincloth of African (Akan) design, which, rather than concealing his genitals, draws attention to them. At his waist, he carries an Akrafena, the sword of Akan medieval warriors, a people of West Africa who formed the Ashanti Empire in the 17th century (M'bokolo, 2008; Darkwah, 1999; Quarcoopome, 1997). However, we cannot assume that Eckhout painted directly from life. First, we know that another artist, Zacharias Wagener, created sketches of the "types", at least for the "Black woman", raising questions about the original authorship of the composition and themes (Belluzzo, 1994; Brienen, 2004). Moreover, as many scholars have noted, these types adhere to European visual conventions, including clichés reminiscent of allegorical representations of America and other continents. In such depictions, standing female figures look sideways at the viewer, hold symbolic objects in their hands, and are surrounded by elements of authority and strangeness, structuring the "European collector's gaze", as James Clifford (2008) discusses. Finally, we know that Eckhout, like other artists, likely completed his works in Europe after creating sketches on-site. This fact further underscores the issue under consideration: the mobilization of visual conventions to establish a structured, articulated framework for the racialized representation of Black individuals through a colonial lens. As Lilia Schwarcz (2018) argues, this process needs to:

> ...demystify the supposed objectivity of the engravings produced at that time, as they reveal underlying interests or even intentional patterns (...). We are, therefore, confronted with a genuine politics of images, which ultimately justified the necessity of domination over peoples whose customs were considered so distinct. (p. 527)

Thus, less ethnology and more colonial fantasy. A fantasy mediated by conventions. It is worth noting that Eckhout's paintings are considered among the earliest to depict the (racialized) inhabitants of the New World in loco. At the same time, the allegorical dimension is evident; in this case, the allegory of race and gender is of particular interest.[40] Regarding the Black woman, there is near unanimity in recognizing her as an allegory of the "beauty and strength" of African women. Her accessories and adornments, however, allow for multiple interpretations. Beside her, the mixed-race child holds a bird of African origin (Agapornis pullarius) and an ear of corn, unmistakably American. These elements have been interpreted as symbols of displacement and colonial exchange (this symbolic layering reflects the broader geopolitical context of the period, specifically the West India Company's attempts to assert its dominance in Africa, including the invasion of São Paulo de Luanda in 1641).

---

[40] Theodor de Bry and others had previously created representations of Indigenous peoples, but not explicitly racialized ones. This distinction arises because the modern concept of race itself was constructed largely through representations of Africans and enslaved individuals in the New World, such as those produced by Eckhout. (Brienen, 2006)

Image 9 — African Woman and Child, Albert Echkout, 1641.
Source: Brienen. 2006

Similarly, the male representative of the Black race in Eckhout's painting is rich with symbolic references. The ivory tusk on the ground to the right clearly points to Africa, as does the date palm. At his waist is the Akrafena sword, while in the background lies the sea. An uninhabited ocean contrasts with other paintings where the background is animated by various activities, such as in the Black Woman painting, which features boats and workers. The emptiness surrounding the male figure seems to heighten the sense of exoticism and savagery, raising questions about the actual setting of the scene. Could it represent Palmares, the famous quilombo?

Barefoot like a slave, the man is armed like a warrior, and his stern, confident gaze reinforces the perception that he is not a captive. According to musician and historian Spirito Santo (2019), there is no doubt that the "African Warrior" is a representation or allegory of Black or African warriors who, capitalizing on the disorder caused by the Dutch invasion, established Palmares (1580–1654) decades earlier. From this perspective, the man depicted is not a slave but perhaps a symbolic representation of Ganga Zumba, the leader of the quilombolas, who, according to Décio Freitas, personally visited Recife after its reconquest by the Portuguese in 1678. Spirito Santo's interpretation, however, contrasts sharply with that of anthropologist Peter Mason (2001), who argues that the figure represents a slave: "The near nudity of the man in the painting leads us to assume that he is a slave. There is, therefore, an obvious incongruence between his condition and his depiction holding an acã [sic] sword, a symbol of *status* for dignitaries and emissaries" (p. 239). Indeed, it is more likely that the figure represents an imagined Akan warrior or dignitary from present-day Ghana, where Dutch colonial presence and interests were also established in the 16th century (Klooster, 2016).

In the construction of enslaved positionality in the colonial world, the commodified nature of the enslaved body has been explored and warrants further discussion. What does this fungibility, the condition of being reduced to a commodity, mean for the identity of Africans in the colonial system? Anna More (2018) and others have contributed to this discourse, alongside critical explorations of the middle passage and its "wake" as analyzed by Christina Sharpe (2016):

> Transatlantic slavery was and is the disaster. The disaster of Black subjection was and is planned; terror is disaster and "terror has a history (...) The history of capital inextricable from the history of Atlantic chattel slavery. The disaster and the writing of disaster are never present, are always present". (p. 5)

In this context, exchange, interaction, and circulation are central to defining the positionality of the enslaved. However, as Peter Mason (2001) points out, "exchange" as reciprocity, in the sense proposed by Marcel Mauss, rather than merely from the perspective of political economy, is crucial to understanding the construction of meaning within the colonial environment. Mason, an anthropologist and leading scholar on Eckhout, argues that three levels, or registers, of exchange define the significance of Eckhout's Brazilian types. The first level is the gifting of twenty-six paintings in 1654 by Johan Maurits of Nassau-Siegen to King Frederick III of Denmark, son of Christian IV. This act reflects the principles of reciprocity governing the exchange of gifts among European royalty, as described by Mauss (2003). The second level of exchange lies within the internal engineering of the works themselves, evident in their related pictorial elements, such as the Asian-style hat worn by the Black Woman or the ivory tusk featured, referencing the broader colonial exchanges that connected different regions and cultures through trade and exploitation. This aligns with Gilberto Freyre's (1995) insights into the orientalist composition of Brazil's colonial sociocultural environment. Notably, the "Negress" is identified as a slave based on a preparatory sketch by Zacharias Wagener, which includes a branding mark with the letter "M" near her breast. Mason (2001) comments significantly: "As a slave, the woman was involved in an economic exchange between cultures; as the mother of a mestizo child, she was involved in a sexual exchange between cultures" (p. 239). The third level reflects the "value" of the exchanged objects themselves. This raises the critical question: What type of objects are these? Mason emphasizes that these works cannot simply be regarded as portraits due to their deeply allegorical nature. Instead, he asks, what is the "visual economy" at work in Eckhout's types?[41] The three dimensions of exchange seem to inherently imply "displacements". As Mason (2001) notes, "The place where these elements are assembled is, therefore, not just any location in Brazil, but the artist's own canvas. In other words, the very act of painting in this case is an act of displacement" (p. 246).

We can, thus, observe that this process involves the deterritorialization and reassembly of visual and ideological elements into an "assemblage" that conveys spatial, geographic, cultural, political, and religious displacement. This a type of disorganization or displacement whose criteria, conventions, and modalities I would like to question, taking into consideration the effects of this relationship of displacement that the work evokes—particularly as they index the European presence—rather than African obviously—within the colonial horizon and the coloniality of power.

---

[41] Here, we adopt the expression "visual economy" to refer to a systematically organized field of vision, one that inherently involves social relations, inequality, and power—an analytical framework that the term "visual culture" cannot fully address. (Mason, 2001, p. 244)

Alfred Gell's anthropological theory of art offers useful insights here, as he contends that artworks act as triggers for social processes rather than mere reflections of them. Gell (2018) emphasizes that "the immediate other in a social relationship does not have to be another human being" (p. 47). In this context, the artwork itself can be a representation, arbitrary and conventional, that manifests the artist's social agency through the "proliferation" of effects. In the case of the "African Warrior", what are these effects, and where do they lie if not within the complex web of exchanges and displacements Mason identifies? Mason puts it as the "given thing" among the princes in a way that the types forge an indexical link between the glory of European crowns and the fascinating colonial world. They operate as the *locus* where colonial elements are reterritorialized and captured within a visual economy of race. This visual economy differently composes the Black woman—with her mixed-race child beside her—and the Black man—with a sword at his waist—as allegorical, fetishized portraits inseparable from the historical conditions that rendered their creation possible. Their fantasy and allegorical verisimilitude constitute the "value" of the works, transforming them into not only fantastical "ethnographic" documents but also operators within the colonial imaginary.

These representations of the Other—be it Eckhout's depiction of the African as savage and fierce or Debret's portrayal of the enslaved in agony—ultimately raise fundamental questions about the construction of freedom, civilization, and Humanity. Such artworks materialize stereotypes, conventions, and visual narrative devices, reducing the complex realities of the colonial encounter—shaped by race and gender—into static forms of representation. These forms retain, as Gell suggests, an indexical dimension[42] that reflects the conflicted agency subjected to this encounter while simultaneously translating and reinforcing the "Western gaze". The "colonial gaze", in shaping colonial subjects, also constructed systems of subjection and political subjectivity as forms of objectification. To interrogate these visual representations is to interrogate the mechanisms of power and control that defined the colonial world and continue to shape its enduring legacies.

---

[42] Indexicality, in the semiotic sense as explained by Gell, refers to the concept from Peircean semiotics where an "index" is a "natural sign". This means it is an entity from which the observer can infer some form of causality or deduce the intentions or capabilities of others. (Gell, 2018, p. 41)

SACRED MATTER

Ayrson Heráclito Novato Ferreira is a contemporary visual artist. Born in a small town in the Brazilian state of Bahia, he has established himself as one of the leading Black artists of his generation. He has presented numerous significant solo exhibitions, including "Pérola Negra" at Blau Projects Gallery, São Paulo (2016); "Genealogy of Materials/Généalogie des Matières" at the Raw Material Company, Dakar, Senegal (2015); "Atlântico Negro" at Central Galeria de Arte, São Paulo (2013); and "Ecologia do Pertencimento" at the Museum of Modern Art of Bahia, Salvador (2002). Additionally, he has participated in equally prestigious group exhibitions, such as the 57th Venice Biennale, Venice, Italy (2017); "10 Rencontres de Bamako", the African Biennale of Photography, Bamako, Mali (2015); and "A Nova Mão Afro-Brasileira" at the Afro Brazil Museum, São Paulo (2013), among others. Heráclito was also one of the curators of the groundbreaking exhibition "Histórias Afro-Atlânticas" [Afro-Atlantic Histories], which brought together over 400 works by nearly 200 artists, dating from the 16th century to the present, at the São Paulo Museum of Art Assis Chateaubriand (MASP) and the Tomie Ohtake Institute. This exhibition emerged as a continuation of the earlier show "Histórias Mestiças" [Mestizo Histories], curated by anthropologist and University of São Paulo professor Lilia Schwarcz and Adriano Pedrosa, held at the Tomie Ohtake Institute in 2014. "Histórias Afro-Atlânticas" was subsequently named one of the best exhibitions of the year by *The New York Times* (Cotter, 2018).

In this discussion, I will focus on one of Heráclito's works that exemplifies his engagement with "translating" Afro-Brazilian religious experiences into amplified artistic experimentation. At the same time, and central to our analysis, the artist demonstrates a commitment to reflecting on "materials", following the recognized influence of Joseph Beuys's work and thought (Rosenthal, 2011; Rodrigues, 2019; Zmário, 2019; Raynner Souza, 2017). The artwork in question is the audiovisual piece "As mãos de Epô" [The Hands of Epô]. Described by the artist as a means to "re-signify the iconography of African deities", the video utilizes the material density of dendê (palm oil), or epô, as a plastic medium for this re-signification. Against the shimmering golden background of the palm oil paste, hands perform a symbolic dance representing diverse orishas in syntactic frames. Figures such as Egum, Oxum, and Iemanjá are ideographically synthesized through the choreography of dancing hands. As the artist explains, it is "a ballet of hands over dendê oil", employing palm oil as a medium for a "semiotics" that analytically deconstructs the choreographic iconography of African deities. In this work, the artist encodes, through metaphorical traces, a sense of grammaticalized symbolism. In his words, it is "quite didactic". This synthetic quality stands out in its paradoxical relationship with the deep cosmological—rather than semiological—dimensions of the orisha religion (Heráclito, 2014, 2020; Salgado, 2014; Souza, 2017).

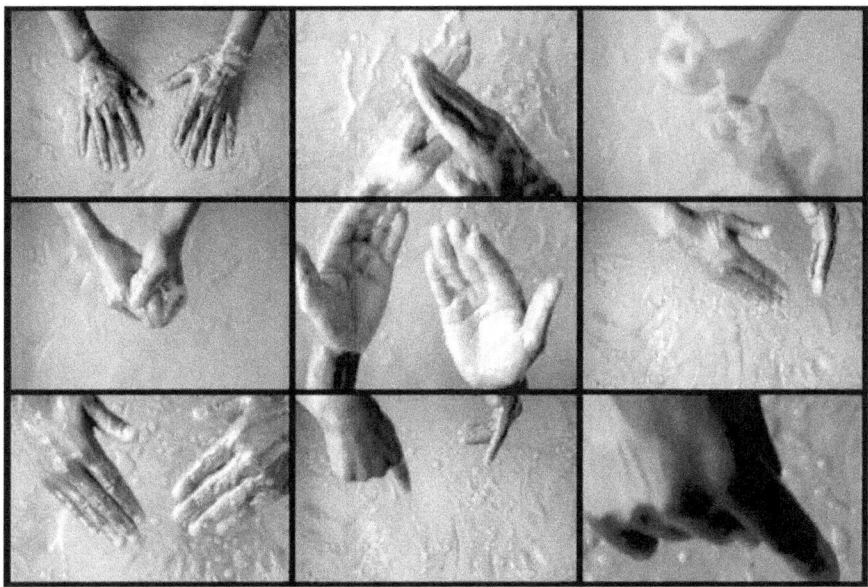

Image 10 — As mãos do Epô, Ayrson Heráclito, 2009.
Source: https://vimeo.com/20802333. Accessed in November 2024.

Before addressing the contradictions inherent in the structure of meaning, which serves as a vehicle for the discussion and experimentation the artist seeks to develop, it is crucial to emphasize the importance of the material dimension in Ayrson Heráclito's work. Both the artist and his critics frequently highlight this aspect, particularly his focus on organic materials as an aesthetic-political means to confront slavery and the colonial past (Heráclito, 2008; Zmário, 2019; Cleveland, 2013). This approach seeks to exorcize the historical trauma of bondage, especially the transatlantic slave trade and the middle passage. Within this material poetics, dendê, or epô, described as the golden vegetable blood, occupies a central role.

Heráclito's exploration of materials aligns with Joseph Beuys's "expanded concept of art", which emphasizes material as both a medium and a philosophical proposition (Rodrigues, 2019; Rosenthal, 2011). Initially, Heráclito's work reflected Bahia's "mestizo and complex" cultural experience (Videobrasil, 2020). Over time, however, his perspective shifted to foreground colonial violence, delving deeply into materials with profound cultural horizons tied to Bahian and/or Black cultural contexts, and/or of candomblé. Through symbolic means, his work seeks to purge the violence of enslavement and the middle passage. In this trajectory, Heráclito has worked with sugar, charque meat (dried beef), and dendê, materials that combine organic, mutable, and perishable properties—qualities that echo Beuys's work. At the same time, these materials draw on Black and Bahian cultural references.

In his master's thesis, which included three artistic installations, Heráclito further elaborated on these themes. Under the mestizo paradigm, he explored the notion of "cultural symbiosis" to identify what he termed the "indicative paradigm of a certain baianidade (Bahian identity)" (Heráclito, 2008, p. 1605). In one of his works, inspired by a poem by the Baroque poet Gregório de Mattos, Heráclito explores the potential of materials to establish syntactic relationships, transforming "objects into sensitive concepts". He manipulates "colonial" materials, including "sulfur, mica, petroleum, beetles, clove oil, formaldehyde, earth, moths, Xerox prints, sugar loaves, fabric, wood, and palm oil", reconfiguring them as mediums of signification (Heráclito, 2008, p. 1610).

The referenced poem by Gregório de Mattos is titled "À Cidade da Bahia", a lamentation for Salvador, Bahia, popularized through the song "Triste Bahia" by Bahian musician Caetano Veloso, recorded in 1971 on the album "Transa". The original poem reads: Triste Bahia! Ó quão dessemelhante [Sad Bahia! Oh, how dissimilar]/ Estás e estou do nosso antigo estado! [You are and I am of our former state]/ Pobre te vejo a ti, tu a mi empenhado, [I see you so poor, you see me so engaged]/ Rica te vi eu já, tu a mi abundante. [I've seen you rich already, you've seen me abundant]/ A ti trocou-te a máquina mercante/ [The merchant machine touched you]/ Que em tua larga barra tem entrado [That has entered your wide bar]/ A mim foi-me trocando, e tem trocado, [They have been trying to change me, and they have changed,]/ Tanto negócio e tanto negociante. [So much trade and so many traders.] (Matos, 2006, p. 103).

Gregório de Mattos e Guerra, born to a Portuguese nobleman, died in 1696 in Recife and is considered both the first Brazilian poet and the greatest Baroque poet of the period. His satirical works critiqued those who were in power during his time, often referencing Black culture and negritude [Blackness]. These references oscillate between blatant racism and the eroticization of Blackness, as complex as it is and contradictory in this colonial environment.

Crioula minha vida,

Supupema da minha alma,
Bonita como umas flores,
E alegre como umas páscoas.
Não sei que feitiço é estes,
Que tens nessa linda cara,
a gracinha, com que falas.
O Garbo, com que te moves,
o donaire, com que andas,
o asseio, com que te vestes,
e o pico, com que te manhas.
Tem-me enfeitiçado, que a bom partido tomara
curar-me por tuas mãos,
sendo tu, a que me matas. (Matos, 2006, p. 185)

Crioula[43] of my life,
Delight of my soul,
Beautiful as flowers,
And as joyful as Easter.
I do not know what spell it is
That you have in that lovely face,
The charm with which you speak,
The elegance with which you move,
The grace with which you walk,
The neatness with which you dress,
And the wit with which you deceive.
You have bewitched me so,
That I would gladly be cured
By your hands,
Though it is you who kills me. (Matos, 2006, p. 185)

We observe that the sexual-colonial fascination with the Black woman, or the Black body, transformed into a "site of irresistible sensuality for

---

[43] T.N.: The terms *crioula* (feminine) and *crioulo* (masculine) in Brazilian Portuguese historically referred to Black people born in Brazil (as opposed to those born in Africa). During the colonial and slavery periods, these terms distinguished between enslaved people born in Brazil versus those brought from Africa. In contemporary Brazil, both terms can be considered offensive and derogatory when used to refer to Black people, as they carry historical connotations tied to slavery and racial hierarchies. The preferred and respectful terms today are mulher negra/preta (Black woman) and homem negro/preto (Black man), reflecting Brazil's ongoing efforts to address racial terminology and promote dignity in language regarding Afro-Brazilian identity.

the captor" (Spillers, as cited in Warren, 2015, p. 9)—has a long tradition in Bahia. This particular poem gains deeper meaning when considered alongside other works by the same Gregório de Mattos.

> Quais são seus doces objetos .... Pretos
> Tem outros bens mais maciços .... Mestiços
> Quais destes lhe são mais gratos .... Mulatos
> Dou ao demo os insensatos,
> Dou ao demo a gente asnal
> Que estima por cabedal
> Pretos, Mestiços, Mulatos.
> (Matos, 2006, p. 61)

> What are your sweet objects? ... Blacks
> Do you have other solid goods? ... Mestizos
> Which of these are more pleasing to you? ... Mulattos
> To the devil with the senseless,
> To the devil with the ignorant people
> Who wait for wealth
> Blacks, Mestizos, Mulattos.
> (Matos, 2006, p. 61)

The works in question—presented in conjunction with the completion of this academic phase—include the installations "À Bahia: 1° Pressuposto do Açúcar" [To Bahia: First Assumption of Sugar], "Segredos Internos: 2° Pressuposto sobre o Açúcar" [Internal Secrets: Second Assumption of Sugar], "O Pequeno Principado: 3° Pressuposto do Açúcar" [The Little Principality: Third Assumption of Sugar], and "Aula: 4° Pressuposto sobre o Açúcar" [Lesson: Fourth Assumption of Sugar]. These works reflect Heráclito's aesthetic-political objectives, as explained by the artist himself:

> I have always been interested in working with "interme-diate" materials, that is, raw materials—substances for reflection. They are intermediate because they are in a constant state of transformation, either physically or sym-bolically. These materials provoke a direct association with a particular theme while simultaneously allowing for a broad range of interpretations. Following the path out-lined by Beuys, I aim to achieve methexis—the concrete

expression of an idea or spirituality. Palm oil is one of these materials. (Heráclito, 2008, p. 1613)

The video installation "Barrueco" can be seen as both a radicalization and a transition from this initial phase, moving toward a new, more African-diasporic vocabulary. This shift marks a departure from a Bahian identity that, while infused with "Black issues", was nevertheless mestizo—that is, not exclusively Black. The title "Barrueco" refers to imperfect pearls, celebrating imperfection, complexity, and "hybridity". Created in collaboration with video artist Danillo Barata, the work incorporates the same elements used in "As mãos de epô", particularly dendê, which appears frequently in Heráclito's works as a means of "reinterpreting our history through artistic creation". Barata elaborates on the use of dendê in Heráclito's work:

> Dendê got his interest because it was a metaphor for the body. Within his poetics, dendê oxygenates this cultural body—the Black, Bahian body—with a strong influence of Black issues. For Ayrson, palm oil symbolized ancestral blood that oxygenated the body and the resilient dried flesh (carne seca). His first concept was to work with dendê as blood, imagining the blood as the ocean, a sea of dendê as a metaphor for the Black Atlantic, the oxygen that propels this resistant body in the Americas. (Barata, 2016, p. 67)

Barrueco draws from Wlamira Albuquerque's poem "Divisor" and engages with the experience of the Middle Passage. The "multimodal" incorporation (Freitas, 2016) of Albuquerque's poem amplifies the work's connection to the transatlantic journey and its enduring impact. The poem reads:

> Era atlântica a solidão negra.
> E nestes dias atlânticos sabemos ser nosso o que está distante,
> submerso em travessias absurdas, em náuseas intermináveis.
>
> Foi atlântico o medo do mar, a adivinhação da tempestade,

a expectativa da rotina.
Foi atlântica a dissimulação de esperança

Nestes dias, sabemos ser nosso o que está distante.
Ela disse ser Esperança da Boaventura,
como os Aleluia, os Bonfim, os da Cruz, os do Espírito
Santo.

Com tantos outros, mergulhamos num flagelo atlântico.
Desde então, estamos todos assentados no fundo do
oceano.
(Albuquerque, 2009, p. 7)

The loneliness was Atlantic and Black.
And on these Atlantic days, we know that what is ours is
distant,
Submerged in absurd crossings, in unending nausea.

The fear of the sea was Atlantic, the divination of the
storm, the expectation of routine.
The dissimulation of hope was Atlantic.

On these days, we know that what is ours is distant.
She said she was Esperança da Boaventura,
like the Aleluia, the Bonfim, the Cruz, the Espiríto Santo.

Like so many others, we plunged into an Atlantic
scourge.
Since then, we are all seated in the deep of the ocean.
(Albuquerque, 2009, p. 7)

As I have already mentioned, a significant part of Ayrson Heráclito's aesthetic strategy is grounded in the work and theoretical approach of Joseph
Beuys, successfully combined with cultural references and the symbolic
universe of the Yoruba and Nagô traditions in Bahia. The performance, or
action—in Beuys's terminology—entitled "Transmutation of the Flesh" exemplifies these principles, particularly the distinction between action and
performance. In the case of "Transmutation of the Flesh", which garnered
considerable attention, the artist creates garments and accessories made of
dried, salted beef and reproduces, in various public or semi-public spaces,

the abuses and mutilations documented in historical records. These records describe the unimaginable and incredibly sadistic tortures inflicted
on the bodies of enslaved individuals by figures such as Gabriel D'Ávila
Pereira and other colonial slave owners (Mott, 2010). Ayrson Heráclito
replicates these torments on the dried meat, including burns and branding
with hot irons. The result is a profoundly sensory experience for the audience, who are confronted with the smell of burning meat and the heat of
fire. As Zmário (2019) describes:

> Layers of sound, smell, and temperature were intricate-
> ly presented in this artistic proposal through actions
> such as branding garments made of dried meat with hot
> irons, walking on embers wearing footwear crafted from
> the same organic material, and cutting and roasting dried
> meat (a highly consumed food in northeastern Brazil). We
> noticed that these actions symbolically reenacted the pub-
> lic tortures and executions of those who were tortured and
> burned alive in the past. The dried meat was displayed as
> a metaphor for human flesh itself, representing the frag-
> mented, dismembered human body. (p. 7)

The connection to Joseph Beuys's work is evident and explicitly acknowledged. The German artist, who transitioned from performative
works to "action" to deepen the relationship with materials and foster interaction with the audience for educational and political purposes, main-
tained that art is life and life is art, asserting that every human being is
an artist. With his concept of "social sculpture", Beuys sought to highlight
the intrinsic creativity of human social activity and envisioned a model of
intervention as a political platform for societal transformation. This vision
materialized in several institutional initiatives, such as the Student Party
founded in 1964, and the Universidade Livre (Free University) established
in 1974 (Rodrigues, 2019; Rosenthal, 2011).

In an interesting and highly relevant way for our discussion, Joseph
Beuys proposes an exploration of the social role of material elements, aligning with his concept of the expanded definition of art and social sculpture
(Rosenthal, 2011). This perspective emphasizes the role of materials as wit-
nesses to processes of transformation and mutability, an idea also deeply
influenced by religious experience. This resonates with Ayrson Heráclito's
approach, as he often identifies himself as a devotee of the orishas. Within

this metaphysical, transubstantial, or transcendental framework, one might interpret the idea that materials accumulate potential energy, which metamorphoses into multiple forms. In this sense, the use of materials should not be seen merely as a symbolic strategy for representation but rather as a method for making theories concrete and tangible. This approach reaches audiences directly—not merely metaphorically or symbolically—inducing social transformation and fostering an awareness of materials as embodiments of plasticity and the intrinsic creativity that underpin both societal structuring and human sensitivity. As Heráclito explains, "I chose the medium of artistic expression that establishes an organic relationship with space: installation, which, in the words of critic Baitello, is a gathering of objects in a defined syntactic relationship, proposing a thesis, illustrating, or materializing an idea" (Heráclito, 2008, p. 1607).

In this particular case, the "idea" oscillates between the register of both the sacred and art. As previously noted, this opens a space for interpreting the artwork beyond the narrow confines of the art world, in line with Alfred Gell's conception of art as an artifact that materializes the extended agency of the artist or cultural tradition—a form of "distributed personhood" (Gell, 2018). In Gell's terms, this is analogous to the concept of the "fetish", understood, like the artwork, as an "index" of personhood, with real practical effects rather than serving merely as a representation of abstract or external content. Sacred objects, like artworks, have objective social effects and connect "people" of various natures, such as "fetishes", gods, priests, and devotees, as discussed more recently by Matory (2018). Similarly, Ayrson Heráclito views his work as an extension of his religious worldview: "I believe in the energy of rituals, in the transformative power they have in the world" (Tessitore, 2018, p. 2). This notion recalls, once again, Antonin Artaud (1987) and his concrete sacred madness:

> I say that the stage is a concrete physical place which asks to be filled, and to be given its own concrete language to speak. I say that this concrete language, intended for the senses and independent of speech, has first to satisfy the senses, that there is a poetry of the senses as there is a poetry of language, and that this concrete physical language to which I refer is truly theatrical only to the degree that the thoughts it expresses are beyond the reach of the spoken language. (p. 51)

The cosmology of the Nagô tradition, from which much of Ayrson Heráclito's visual grammar is derived, provides a critical framework for understanding his work. Central to this discussion is the significance of dendê, epô. It would be important, in this case, to recognize the àse as the fundamental principle of Yoruba philosophy. As Santos (2017) explains, àse is "the force that ensures dynamic existence, enabling events to occur and transformations to take place" (p. 40). Àse, or in Brazilian Portuguese writing, axé, is the vital principle of all existence; everything that exists does so because of àse, which must be continuously accumulated and nurtured. In this cosmological framework, àse manifests through various material elements that allow its manipulation, containment, or symbolic transmission. However, this relationship cannot be reduced to a simple symbolic–material dichotomy, as the boundaries between the two seem blurred, as we will see further. For instance, àse is "seated" in the terreiro, the temple of the orishas, with all its architectural, ecological, and mystical complexity. It is present in the ancestors, their legacy, and, most importantly, the orishas. However, an essential characteristic of the Nagô system is that "every spiritual or abstract element corresponds to a material or corporeal representation or location" (Santos, 2017, p. 41). Substances and materials thus serve as both materializers and transmitters of àse. These materials are categorized into three distinct categories: (1) red blood, (2) white blood, and (3) black blood. Each category of blood can further be divided into vegetal, animal, and mineral forms. For example, red blood can be either vegetal (honey, the blood of flowers and, mainly, our well-known epô, or dendê); animal (the blood of humans or animals); or mineral (copper or bronze). This can be also used to refer to Black and white blood, divided and multiplied as such. These categorizations extend to the orishas, which share properties and modalities among the three types of blood, resulting in complex cosmological and ethical implications. Red blood appears to be more fully associated with the power of àse's realization, while white symbolizes generic, non-individualized existence, and black represents the secret and the unknown.

Roger Bastide (2001) draws on the traditional anthropological concept of "participations" to understand not only the Nagô-Catholic syncretism found in Bahia and Cuba but also, and more importantly, the *modus operandi* of African thought forms as an epistemology. The debate on "participations" reminds us of James Frazer (1982) and Lucien Lévy-Bruhl (2008). Frazer focused on explaining mythological regularities observed across different peoples, finding connections as peculiar as they are enduring. The oak tree, the summer, the king who must die and be reborn annually, and the virile god dismembered by his worshippers. Frazer developed the theory of sympathetic magic to address these phenomena, also noted by Lévy-Bruhl. Why, Frazer asks, do "primitive" people believe that manipulating certain objects influences other objects, human life, or the will of the gods? Sympathetic magic, whether through contagion (contiguity) or similarity (substitution), constitutes a way of operation of the "primitive" thinking. It does not systematically oppose recognizing things in their empirical individuality but instead interprets them through cosmological and mythical divisions or participations. As it appears in Lévy-Bruhl (2008), it is the law of participation or the principle that organizes the logical connections or causal chains.

This notion relates to Emile Durkheim's (2003) concept of "categories of understanding"—seen as a "collective representation", that is, a symbolic for or a category of classification. This connects with Lucien Lévy-Bruhl's idea that so-called primitive thought does not adhere to the principle of non-contradiction. Instead, it possesses a mystical quality, driven by affection, which somehow opposes the Western mindset, but also guides itself as a logical form, "rational" in its own terms. This perspective leads to Roger Bastide's argument (2001): Africans either think through participation, or do not take into account the "objective" contradictions. For example, within these frameworks, there is an identity among dendê, blood, axé, and a deity. Participations, which can only form within predefined categories, rely on a religious epistemology where symbols—such as the three types of blood—serve as operational elements. However, whether these classificatory and operational structures, which are not merely logical but also affective and mystical, constitute a "grammar" or "language" is a different matter. The question of whether they are governed by the semiological principle of separation or representation (sign/signifier) remains open for discussion, as we will see further.

From an anthropological standpoint, a well-established approach to the problem of "primitive" symbolism can be found in Victor Turner (1974). Claude Lévi-Strauss, in "The Savage Mind" (1989), examines what he calls the "science of the concrete"—the structure of so-called primitive thought, analogous to myth, defined through its comparison to the activity of bricolage. He distinguishes between the bricoleur and the "engineer", representing Western thought. The engineer works within predefined plans, selecting materials that fit preexisting structures. In contrast, the bricoleur deals with diverse, heterogenous objects or remnants, whose concrete and virtual relationships are usable or perceptible only through their ad hoc conformation to a symbolic type defined structurally. Or, as Lévi-Strauss further posits, primitive thought is characterized by a (structural) form seeking content rather than a set of items arranged according to relationships subordinated to a prior intentionality. This distinction impacts how he understands art. "Art thus proceeds from a set (object + event) to the discovery of its structure. Myth starts from a structure by means of which it constructs a set (object + event)" (Lévi-Strauss, 1989, p. 41).

Victor Turner approaches symbols within a ritual context as elements of pragmatic symbolic action or mobilization. For him, symbols are the molecules of ritual construction, viewed as a process rather than a purely structural (ahistorical and without a subject) phenomenon. As elements of a practical–mythical operation, symbols, valued for their material contingency, have the ability—at least among the Ndembu people—to reveal or make visible, or in Turner's terms, "embody", deep elements of culture. What is embodied, more concretely, are the mediated contradictions inherent in the very social structure of the Ndembu. As Turner (1974) states, within the semantics of the symbol, we find "the union of ecology and intellect, resulting in the materialization of an idea" (p. 43). Turner, in dialogue with Claude Lévi-Strauss, insists that beyond the structural dimensions—organized as homologies and formal correlations at a non-conscious level—there is an experiential dimension. Symbols are not merely categories of understanding designed for thought; they are "sensibly perceptible" objects encountered in experience. In this sense, symbols are not just elements of social structure but also social action (Turner, 1974).

In contemporary anthropology, Roy Wagner argues for the autonomy of symbols in the field of the "invention of culture". He sees symbols as analogies that both build upon and subvert other analogies, understood as central metaphors. These metaphors operate through successive framings, through which culture reinvents itself. A metaphor, or "cultural trope", symbolizes itself and expands into increasingly broad and dynamic framings. In doing so, it constitutes culture through the "perception of meaning" within cultural reference points. For Wagner, culture is self-referential, operating without strict adherence to structural (binary) models, thus allowing for contingent and "holographic" agency. That is, he argues that the symbols, the metaphors, operate in the field of cultural invention as perspectives through which the objects can bear a meaning. In his words, "the argument that basic cultural framings are formed as large-scale tropes, essentially as myths, implies that cultural meanings exist in a constant flux of continuous recreation" (Wagner, 2017, p. 169). Symbols, therefore, have agency; they do or produce something, much like indexical works in

Alfred Gell's theory, which trace human agency as distributed personhood, or like Beuys's expanded concept of art.[44]

We have seen earlier in the chapter how Ayrson Heráclito situates his work as a bridge between Nagô religious cosmology and self-aware, reflective artistic expression. The ritual object, in this case, acts as a sacred-processual symbol that materializes a category. The artistic object, on the other hand, functions as a representational artifact—or, more precisely in Heráclito's context, as a trigger for experience and a reconfiguration of sensitivity and perception. It assumes the practical and interventionist form of action, as in Beuys's concept of art, or in Heráclito's performance "Transmutação da Carne", discussed earlier.

However, an analogy between artistic form and ritual form becomes apparent if we adopt the perspective of Alfred Gell's anthropology of art. Gell sees both ritual objects and artistic objects as indices with practical effects. The critical question here lies in the nature of this object or practice: Are they signs representing something else? Are they instances of "distributed personhood", collecting social or metaphysical agency as a bundle of para-semiotic and/or ritualistic symbols and perceptions? Are they substances or sacred materials, communicating on profound and complex cosmological and metaphysical levels, acting at the intersection of the empirical and the transcendental worlds?

In the next section, I will delve deeper into these questions, proposing a model for addressing the issue of Black art—suspended in its ambiguity as art "by" Black people or "about" Black people. This model will take into account the tensions between representation and immanence, particularly through a comparative consideration of two vastly different artists, Eckhout and Ayrson Heráclito.

REPRESENTATION AND IMMANENCE

In the previous chapter, we explored how the insoluble antagonism between Blackness and the world, as articulated by Frantz Fanon and discussed by other scholars, can serve as an interpretative paradigm for the ontological precariousness of Black existence. Blackness is thus framed as absolute negativity and/or objecthood (Fanon, 1983; Gordon, 1999). Overdetermined in its materiality by a libidinal economy, Black consciousness is saturated

---

[44] We also know, as succinctly summarized by Stuart Hall, that the semiotics of representation has been challenged by the historicism of historical materialism and by the theory of discursive formations, as in Foucault (Hall, 2016). This tension highlights the conceptual importance of "power" and "subject" as key categories within the sociological production of meaning.

in the flesh, experienced as a thing or object that nevertheless resists, striving "to be" in a fully objective sense—without presupposing the semiotic division as the foundation of meaning. In this sense, we inhabit a presignified world, imprisoned, as repeatedly noted, in the materiality of existence, as "a thing among other things" (Gordon, 1999).

This returns us to the core of my inquiry: How can Blackness be represented, and how do the works of the two artists under consideration help address these questions?

This chapter is part of a broader effort developed throughout this book, which seeks to situate two moments or positions within the political forms of Black subjectivity and imagination: "ancestrality" and "social death", as I initially outlined. What has emerged so far is the possibility of understanding the unfolding of these metamorphoses as (re)configured through the tension between representation and immanence. This issue, introduced in the previous chapter through the concept of the "Black border", will be revisited in its transformed form in Chapter 5, which focuses on slave autobiographies and further examines the relationship between "subject" and "representation". Can Black culture be represented? If it is represented, does it remain Black? Does the subject, or Black "consciousness", constitute itself within these representations, or are they mere reflections, mirrored through the white gaze? Can Black art produce true self-consciousness? Or, alternatively, does the autonomous and robust condition of a genuine civilizational and "mythopoetic" alternative, as Abdias do Nascimento might suggest, lie in this epistemological rupture that denies representation?

Of course, the impossibility to which Gordon and Fanon refer is primarily the impossibility of articulating a subject—the Fanonian ontological precariousness—or, as I would argue, the impossibility of completing the ontological cycle, as well as the political cycle of constituting a person, as previously discussed. What I propose here is that, beyond this impossibility, the rupture with representation constitutes an epistemological dissidence, actively rejecting the representational division that forms the cornerstone of Western epistemology and the theory of the sign. This is evident in Ayrson Heráclito's work, which consciously aligns itself with a religious dimension where signs are the thing itself and not merely a representation. Conversely, in Albert Eckhout's work, we see an almost diametrically opposed situation as the African Warrior is nothing more than his representation. He is an allegory, not of himself or of a reflective instance of subject formation, much less of his consciousness, but rather a projection riddled with contradictions, a re-presented object meant to be read and interpreted, fashioned with historically conventional visual resources (even if it retains a colonial indexicality, as I said). In this sense, representation appears to be the quintessential colonial epistemological device for constructing race and Blackness as defined by the overarching anti-Black antagonism.

But what does it mean to represent something? This is an old question with many answers. In anthropology, one possible answer lies in the influence of structural linguistics, which achieved great prominence through the work of Claude Lévi-Strauss. As Edmund Leach (1973) discusses, Ferdinand de Saussure's distinction between langue and parole was adapted by Lévi-Strauss to account for the unconscious and universal dimensions of signification structures, which ultimately underpin culture and the human condition. These structures, like the Saussurean sign, are binary, divided between signifier and signified. A regime of truth in which the sign refers to something it is not (Hall, 2016; Leach, 1973).

The operations of meaning, as applied through a classificatory framework, unfold along paradigmatic (metaphoric) or syntagmatic (metonymic) dimensions, bringing us back to Frazer (1982) and sympathetic magic. However, as Celso Azzan (1993) points out, Lévi-Strauss's logic of meaning is not a semantic logic but a syntactic one, where structural position determines meaning. This is evident in Lévi-Strauss's analysis of myths, where he dismisses the nominalist illusion that identifies sound with meaning, word with thing. Through the notion of the arbitrariness of the sign, a concept borrowed from structural linguistics, Lévi-Strauss identifies meaning as arising from the relationships between parts—mythemes—not from presumed objective content that the myth represents or conveys. Myths derive their meaning from their formal structure, not from the correspondence between message and truth, as in the discourse of semantic nature, or, as it is worth saying, historical.

Classically, representation is defined as something that substitutes for something else. As the poet Décio Pignatari (1969) reminds us, the etymology of the word "sign" derives from cut or section. A sign exists in separation, and its power to create meaning derives from this separation. But is this not the effect of an epistemology—to avoid saying ideology—alienated and split into binary divisions between body and soul, reason and emotion, essence and appearance, thing and concept, subject and object, form and content?

Pierre Clastres, in "On Torture in Primitive Societies", associates a "non-separated" regime of signification, a regime that is not split or divided, with a political regime. He states:

> Every law, as we said, is written. Thus, the triadic con-
> nection already identified: body, writing, and law is re-
> constituted in a certain way. The scars inscribed on the
> body represent the written text of the primitive law; in
> this sense, it is a writing upon the body. Primitive soci-
> eties, as the authors of Anti-Oedipus assert with vehe-
> mence, are marking societies. In this regard, primitive
> societies are indeed societies without writing. However,
> they lack writing only insofar as writing signifies, above
> all, the separate, distant, despotic law, the law of the State
> (...). (Clastres, 1990, p. 130)

Societies that do not have state, those without politically centralized
institutions positioned "against" society, are possible because they do
not separate meaning from its medium or the name from the thing itself.
The cosmogonic reconciliation of the world with its "presentation" and
non-representation serves as the safeguard that prevents political power
from becoming autonomous in South American stateless societies.

To a great extent, the claim for "ancestrality" animates the formation of
political subjectivities and the imaginary of Blackness in Brazil, as discussed
in Chapter 1. In contrast to the Fanonian approach, which recognizes the
regime of signification only to deny it to Black people, ancestrality calls for
immanence and for a return or reconciliation with a non-separated regime
of signification. This idea appears to materialize in Ayrson Heráclito's engagement with sacred materials, though perhaps not entirely consciously,
as it is also informed by Joseph Beuys's "theory of art", which to some extent is still committed to metaphor. This is why I identified a contradiction
in "As Mãos de Epô", between an interpretive semantic or metaphorical
register, in which the hands function as signs, and a paradigmatic register,
as mentioned earlier, that approaches the ideogrammatic, where the ballet of hands forms a grammar or code. This tension could be understood
precisely as a tension between representation and immanence in Ayrson's
work. Like any great artist, he transcends the conventional mediums he
employs and burns the slave ships behind him.

Within the framework of Ancestrality, we find in the liberation philosopher Eduardo Oliveira (2002) a synthesis of this ancestral demand for
immanence:

Influenced by Western culture, we are driven to seek alternatives for our future, perpetuating the eschatological mindset of finding paradise in what is yet to come. This cultural trap has deprived us of recognizing our own history and the creative models we have invented over time and across various territories of the planet. Hostages to dichotomies such as reform–revolution, modern–archaic, progress–tradition, we fail to value the socio-economic and political-cultural models crafted by the complex African tradition. This tradition, nevertheless, spread across the globe, carrying with it an inclusive, immanent, dynamic, and alternative worldview. (p. 16)

As I suggest, the perspective of Africanity exists in tension, mediated by various transformations, with the field that centralizes social death and slavery as key categories for political subjectivity and aesthetic imagination. Structured as a representation—an allegory—Albert Eckhout's monumental painting materializes a network of colonial exchanges that fixates on Blackness and the Black body, race, and gender as inventions rooted in fundamental separation. This separation, within the realm of representation, divides content from its ontologically distinct form, mirroring another foundational cell of capitalist hetero-patriarchal modernity. In this context, the African is the enslaved person, a human being converted into a commodity. In Heráclito's work, however, representation is at least challenged by the emphasis on materials, action, and the incorporation of what Alfred Gell would identify as the agency of artistic artifacts and sacred fetishes. These elements exert transformative influence over subjects, spaces, and senses, converting immanence into a material form of transcendence that is simultaneously aesthetic, ethical, and historical (Gell, 2018; Matory, 2018).

CHAPTER 5
THE SCENE OF OBJECTION: NARRATIVE, POLITICAL ECONOMY, AND PERFORMANCE

"Pois não vês que morremos todo dia Debaixo do chicote, que não cansa?"
— **Castro Alves, "Os Escravos," 1883**
"Do you not see that we die every day Under the whip that never tires?"
— **Castro Alves, "The Slaves," 1883**

"PERSONHOOD" AND SUBJECTIVITY

To a large extent, the social forms of knowledge, understood as socially configured epistemologies—whether representational or immanent, as discussed throughout this book—define the forms of being. Ontology and epistemology are thus critically entwined as subjects of reflection, offering, in this framework, a way to ask and answer fundamental questions: Who are we, and how do we recognize ourselves? These questions hold particular significance for the descendants of enslaved Africans in the Americas. Considering the forms of representation or symbolization as modes of being appears to be a viable approach to reclaiming a sense of self that often seems elusive. This elusiveness becomes apparent when examining the historical contexts that shaped modern nation-states, with all their contradictions, subjects, and languages.

Yet, under the oppressive weight of race and its attendant prerogatives, these formations are rendered almost natural. Race, along with its correlating violences, situates individuals within the phenomenological plane of everyday interactions, as Fanon (2005, 1983) noted. Simultaneously, it intertwines with the afterlife of slavery—a traceable legacy that guides our journey through the shadows of History, back toward Africa or through the haunting middle passage (Hartman, 1997).

None of this is pacific, of course. Movements such as the American Descendants of Slavery (ADOS), while jarring, are not entirely surprising. One of its founders, Antonio Moore, articulates the matter succinctly: "You don't voluntarily immigrate into a community that is supposedly segregated, and then claim the struggles of people who have been here chained to chattel slavery for multiple generations" (Adjei-Kontoh, 2019, p. 1).

Moore's remarks aimed to challenge the inclusion of individuals like former Senator Kamala Harris, whose parents immigrated from Jamaica and India, (like other Black individuals)—whether immigrants or descendants of immigrants from the Caribbean, Latin America, or Africa—into the political and historical narrative of African American struggles. According to this movement, it is the historical experience of slavery in the United States, rather than race or African ancestrality, that defines identity and its associated political, historical, and ontological ties (Adjei-Kontoh, 2019).

As the group states on their website:

> ADOS—which stands for American Descendants of Slavery—seeks to reclaim/restore the critical national character of the African American identity and experience, one grounded in our group's unique lineage, and which is central to our continuing struggle for social and economic justice in the United States.(...) #ADOS #AmericanDOS sets out to shift the dialogue around the identity of what it is to be African American in an effort to move the discussion from melanin, and properly center the discussion around lineage." (https://ados101.com/)

The Weberian theory of ethnicity might find fertile ground for development here. However, the Garveyist "race first" theory or the Third-Worldist connections of the Black Panther Party would likely falter in shame. Slavery—particularly slavery understood within the framework of the formation of the U.S. nation-state—provides the structural foundation for this mobilization. In this context, two key points underlying the original motivation for writing this book converge, with some perplexity, though: (1) the role of slavery in Black ontology and epistemology across the Americas; (2) the (in)communicability or (in)congruence of the experiences and politics of Blackness in the United States and Latin America, as explored by intellectuals such as Frank Wilderson and Lélia Gonzalez.

The question of who we are and how we recognize ourselves remains an ongoing problem. This is particularly evident when these questions and their answers are constructed within and against the anti-Black world—a world that paradoxically is also the Black world, existing in exile or ejected from itself. In this context, self and world become problematic terms. This problematic configuration deserves my attention from a Black, Afro-Brazilian standpoint, which is central to the issue pursued here. How can one establish a stable standpoint to define this positionality? Should it be based on the history of absolute negation, which defines Blackness as social death and social death as the fundamental structure of slavery and its afterlife? Or should it draw upon the mythopoetic connections to Africans, rooted in popular culture, subjectivity, and the social and familial lives of Black Brazilians? These questions, repeated in various forms and registers here, seek to answer the question of who I am by interrogating where I come from.

Historically, the ways these questions have been formulated are tied to formal structures of meaning, traditions, tropes, grammars, styles, subjects, and settings. With Fred Moten's (2003) proposition in "In the Break" as a starting point, I aim to articulate, through a specific and limited corpus—slave narratives—the disjointed correlation between objection/negation/objectification and the construction of subjectivity. This issue is crucial for recognizing the slave's "personhood" and the structural forms this concept might assume as a condition of enunciation for a subject who initially appears as a subject of representation. However, this introduces another recurring problem: Representing oneself within a particular epistemological framework often entails becoming an object to oneself within a "scene" defined by absolute violence. As Moten (2003) writes: "Blackness—the extended movement of a specific upheaval, an ongoing irruption that arranges every line—is a strain that pressures the assumption of equivalence of personhood and subjectivity" (p. 1). In this sense, autobiographical and fictional narratives by enslaved individuals offer a way to engage with this problem. These narratives allow the enslaved to represent themselves as the Other, the "foreigner" described in distinct ways by Toni Morrison (2019) and Claude Meillassoux (1995).

Yet, the issue extends beyond the literary realm, as the politics of representation are intertwined with political economy, a socio-historical trope of significant relevance.

From the perspective of slavery's political economy, which must confront historical materialism, the central problem is the socio-juridical ontology of the enslaved: Were they a person or a thing? Were they subjects of their own emancipation or mere cogs in the economic machinery of slavery? In this sense, both Brazilian historiography and the Afro-pessimist critique of Marxism are called upon to contribute to this epistemological reckoning under the shadow of the anti-Black world. They offer an opportunity to reinterpret Black subjectivity, social death, and the ontology of the Black subject from an alternative point.

However, and finally—as should now be evident—both political economy and literate narrative structures operate within the same framework, aligned with modes of signification and epistemologies rooted in representation, sign theory, or value theory. The solutions they offer are, therefore, preconditioned by the objectivity inherent to Western, bourgeois modes of subjectification, as we will see. Yet, alternatives exist. In the final section of this work, I will explore these alternatives, which operate outside the representational logic of signs or value and instead follow the immanent logic of performance. These performances are grounded in community repertoires—oral, cosmological, or mythopoetic (Martins, 1997). One such example is the popular performance known as "Nêgo Fugido", which occurs annually in July in Acupe, Recôncavo of Bahia. This performance demonstrates how knowledge can be signified, produced, and reproduced outside the structural modalities defined by the anti-Black world. Similarly, I will examine the Mardi Gras Indians of New Orleans, as the reenactments, situated within the American South, offer a comparative context. Their themes and modalities resonate with those of their Bahian counterpart, showcasing analogous performances of Black identity within the African Diaspora in the New World.

"WHERE THE SELF THAT WAS NO SELF MADE ITS HOME"[45]

A central question in the discussion presented in this section is the potential correlation between fiction and non-fiction in imagining the world of slavery and its subjective forms. This imagination is at times autobiographical and at other times historical. The dividing line between factual biographical narratives, grounded in memory, and fictional narratives that reconstruct a voice speaking from a presumed past is problematic. This tension, however, can be seen as productive. Walter Benjamin's propositions in "On

---

[45] Excerpt from "Beloved" by Toni Morrison (2007). The full excerpt reads: "No question. And no matter, for the sadness was at her center, the desolated center where the self that was no self-made its home. Sad as it was that she did not know where her children were buried or what they looked like if alive, fact was she knew more about them than she knew about herself, having never had the map to discover what she was like" (Morrison, 1988, p. 140).

the Concept of History" highlight the consciousness of a historical subject who, in a "moment of danger", grasps at a fleeting flash imbued with meaning and dramatic intensity. Similarly, Michel-Rolph Trouillot contends that the consciousness of History is itself historical, subject to the immediate flash of the present, demanding a response through transient forms of meaning-making, such as slave autobiographical narratives. Historical reminiscence emerges in contexts of struggle, where the enemy's victory threatens even the dead. The state of exception we live in represents a "consummated order" and a regime of truth rooted not only in specific historical content but also in a validated mode of telling history. This dangerous history centers on a subject, "the struggling, and combatant class itself" (Benjamin, 1996, p. 228).

Trouillot (2016) argues that part of official historiography clings to factuality as a "naive positivist illusion", disregarding the dual meaning of "history" in its vernacular sense: both the events that occurred and their narration. This duality disentangles what happened from how it is told as inherently difficult. The distinction between a fictional or "false" narrative and a historical one ultimately becomes a question of authority, often determined by conventional modes such as authenticity (Clifford, 2008). As Benjamin (1996) asserts, "History is always produced in a specific historical context. Historical actors are also narrators, and vice versa" (p. 52). In contemporary political disputes, as seen in the ADOS movement, the authenticity of a "lineage" that guarantees rights to certain subjects while excluding others is at stake. This lineage requires determining a foundational context or scene where a coherent drama unfolded—namely, Black slavery in the United States. However, it becomes evident that this scene—like a crime scene distorted by corrupt and violent police—is often manipulated to obscure evidence and blur attributions of authorship. The primitive scene, which generates rights by repositioning the subject within a lineage, is simultaneously arbitrary and fictional because Black slavery in the U.S. was neither historically produced nor subjectively experienced as a national isolation. It was deeply interconnected with the transatlantic slave trade, the African diaspora, and the successive migrations and displacements driven by racialized global capitalism (Sundiata, 2003; Garvey, 2004; Gilroy, 2001, 1987). This connection is vividly illustrated in the narratives of Frederick Douglass (n.d.), Olaudah Equiano (n.d.), and Mahommah Baquaqua (2017).

Defining a foundational scene for the emergence of a subject in history or an authentic historical narrative involves actively producing an archive. This requires choosing certain elements while excluding others and subjecting sources to criticism and selection. As David Scott (2008) notes, the archive does not exist passively, awaiting access; it must be actively constructed by a subject in a moment of fear and danger. On a broader scale, history cannot be conflated with memory, as the latter preserves validation criteria beyond factual authenticity. Memory is also tied to affective, fragmentary, allusive, non-linear, and loosely referential dimensions. In the case of Black people of the diaspora, memory serves as an antidote to dehumanization and annihilation, deeply rooted in the denial of lineage or kinship, as both Orlando Patterson (2008) and Claude Meillassoux (1995) argue. Reconstructing a connection, a narrative, or a place where the body, as a "memory machine" (Scott, 2008, p. 15), can remember is thus essential.

Within the historical setting and its structural dispositions, Black slavery becomes the primal scene for the narrative of a subject seeking their place in history. Saidiya Hartman revisits the notion of the archive, always provisional, as it is built to construct the conditions of possibility for representing the subaltern. Hartman aligns with Gayatri Spivak's assertion when she says: "There is no access to the subaltern consciousness outside dominant representations or elite documents" (Hartman, 1997, p. 10). This consciousness also emerges within scenes produced by enslaved autobiographical or fictional narratives, leading Hartman to acknowledge the need for "historical fiction". In "Venus in Two Acts", Hartman explores the ubiquitous figure of the enslaved Venus found in locations such as the "barracoon, the hollow of the slave ship, the pest house, the brothel, the cage, the surgeon's laboratory, the prison, the cane-field, the kitchen, the master's bedroom" (Hartman, 2008, p. 1). Here, she examines the limits and perversities of the archive and the libidinal economy of slavery. Venus, a ubiquitous yet obscure figure, embodies countless Black girls imprisoned within the archive, glimpsed indirectly through "death sentence, a tomb, a display of the violated body, an inventory of property, a medical treatise on gonorrhea, a few lines about a whore's life, an asterisk in the grand narrative of history" (Hartman, 2008, p. 2). How, then, can we render the violence of the archive visible without reenacting the violence of its violation? This violence and staged violation, buried at the heart of history and in the bodies of countless Venuses, persists as untold stories, scandalous and terrifying silences. Until someone decides to tell a story. Someone like Toni Morrison. In "The Origin of Others" (2019), she states:

> Amid all this struggle, chaos, and the indestructible conflict caused by the distribution of power within racial and

gender classifications, I sought to draw attention to specific individuals who are striving to escape violence and mitigate their failures—one narrative at a time. Individually, one by one. (p. 103)

Among the narratives we will examine, one explicitly balances the tension between truth and fiction. "Incidents in the Life of a Slave Girl" begins, not coincidentally, with the statement: "Reader, be assured this narrative is no fiction" (Jacobs, 2019, p. 9). The narrative in question is extraordinary enough to provoke skepticism: Seven years hidden in a tiny attic; a period so prolonged that the narrator's body was permanently deformed. It also seems implausible, from a certain perspective, that an enslaved Black woman could produce such a complex and articulate narrative, filled with moral exhortations and dramatic twists (O'Neill, 2018). Harriet Jacobs's text is regarded as foundational to the development of African American literature in the United States and, having been published in 1861, serves as a powerful precursor to Black feminist thought, providing a model for self-reconstruction through narrative. O'Neill suggests examining this text alongside fictional narratives such as "Kindred" by Octavia Butler (2019), and "Beloved" by Toni Morrison (2007), which are included in this analysis, and "Sister Mine" by Nalo Hopkinson, which will not be analyzed here. In all these cases, the author identifies the critical use of "Black speculative fiction" or "visionary fiction" (idem). The key word in this approach is imagination, which enabled Harriet, or Linda (her pseudonym), to reimagine herself through the lens of freedom and transform her nearly surreal experiences into a coherent narrative.

We now turn to the narratives in question and their main characters, protagonists, or narrators. First, the two Cubans: the cimarrón[46] Esteban Montejo and the "slave poet" Juan Manzano, whose stories are markedly distinct. Manzano, who identified as "mulatto", was a "house slave" and treated as a pet by his elderly mistress, who "took him on as a form of entertainment" (Manzano, 2015, p. 32) until his sufferings began, which were numerous and profoundly cruel. Montejo, born a Crioula like Manzano, was described as a bold and combative personality by the anthropologist Miguel Barnet, who compiled the narrative based on interviews conducted when Montejo was 104 years old. Published in 1966, the book portrays Montejo as a kind of prerevolutionary rebel and an eyewitness to significant events in Cuban national history (Barnet, 1986). Another "transcribed" figure is the "Brazilian" Mahommah Gardo Baquaqua, an African

---

[46] Fugitive slave who takes refuge in the woods or mountains.

native of Zoogoo and protagonist of numerous adventures. Like the other African in this group, Olaudah Equiano, Baquaqua's life was deeply marked by maritime experiences, shaping a transatlantic Black cosmopolitan identity (Baquaqua, 2017; Gilroy, 2001; Okonkwo, 1980). Baquaqua's voice, or the voice inscribed on his behalf by the compiler Samuel Moore, joins the nineteenth-century abolitionist chorus, alongside figures such as Frederick Douglass, an iconic representative of the Anglo-Saxon abolitionist movement. Olaudah Equiano (n.d.), however, distinctively portrays himself as a subject on a spiritual journey toward perfect Christianity, distancing his narrative by nearly a century from the others .

Notably, few slave narratives were written in the first person, and even fewer were authored by women. In addition to Harriet Jacobs, we will consider three fictional female narratives: the aforementioned "Kindred", a speculative fiction novel recounting the time-travel journeys of Dana, a Black woman from the 1970s who returns to the past to save—and ultimately kill—a white ancestor; "Beloved", Toni Morrison's breathtaking work fictionalizing the real story of Margaret Garner, who killed her children in 1856 to prevent their return to slavery (Morrison, 2019); and, finally, two Brazilian narratives. The first is Ana Maria Gonçalves's account of Kehinde, an African woman from Savalu and a fictionalized version of Luiza Mahin, mother of the abolitionist Luís Gama, who was sold into slavery by his own father. The second is "Úrsula", a novel written by Maria Firmina dos Reis, a freeborn Black woman from Maranhão, Brazil, and the daughter of an enslaved mother (Gonçalves, 2016; Reis, 2018).

Narrative conventions are a crucial aspect to consider, as is the work of mediation or intercession, as noted by Stephanie Youngblood (2013). Except for Equiano's text, all the narratives are set in the 19th century, a period shaped by abolitionist discourse. This is epitomized by Rufus, the white ancestor and slave owner in Butler's novel, who sarcastically dismisses abolitionism as "the biggest nonsense" when confronted with a 20th-century history book discussing free Black individuals (Butler, 2019, p. 226). Jacobs, Douglass, and Manzano wrote explicitly aligned with the abolitionist agenda, aiming to touch and mobilize white public opinion regarding the injustice of slavery. Jacobs (2019) addresses her plea to the "women of the North", stating: "I do earnestly desire to arouse the women of the North to a realizing sense of the condition of two millions of women at the South, still in bondage, suffering what I suffered" (p. 10). Douglass, unmatched in exposing the moral contradictions of slavery—though his work was, as Morrison termed, sometimes full of "romanticization"—frequently appealed to religion in an effort, quite futile, to reason with slave traders and enslavers:

> We have men-stealers for ministers, women-whippers for missionaries, and cradle-plunderers for church members. The man who wields the blood clotted whip during the week fills the pulpit on Sunday and claims to be a minister of the meek and lowly Jesus. The man who robs me of my earnings at the end of each week meets me as a class-leader on Sunday morning, to show me the way of life, and the path of salvation. He who sells my sister, for purposes of prostitution, stands forth as the pious advocate of purity. He who proclaims it a religious duty to read the Bible denies me the right of learning to read the name of the God who made me. He who is the religious advocate of marriage robs whole millions of its sacred influence and leaves them to the ravages of wholesale pollution. The warm defender of the sacredness of the Family relation is the same that scatters whole families, separating husbands and wives, parents and children, sisters and brothers, leaving the hut vacant, and the hearth desolate. (Douglass, n.d., p. 43)

The unparalleled fervor of Douglass against slavery delves into the contradictions of Christianity, with its unequivocal universalist message, and the inconsistencies of economic and political liberalism. Much like Equiano a century earlier, Douglass meticulously demonstrates how the slave trade and African slavery, by keeping millions of human beings oppressed and alienated from "civilization" and the market, hindered the full development of European, particularly British, commercial interests. This abolitionist fervor also appears in Manzano, though with a different tone or emphasis. As Alex Castro (2015) notes in the excellent introduction to the Brazilian edition, Manzano, like other autobiographers in our study, does not exactly write in his own voice . Montejo's autobiography was written by Barnet; Jacobs's narrative was "revised" by Maria Child; Baquaqua's account was compiled by Samuel Moore; and Manzano's narrative was commissioned at the request of a group of Cuban literati, including Nicolás de Prado Ameno, the son of one of his owners, the marchioness de Prado Ameno. As Lopes points out, Manzano, or his "editors", faced the complex task of condemning slavery without condemning slaveholders. Carmen Cosme (2014), in her thesis, argues more specifically that Manzano's text, commissioned by Domingo del Monte, a Cuban abolitionist, was later edited by Anselmo Suárez y Romero. To appeal to white readers' sensibilities, the text adopted a picaresque style, which Cosme (2014) describes as a "biographical simulation set in sordid social environments" (p. 4). Manzano's narrative, filled with silences and ambiguities, including sexual ones, describes his relationship with the marchioness, whom he referred to as "mommy".

As I previously mentioned, the narrative and subjectivity of Manzano present a striking contrast to Montejo, who is depicted as embodying a "wild spirit", in opposition to the docile and acculturated Manzano, the prototype of the house slave. Manzano, the son of a mixed-race house slave and a free Black man, like all the other authors considered here, experienced relatively privileged conditions during his childhood. Yet, as both Manzano and Jacobs frequently remind us, the cruelty and injustice they describe in detail offer only a pale glimpse of the much worse conditions endured by field slaves. Furthermore, all the authors we analyze here achieved literacy and freedom—either through escape or manumission—and, in some cases, such as Douglass, gained significant political influence and social recognition. These accomplishments were far removed from the lives of the vast majority of enslaved individuals, who died illiterate and anonymous in bondage.

These relative privileges reveal hierarchies and differences within the world of the enslaved, often marked by lighter skin, as in the cases of Jacobs and Manzano, or by extraordinary intelligence and resourcefulness, as seen in Douglass and Equiano. However, none of these distinctions spared them from the brutal violence, exploitation, and contempt intrinsic to slavery. Indeed, perhaps because of this proximity to privilege, Montejo, or rather Barnet (1986), does not hold back in his criticism and disdain for house slaves.

> If a little black boy was pretty and lively, they sent him inside, to the master's house. There they began to sweeten him up, and...what do I know! The fact is that the little black boy had to spend his time shooing flies because the masters ate a lot. And they put the little boy at the head of the table while they ate. They gave him a big long fan made of a palm frond. And they told him: "Shoo, so those flies don't fall in the food!" If a fly fell on a plate, they

scolded him severely and even whipped him. I never did this work because I never liked to be near the masters. I was a cimarrón from birth. (p. 22)

Maria Firmina dos Reis's novel also aligns with the abolitionist discourse, albeit with greater subtlety, as it is not a *stricto senso* slave autobiography, nor does it center enslaved individuals as main characters. However, with remarkable skill and tact, the enslaved supporting characters are portrayed not only in a humanized manner but also heroically. Considered by Eduardo de Assis Duarte to be the first abolitionist novel in Brazil, "Úrsula", published in 1859, precedes, for instance, the romantic and extravagant works of Castro Alves, who was active in the 1880s (Reis, 2018). In "Úrsula", early in the narrative, the enslaved character Túlio, described as "unfortunate but virtuous", is, in fact, the savior of Tancredo, the romantic hero in love with the unhappy Úrsula, who is ensnared by a web of hatred and past passions. The novel ends tragically with the unjust deaths of the two lovers, defeated by the malice and desire of Úrsula's cruel uncle. However, beyond Túlio, other Black characters are featured in an uncommon way, notably the incredible Mãe Susana, whom Assis Duarte highlights as the most poignant and lucid voice in the narrative. She explains to Túlio the meaning of "true freedom" in African lands, untainted by the experiences of slavery or even manumission within a slaveholding society (Duarte, 2018).

A similarly tragic ending is found in the remarkable "A Cachoeira de Paulo Afonso" by Castro Alves. Through a series of 32 poems of varied forms and styles, Alves narrates the ill-fated love and tragedy of enslaved individuals in a slaveholding society, showcasing his technical expertise and abolitionist virtuosity. Alves, who died romantically young at the age of 24, imbues the work with a dramatic and vivid greatness. The natural scenery is breathtaking, echoing the artistic impressions of 19th-century travelers like Thomas Ender, framing an experience of overwhelming beauty, peace, and harmony: "Hora meiga da tarde! Como és bela/ [Gentle hour of the afternoon! How beautiful you are.] Quando surges do azul da zona ardente! [When you emerge from the blue of the blazing zone]" (Alves, 1983, p. 3). The beautiful mucama, described as the "delicate slave flower", and her lover, none other than the legendary bandit and former enslaved from Bahia, Lucas da Feira,[47] are placed within this tropical greatness. At this

---

[47] I am assuming here, although provisionally and speculatively, that the Lucas mentioned in the poem is the same "slave bandit", Lucas da Feira. The poet was born in the same year Lucas was executed by hanging, 1847.

point in the narrative, Lucas is still portrayed as enslaved (Lima, 1990). The majestic Paulo Afonso waterfall in Bahia serves both as the setting and a character in this work.

> Que bela testa espaçosa,
> Que olhar franco e triunfante!
> E sob o chapéu de couro
> Que cabeleira abundante!
> De marchetada jiboia
> Pende-lhe a rasto o facão...
> E assim... erguendo o machado
> Na larga e robusta mão...
> Aquele vulto soberbo,—vivamente alumiado,—
> Atravessa o descampado
> Como uma estátua de bronze
> Do incêndio ao fulvo clarão. (Alves, 1983, p. 11)

> What a broad and noble forehead,
> What a frank and triumphant gaze!
> And beneath the leather hat,
> What a mane, so full and untamed!
> A machete with an ornate sheath
> Hangs by his side, trailing behind...
> And thus... lifting the axe
> In his wide and sturdy hand...
> That majestic figure,—vividly illuminated,—
> Crosses the open plain
> Like a bronze statue
> In the fiery, amber glow of the blaze. (Alves, 1983, p. 11)

As in "Úrsula" and many other novels and poems of the time, love between two individuals is marked by tragedy, as a "horrible secret" looms over the couple's happiness. The "flower of the enslaved" had been violated—a violation that is attributed to Lucas's revolt, his escape, and subsequent turn to banditry. However, as the poet starkly defines, what does rebellion or crime mean for an enslaved person? "E vens falar de crimes ao cativo? / [And you speak of crimes to those in bondage?] / Então não sabes o que é ser escravo". [Then you do not know what it is like to be a slave]" (Alves, 1983, p. 36). The primal crime is slavery itself, which, among its many horrors, produces perverse arrangements and cursed ties between enslaved individuals and their masters.

The violator of the enslaved woman Lucas loves is his white brother—born of the same father, who had previously violated Lucas's mother. Thus, Lucas's white brother is both his rival and the destroyer of his beloved, just as their shared father had been the destroyer of Lucas's mother. Violations, rapes, abuse, and harassment like these are consistently portrayed as the daily reality of slavery by all the authors under consideration. Historical narratives affirm this as well, despite efforts to "rehabilitate slavery". Even in Gilberto Freyre's work, sexual and homosexual abuse is thoroughly documented (Freyre, 1995; Mott, 1988; Aidoo, 2018). Yet hearing the voices of those who lived through and experienced such realities has a profoundly different resonance: "ghosts without skin stuck their fingers in her and said beloved in the dark and bitch in the light". (Morrison, 2007, p. 320). In "Kindred" and "Incidents in the Life of a Slave Girl", this theme is central. In the former, it serves as a leitmotif of the protagonist's desperate and ultimately futile struggle to keep the "past at bay". In Jacobs's narrative, it is a more persistent and structurally defining element. Linda's entire fight is centered on escaping the constant harassment of Dr. Flint, her enslaver, and on saving her children from slavery (O'Neill, 2018). Despite being relatively privileged—never having been whipped, for example (a fate Dana in "Kindred" and Manzano, despite his intelligence and grace, could not avoid)—Linda is, however, constantly harassed, threatened, and blackmailed to yield to Flint's advances. She ultimately chooses to enter a relationship with another white man, the father and enslaver of her mixed-race children, rather than submit to Flint's unbearable desires. Jacobs's sexual decisions are a source of constant embarrassment and shame, and she is accused of immorality, even by other Black women. Similarly, Kehinde, or Luiza, in "Um defeito de cor", enters a relationship with a white man after gaining her freedom. In this case, however, she does not seem to succumb to the temptation of moral self-condemnation: "He was quite affectionate and made me feel at ease, as if he truly enjoyed being with me, as if he saw me as a woman and not as a Black woman" (Gonçalves, 2016, p. 342). Relationships with white individuals—whether sexual or otherwise—are thus consistently depicted in these narratives. This is a point worth emphasizing: the relationship with white people as a central element in the structured subjectivity of enslaved individuals. While seemingly obvious, this aspect sometimes appears neglected, both from the perspective of political phenomenology and epistemological politics, as Fanon (1983) so incisively demonstrated.

Jacobs, Equiano, and Dana often succumb to the dishonesty of white individuals. Traders in the West Indies repeatedly cheat and rob Equiano, even attempting to re-enslave him amidst his tumultuous adventures. Flint, like Rufus, deceives Dana and Linda, promising to help them, pledging to free their children or treat other enslaved individuals better. Even the unfortunate Manzano, the "little mulatto of the Marchioness", so aligned with the white world that he seeks to distance himself from other Black individuals, is betrayed and deceived many times, often brutally punished unjustly. He is even forced to lie to satisfy his tormentors' thirst for the truth: "For nine nights I endured this torment. I told nine thousand different stories, because when they said: 'tell me the truth,' and whipped me, I no longer had anything plausible left to say to stop the punishment" (Manzano, 2015, p. 63). Nevertheless, all these authors, at various moments, recount finding friends among white people and praise the kindness, charity, and Christian spirit of some. Equiano—who himself participated in the slave trade—despite being betrayed many times, found "friends" among his owners, such as Mr. King, who ultimately granted him freedom. Dana, married in the 1970s to a white man, paradoxically develops empathetic feelings for Rufus, her ancestor and oppressor, much like Manzano, who admits: "I loved her despite the harshness with which she treated me" (Idem, p. 79).

In many of these cases, it is evident that the authors, aware that their potential readers were predominantly white, understood that it would neither be prudent nor safe to openly challenge or confront those with absolute power over the bodies—if not the voices—of the (formerly) enslaved narrators. This engagement does not extend, however, to Baby Suggs, Sethe's prophetic mother-in-law in "Beloved", who knew she would not be read by any white person. Baby Suggs also understood

> that anybody white could take your whole self for anything that came to mind. Not just work, kill, or maim you, but dirty you. Dirty you so bad you couldn't like yourself anymore. Dirty you so bad you forgot who you were and couldn't think it up. (Morrison, 2007, p. 333)

Not only from a feminine perspective does sexuality, with its tense balance of terror and pleasure, affection and abjection, play a central role, but also through silences. Douglass and Equiano are notably reserved about their sexual and romantic lives. Manzano, often portrayed in the text as sentimental and tearful, hints at a silence surrounding distressing topics:

"Since the age of twelve, I leap to fourteen, leaving behind what demonstrates how unstable my fortune was during that time" (Manzano, 2015, p. 37). Esteban Montejo, in contrast, is far more forthcoming, dedicating numerous pages to discussing women, lovers, passions, and the frustrations of desire during his time hiding in the woods, even recounting erotic games with an ethnographic voyeurism. Most surprising, however, is his reference to homosexuality within the slave quarters (senzalas):

> To make a long story short, life was lonely anyway because women were pretty scarce. And to have a woman you had to be twenty-five years old and lay her in a field. Even the old folks didn't want the young men to have women. They said that twenty-five was when a man ought to have experiences. Many men didn't suffer because they were accustomed to that life. Others had sex with each other and didn't want to have anything to do with women. Sodomy, that was their life. (...) In my opinion it didn't come from Africa. Old men didn't like it at all. They wanted to have nothing to do with them. It never mattered to me, sincerely. I believe that everyone marches to his own drummer. (Barnet, 1986, p. 40)

Finally, attention is drawn to the cases of the Africans Kehinde, Baquaqua, and Equiano. Their descriptions of Africa and the Middle Passage represent fundamental tropes in the political imagination of the contemporary African diaspora, vividly depicted in their accounts. Regarding Africa, these descriptions sometimes resemble ethnographic detail in their depth. Lovejoy attempts to relativize or even challenge the claims of identity and ethnic stability or coherence for Baquaqua, casting doubt on whether the African himself authored such a vivid account of numerous adventures across three continents. Nonetheless, he acknowledges Baquaqua's (2017) "strong identification with Africa and his homeland", Zoogoo or Djogou (p. 15).

A member of a prominent Islamic family who succumbed to bondage due to recklessness caused by alcohol abuse, Baquaqua was baptized as a Christian in 1848. Yet, he retained a fervent desire to return to his homeland, which he describes as follows:

> The city of Zoogoo is located in the heart of the most fertile and pleasant region of the country. Despite its extremely hot climate, it remains agreeable. The area features a diverse landscape of hills, mountains, plains, and valleys, all richly irrigated. About a mile from the city flows a stream of water, strikingly white like milk and remarkably beautiful. (Idem, p. 18)

Kehinde, or Luiza, weaves her personal story into interpretive cosmological frameworks from the Fon tradition, in addition to describing the customs and culture of her people: "[...] My name is Kehinde because I am an ibêji and was born last. My sister was born first, which is why her name is Taiwo. Before us, my brother Kokumo was born, and his name means 'you will no longer die; the gods will hold you.' Kokumo was an abiku, like my mother" (Gonçalves, 2016, p. 19). This mythical configuration of kinship follows the protagonist throughout the narrative and being Ibêji (twin) and the daughter of an abiku significantly influences the plot. It serves as an internal explanatory model for the unfolding story, particularly shaped by the search for a missing child—a recurring theme tied to the reconstitution of family bonds, or "kindred", severed or sustained by slavery. Gonçalves employs African proverbs as epigraphs for the chapters of the voluminous 951-page book, situating the narrator as the protagonist of iconic moments in Black history, such as the 1835 Malê revolt. The narrative alternates between historical and mythical interpretations, enriching its scope.

The third African figure in our discussion, Equiano, who, as evidence suggests, wrote his account in his own hand and had greater control over its content, also begins his narrative, toward freedom and Christianity, by describing his homeland:

> That part of Africa, known by the name of Guinea, to which the trade for slaves is carried on, extends along the coast above 3400 miles, from the Senegal to Angola, and includes a variety of kingdoms. Of these the most considerable is the kingdom of Benin, both as to extent and wealth, the richness and cultivation of the soil, the power of its king, and the number and warlike disposition of the inhabitants. It is situated nearly under the line, and extends along the coast about 170 miles, but runs back into

the interior part of Africa to a distance hitherto I believe unexplored by any traveler; and seems only terminated at length by the empire of Abyssinia, near 1500 miles from its beginning. This kingdom is divided into many provinces or districts: in one of the most remote and fertile of which, called Eboe, I was born, in the year 1745, in a charming fruitful vale, named Essaka. (Equiano, n.d., p. 1)

These African individuals describe the middle passage with harrowing detail: the overwhelming fear of an unknown fate; the unbearable filth and stench; the pain, despair, madness, and suicide attempts. Yet, I choose not to dwell on these aspects, just as I have not lingered on the terror and subjugation so vividly recounted in the narratives of Douglass, Manzano, and Equiano. This is not only because others have examined these elements extensively but also to avoid succumbing to what Saidiya Hartman (1997) terms the "violence of the archive".

I aim to conclude this section with Equiano, returning to the theme of representation—or the articulation of African or enslaved subjectivity—within and under the constraints of conventional European and white structures and models. It is also crucial to highlight what may already be evident: the diversity, not so much of experiences or circumstances, but of personalities—"personhood"—of the individuals portrayed. This individuality persists despite the mediation or intervention of editors, compilers, and interviewers, serving as a testament to the indomitable Humanity of the enslaved, perceptible even through the uniformity of narrative styles. While following conventions, these narratives often strive to evoke empathy—such as the appeal to female compassion in "Incidents"—or highlight contradictions in Christianity, as seen in Douglass. How can we fail to recognize, within the idiosyncratic traits of Montejo's fearlessness and ambition, reminiscent of elder Black figures (pretos velhos) I have known, and Manzano's despair and disorientation, rejected by Black peers and scorned by whites, the same flicker of individuality—strength and frailty—that makes us human?

Lisa Lowe (2009), in "Autobiography Out of the Empire", draws attention to the limitations of narrative genres in representing racial difference and its historicity. Discussing Equiano's narrative, Lowe interprets it as a mediation between distinct historical structures—slavery and free labor—and the corresponding subjectivities shaped by these interconnected systems. In this sense, Equiano's autobiography stylizes the "conversion from chattel to liberal subject" (Lowe, 2009, p. 28). As the first published text by an enslaved African, widely circulated at a time when the emergence of the enslaved subject and their relationship to freedom became possible or necessary, Equiano's narrative embodies a "structure of feeling" (Wiliams, 1979) tied to the very invention of modern freedom during the Enlightenment. It inaugurates the enduring trajectory of metaphors opposing master and slave as a dialectical relationship. "This dialectical overcoming is the central mechanism of liberal historiography, in which the violent human negation of colonial slavery is both acknowledged and assimilated in a narrative that overcomes the violence in a consolidation of the polity" (Lowe, 2009, p. 105). Thus, the genealogy of liberal freedom becomes the genealogy of race and its redemption—a perspective echoed, in some ways, by Orlando Patterson (2008):

> That is the problem of freedom. Beyond the sociohistorical findings is the unsettling discovery that an ideal cherished in the West beyond all others emerged as a necessary consequence of the degradation of slavery and the effort to negate it. The first men and women to struggle for freedom, the first to think of themselves as free in the only meaningful sense of the term were freedmen. And without slavery there would have been no freedmen. (p. 342)

What I would add here is that this historical conception of freedom, particularly in moments of danger, was crafted using the very resources and structures developed and controlled by the same oppressors who made the dream of freedom a savage, inglorious, uncertain, and unrelenting struggle, as we have seen in the narratives. It was through the white man's language, his conventional expressive forms such as autobiography, appealing to his sentiments and seeking his empathy, that the enslaved voice—revealing subjective forms both uniquely particular and universally human—could be constituted and reach us, in this form, at this historical moment.

Stephanie Youngblood (2013), drawing on Jacques Derrida's notion of intercession, interprets Manzano's autobiography as a narrative in which the self (that was no self) can be narrated while simultaneously rejecting the very objectification it entails. The problem, as presented earlier, lies in this: How can one narrate oneself without becoming an object of representation, externalized, alienated, and constructed as the other of oneself, using tools foreign to the presumed ontological foundations of a subject entirely defined by negation? How can one balance the narrating subject and the narrated object? And how can this balance be achieved without falling into the kind of "othering" deplored by Morrison, often based on facile colorisms? (Morrison, 2019). This is where the notion of intercession proves useful. To intercede is to speak for someone, "by the name of" someone—someone who cannot speak for themselves because they are not, strictly speaking, a "subject". Such individuals lack the structural prerogatives and a stable position within a representational system to be read as coherent voices or subjects. This is especially true within the juridical and representational framework of the slaveholding system, which we will discuss further. This configuration is not merely representational and symbolic but deeply rooted in political economy and representational (political) structures: "The intercessory act as speaking in or by the name of others emerges in the inability of the narrator to participate in the market as a figure who, in his own name, can move himself out of slavery into freedom" (Youngblood, 2013, p. 418).

In this way, there is an analogical dependency, so to speak, between the position of the subject within a narrative structure and their position within a structure of antagonisms that is both political and economic. These antagonisms rest on statutory dimensions with truly civilizational implications. All of this refers to these subjects' relationship with the white world, the machinery of the transatlantic slave trade—which produced the first brutal deterritorialization—and the mercantile economy of the plantation, the colonial-slave mode of production. Paradoxically, it also relates to the promises of universal freedom and epistemological transparency, rooted in a newly invented shared Humanity. These tortuous correlations and incongruities, this odious and cruel ancestor, akin to Rufus for Dana, represent the antagonistic avatar I must confront and kill:

> I could feel the knife in my hand, still slippery with perspiration. A slave was a slave. Anything could be done to her. And Rufus was Rufus—erratic, alternately generous and vicious. I could accept him as my ancestor, my younger brother, my friend, but not as my master, and not as my lover. (Butler, 2019, p. 416).

THE SLAVE AS A SUBJECTIVE AGENT

Shifting the focus from the narratives of enslaved individuals, with their poignant richness and acute contradictions, I interrogate the same issue as articulated within a related yet distinct domain. Specifically, I consider the paradoxical obliteration of freedom embodied in the figure of the freed person. This individual, unable to carve out a space for autonomous representation, was similarly precluded from being recognized as an autonomous subject of economic exchange. Such recognition, tied to the status of "property owner", was a prerequisite for citizenship. This inability to be acknowledged as an economic subject capable of ownership clashes directly with the conditions necessary for representation. Furthermore, the ontological void ascribed to Blackness renders aspirations for participation—whether in the public sphere or political society—at best naïve, and at worst, entirely absurd.

> Let us put a finer point on it: violence towards the black body is the precondition for the existence of Gramsci's single entity 'the modern bourgeois-state' with its divided apparatus, political society and civil society. This is to say violence against black people is ontological and gratuitous as opposed to merely ideological and contingent. (Wilderson, 2003, p. 229)

In this sense, to address the issue of subjectivity and enslaved personhood, we must reconsider the political economy of modern slavery in the Americas. Let me be clear: the question is not whether enslaved individuals were human—this is self-evident, as they were no less human than ourselves or their white masters. Instead, the critical inquiry lies in the meaning of "Humanity" itself, a concept far from obvious. Even less clear are the distinctions between thing and person, agent and patient, subject and object (Strathern, 1990). As explored in this chapter and throughout this book, "Humanity" as historically constructed was predicated on Black dehumanization. Political structures that facilitated economic exploitation simultaneously undermined the structural conditions for Black self-representation. Consequently, Blackness can be described as an embodied negation, with social death serving as the defining trait of a subject defined precisely through violation. A more practical question arises: Who were the enslaved men and women? Earlier, we engaged with this issue from a first-person perspective, albeit alienated. Now, let us reconsider it from another standpoint, beginning with alienation itself.

This approach leads us briefly to the classical debates within Brazilian historiography on slavery and its influence on sociological and political readings of slavery's legacy in Brazil, especially in shaping political subjects and sensibilities. More specifically, we turn to how political economy has contributed to defining or describing subjectivity.

While some may consider this topic outdated, it remains far from resolved in my point of view. Jacob Gorender, a prolific and incisive author who worked outside and often against academia, approached this issue through the lens of historical materialism. His concept of "colonial slavery" sought to transcend the binary, favored by certain leftist perspectives, of feudalism versus capitalism in Brazil (Maestri, 2016). This dichotomy informed not only interpretations of Brazil's historical processes and social formation but also political strategies—a concern for Gorender, a longtime militant in the Brazilian Communist Party (PCB) for over 30 years. Maestri describes Gorender's concept of colonial slavery as a "Copernican revolution", defining it as a new mode of production distinct from feudalism and capitalism, with its own historical categories. Central to this framework is the autonomy of enslaved individuals and the role of the so-called "peasant gap", referring to the production of foodstuffs by slaves, former slaves, and their families. Gorender viewed this "gap" as residual rather than structural to the economic model, a perspective that has significant implications for understanding slavery's broader social and economic meaning and its role in perpetuating an unequal reproduction of society (Gorender, 2016, 1990).

Equally central is the category of "slave", which serves as an explanatory rather than an explained concept in analyses of colonial Brazil. Here, Gorender echoes Karl Marx, who wrote in the "Grundrisse": "[...] a mode of production corresponding to the slave must be created" (Marx, 2011, p. 52). Gorender took on this task, arguing that slavery, defined as the ownership of one person by another, should be recognized as the foundation of a distinct mode of production, economic order, and historical social formation. This subject, however, inhabits a familiar contradiction: defined simultaneously as "thing" and "person", as well as a very specific type of "worker" whose wealth extraction relies not on economic coercion but on direct physical violence. As Gorender (2016) notes, "the economic becomes accessory, while the extra-economic becomes essential" (p. 115).

In this sense, the subjugation of the enslaved was personal and their alienation total, resulting in the complete negation of autonomy. This negation of autonomy coexisted with colonial dependence on external markets. Colonial slavery acknowledged market mechanisms, although distorted by colonial protectionism, but lacked capitalism's central category: free labor as a commodity. Instead, the enslaved individual themselves became the principal commodity, embodying this paradox. "As freely alienable merchandise, the slave became the object of all types of transactions common to mercantile relations" (Gorender, 2016., p. 109). Free labor and its presumed subject—the worker—were either absent or residual, which, according to contemporary Afro-pessimist readings, precludes a political-economic foundation for Black radicalism (Wilderson, 2003, 2010). Conversely, in the slavery system, the worker was the commodity itself, in its most personal and paradoxically human dimension.

Beyond his critique of the "peasant gap", which other scholars such as Ciro Flamarion Cardoso have interpreted as a proto-capitalist feature within a slave economy—a claim Gorender categorically denies—another critical aspect of Gorender's perspective that is particularly relevant here involves the nature of enslaved agency, autonomy, and subjectivity. Gorender addresses this topic extensively in "A Escravidão Reabilitada" and, to a lesser extent, in "O Escravismo Colonial". Writing from outside institutional academia, Gorender reacted strongly against what he termed the "rehabilitation of slavery". This rehabilitation, according to him, was advanced by scholars who portrayed slavery as a malleable and flexible system, emphasizing spaces of freedom such as the enslaved family. This framework suggested an interplay of "negotiation" and "conflict", which, to Gorender's great frustration, lent slavery an almost contractual quality, moving away from its foundations of violence and coercion (Gorender, 1990).

It is important to note that much of historiography recognizes slaves as full subjects—not only possessing autonomy but also maintaining familial, genealogical, and cultural ties. This directly counters their portrayal as utterly uprooted, socially dead, or the fragmented, anomic personification of a precarious life. However, the scholars Gorender critiques as belonging to the so-called "São Paulo school", notably Florestan Fernandes, are accused of perpetuating the "coisification" [reification] of enslaved individuals—an interpretation that seems inconsistent with the findings of subsequent historical research (Fernandes, 1978; Arruda, 1996). In contrast, the scholars Gorender associates with the "UNICAMP school", such as Robert Slenes, denied the reification of enslaved individuals and instead emphasized their Humanity. Slenes argued, for instance, that enslaved people were capable of reconstructing familial and ethnic ties. However, Gorender critiques this position as well, suggesting it downplays the centrality of violence and conflict in colonial slave societies. He draws parallels to Gilberto Freyre, who, despite acknowledging slavery's cruelty, emphasized the possibility of negotiation, freedom, and even "reconciliation" or "synthesis" between Black and white worlds, mediated through sexual desire and miscegenation. As discussed in Chapter 2, Gorender (1990) vehemently rejects such notions, stating: "the enslaved-victim gives way to the enslaved-subject, and the result is the same: the nullification of resistance" (p. 26). In Gorender's view, both the "São Paulo school", which denied Black agency, and the "UNICAMP school", which emphasized negotiation within slavery, were fundamentally flawed. Scholars like Kátia Mattoso, João Reis, and Robert Slenes are harshly criticized for reproducing a perspective akin to Freyre's. Gorender argues that this perspective aligns with the dominant planter class's ideology, which framed slavery as a system that was not fundamentally structured by violence but instead fostered consensus and "social peace" (Mattoso, 1990; Slenes, 2011; Reis & Silva, 1989).

To fully grasp Gorender's critique, it is necessary to revisit Fernandes's dehumanizing argument, which the "rehabilitation" scholars opposed. Fernandes asserted that during the disintegration of the slave system, dominant classes sought to ensure a smooth transition to free labor, particularly in São Paulo. This transition framed freed individuals as independent agents, thrust into a competitive economy as individual actors. From this perspective, abolition was a cruel expropriation—a white condemnation of the old regime in which Black individuals played only a supporting role. The freed masses were reabsorbed into systems that recreated conditions analogous to slavery, further entrenching Black individuals' subjugation in the production process (and broader social life). Fundamentally, Florestan Fernandes argued that the socio-psychological conditions created by slavery severely disadvantaged freed people, leaving them poorly prepared for an individualistic, competitive way of life. According to Fernandes, Black individuals faced stark choices: marginalization into vagrancy and criminality, driven by the presumed irrationality of their behavior. This irrationality, he argued, stemmed from the structural degradation of enslaved life—marked by constant sales, familial separations, sexual immorality, and the coercive association of labor with violence—the moral condition of individuals and freedom (Fernandes, 1978). Indeed, it is precisely against this anomic and dehumanizing perspective that authors like Robert Slenes write. Slenes argues that the enslaved family was not merely a tool for domestication or a mechanism to keep "the peace in the senzalas" through concessions such as granting small plots of land for cultivation—the so-called peasant gap. Instead, he emphasizes that enslaved families and other social and community ties created genuine spaces of freedom. As Slenes (2011) writes: "[...] everyday life in captivity nevertheless tended to value the construction of social identities beyond those imposed by bondage" (p. 63).

In this context, sexual life and family ties represent the crux of a heated debate among historians, grounded in evidence from sources such as those discussed by Slenes. These sources, primarily demographic, aim to demonstrate that many enslaved individuals indeed formed family units. Let us also recall the distinct experiences of figures like Manzano and Jacobs, who were descendants of enslaved families, as well as Esteban, who bore witness to the sale of enslaved children as though they were "piglets" (Barnet, 1986). However, as Gorender (1988) asserts, it is crucial to differentiate between "social reification, which is distinct from subjective reification. The social condition clashed with the person of the slave (personhood = human subjectivity)" (1990, p. 23). In this regard, following an anthropological perspective as discussed in Chapter 1, I would argue that personhood ≠ human subjectivity. While the slave condition negated personhood, it could not entirely negate subjectivity. The peasant gap and the subjective gap collided against the fluid and brutal boundaries of this paradoxical conjunction, which is also reflected in the superstructural legal framework. For now, it is pertinent to highlight Gorender's insight into the distinction between the socially imposed objectification, or social death, and the inescapable phenomenological contradiction, acknowledged by all parties involved—enslaved individuals, slaveholders, and historians—that the enslaved were bearers of human consciousness, although alienated and alienable in their fungibility. This human condition, ostensibly denied for economic purposes, was further undermined by moral contradictions and caprices. In this sense, as Gorender (2016) states, the enslaved, like other workers, were required to embody the relations of production, which provided the objective conditions for the development of subjectivity and personality, defining a "historical mode of human existence" (p. 216). Paradoxically, this objectification served as the historical condition for their existence as subjects, particularly as subjects of the labor process. Even under coercion or violence, their objectification did not negate their role as the "subjective agents" of production, albeit through the most brutal forms of subjugation (Maestri, 2005).

This highlights a broader formal question concerning the very status of being a slave—a juridically and politically regulated ontology designed to encompass economic imperatives. This framework concedes that economic considerations possess a structurally determining level, representing the "internal secret" of social life (Schwartz, 1995). Thus, the legal structure provides a lens which allows us to understand the socially accepted definitions and normative values that formally regulated, under the sanction of the state, both the production of enslaved individuals and the social relations inherent to slavery as a mode of production.

Published in 1758, nearly three decades before the earliest autobiography considered here, Olaudah Equiano's manual "Etíope Resgatado, Empenhado, Sustentado, Corrigido, Instruído e Libertado" was written by Jesuit priest and Portuguese lawyer Manuel Ribeiro da Rocha, who lived in Bahia. The manual seeks to justify African slavery and provide guidance to slave owners on how to treat their enslaved people in a "Christian manner". Like Equiano Rocha's work draws heavily on Christian religion, faith, and the Holy Scriptures as its primary sources. The attempt to provide an enlightened justification for slavery reflects the contradictions and paradoxes of the Enlightenment era, as Susan Buck-Morss (2017) also discusses in relation to Hegel's work. Rocha, much like Equiano, demonstrates an interest in economic issues and seeks to establish an alignment between civilization and economic order. However, as França and Ferreira (2017) aptly note in their introduction, Rocha should be understood as "a respectful and creative interpreter of the Catholic tradition rather than a precursor of abolitionism" (p. 26). In this respect, Rocha diverges significantly from Equiano (n.d.), who asserts that "the worth of a soul cannot be told" (p. 97).

For Rocha, the condition of enslavement is, above all, a miserable one, and enslaved people deserve the compassion of Christians. Moreover, he recognizes slavery as a human condition that violates natural laws, and the divine intentions established by God for Humanity. Importantly, there is no presumption in Rocha's work that Africans are less than human or excluded from God's grace. Rather, enslaved people are portrayed as unfortunate victims of an unjust economic relationship, bearing all the personal and moral consequences of this injustice. In this sense, the author's argument departs from racial justifications for slavery and aligns more closely with the colonial mercantilist framework.

> The greatest misfortune that can befall a rational creature in this world is slavery, for with it come all the miseries and discomforts that are contrary and repugnant to the nature and condition of humankind. For while humans are only slightly lower than angels, through slavery they

are so degraded that they become little more than beasts. Though alive, slavery renders them as if dead; though free, it subjects them; and though born to rule and possess, slavery renders them possessed and dominated. (Rocha, 2017, p. 41)

In fact, the depiction of war and the notion of just wars emerges as a fundamental frame of reference. Like other authors such as Patterson and Meillassoux, Rocha views the enslaved person as someone who, having been defeated in war, faces a stark alternative: physical death or social death as a slave. The presumably more cowardly choice—if it can indeed be called a choice—serves as a justification for slavery, marking a kind of rebirth for the individual who relinquishes freedom and selfhood to live as a slave, an appendage of their master (Patterson, 2008; Meillassoux, 1995). The issue lies in whether the war in question is deemed "just" or "unjust", a debate familiar in the context of Indigenous peoples in the Americas (Todorov, 1993). If captured in a "just war"—fundamentally justified by religious reasons—the resulting enslavement would also be considered just. A similar type of debate surfaces in the context of the Iberian Reconquista and the Islamic expansion in Africa, given that Islam, in theory, prohibits the enslavement of fellow Muslims (M'bokolo, 2008).

For Rocha (2017), the critical question revolves around whether enslaved individuals were acquired legally or illegally.

It has often reached the ears of merchants and other inhabitants of Brazil that learned and God-fearing individuals condemn the trade, purchase, and possession of African enslaved people. This criticism stems from the claim that they were not legitimately captured in public and lawful wars but rather through covert and sudden raids carried out and tolerated by those barbarian rulers and their subjects. (p. 63)

Even if the origin of enslaved people were deemed illegitimate, Rocha argues that if someone purchased them in good faith, the right to ownership should be preserved. As a compromise, he candidly proposes that enslaved individuals, besides being treated humanely, should be manumitted once they reimburse their masters for the cost of their purchase. This reveals an evident contradiction: the contract of sale was not sacred between the buyer and the enslaved person but rather between the buyer and the trader. Ribeiro states, "The law that prohibits the purchase of free individuals does not prohibit, but rather permits, selling freedom to enslaved people in exchange for money" (Rocha, 2017, p. 81). Contrary to Equiano's view that the human soul is priceless, Ribeiro considers the soul to have a value, which he terms "rescue". Father Manuel Xavier, S.J., in a somewhat cynical and metaphysical tone, reflects this in a poetic epigraph of Ribeiro's book: "Freedom will be that which is used to be sold" (Rocha, 2017, p. 45).

By the 19th century, in Imperial Brazil, under the pressures of abolitionist movements, European political ideologies, and the process of constructing a national state, the religious framework prominent in Ribeiro's and Equiano's writings had significantly shifted. As the "Manual Jurídico da Escravidão" (Campello, 2018) highlights, slavery was no longer simply an interpersonal power relationship, but a social system legitimized by law. At the time of Brazil's independence, there were 1,140,000 enslaved people in a total population of 3,690,000—approximately one-third of the population. The legal tradition regarding slavery, as the "manual" reminds us, was deeply rooted in Roman and medieval law, which, while generally applied to a related but distinct phenomenon—servitude—still allowed for slavery, particularly in cases of war as an alternative to death, thereby underpinning the concept of a "just war".

The "Ordenações Filipinas" of 1603, considered the most pertinent legal codification for the colonial context, moved beyond the category of "servants" to refer explicitly to enslaved people, granting African enslaved individuals the legal status of commodities. The Empire largely inherited colonial slavery legislation, culminating in the 1824 Constitution, granted after significant turmoil by Emperor Dom Pedro I. A profound contradiction marked this constitution: How could slavery be reconciled with a supposedly liberal constitution? Slavery, notably, was not explicitly mentioned in the constitution, though there was an implicit reference. Article 6 states: "Brazilian citizens are: I. those born in Brazil, whether free born [ingênuos] or freed, even if their father is a foreigner..." (Campello, 2018, p. 55). According to the author, this meant that "enslaved people were not part of the political community of the country" (Idem, p. 56).

This paradox is a recurring theme throughout Campello's work: there was no clear legal foundation for slavery in Brazil. During the Empire, the State and society tolerated what was essentially a "manifest illegality" and a glaring injustice. Numerous contradictions arose; for instance, if enslaved people were not citizens, how could they bear arms in wars to defend the country? While the legality of slavery remained ambiguous, property rights were enshrined as one of the main individual rights, which, in turn, justified not slavery itself but the rights of slaveholders. Thus, enslaved individuals became a precondition for the bourgeois subject and its corollaries.

Who, then, was the enslaved person in this context, if not a citizen? Defined as a thing—"a material object subject to valuation" (Campello, 2018, p. 127)—how could the enslaved person hold civil status within the *polis*? The legal status of the enslaved person, Campello argues, was defined by a combination of two ontological attributes: persona (person) and res (thing). Drawing on Roman law, Counselor Joaquim Ribas, cited by Campello, distinguishes between *dominium*—referring to ownership of things (*res*)—and potestas—referring to authority over persons (persona), as in the case of paternal authority over children. In the case of the enslaved person, these two concepts converged: *dominium*, because the enslaved person was an alienable commodity, and *potestas*, because they were a conscious human being. This duality had various legal consequences. For instance, enslaved people were entitled to adequate food but were not allowed to represent themselves legally against their masters. As Campello explains, "slaves had a legal status for the purposes of applying civil and commercial laws as movable goods subject to a special legal regime" (Idem, p. 136).

The distressing analogy between domestic animals, livestock, and slaves was a recurring notion, where enslaved people were often viewed as "human animals". Much like today, when we acknowledge the personality, intelligence, and emotions of our pets while still trading or selling them and their offspring, this was the prevailing logic of slaveholding societies. Similarly to animals, slaves were not legally recognized as having families or familial bonds—a perspective already present in Roman law. Under Roman legal principles, enslaved individuals did not have families; they could not marry but were limited to contubernium, a natural or de facto union. More significantly, enslaved people were denied patriarchal authority, reflecting a broader connection between slavery and the negation of kinship, especially within patriarchal frameworks. In Brazilian law, likewise, the captives were not granted the civil right to exercise paternal authority. Additionally, they could not accumulate or transmit wealth. In the rare instances when this occurred, it was only by the grace of their masters who could permit or revoke such privileges at their discretion. As we can observe, slave narratives often recount instances in which masters ignored, denied, or outright lied about such allowances, stealing money or property from enslaved people without any legal recourse available to the victims (Campello, 2018).

Fundamentally, slaves were inscribed into normative codes as "things", governed by contractual and commercial relationships of purchase and sale. While they were acknowledged as human beings, they were not considered parties to these contracts but rather as mere objects within them, along with their labor and the products of their labor. In the case of enslaved women, this included their children. Historiography and narratives provide numerous examples of this alienation, such as in "Úrsula", where enslaved people constitute the only property of poor individuals—like Úrsula's mother, who is a woman with disability; these are the people who guarantee the subsistence of their master through their labor. This dynamic is echoed in the broader historiography of slavery in Brazil as well. Thus, while economic relations often manifested as total social facts (Mauss, 2003; Patterson, 2008), they also structured the positionality of the slave as formal regulatory frameworks.

THE SOCIAL BEING OF THE SLAVE AS NON-BEING

Throughout this discussion, I have frequently referred to the works of Claude Meillassoux (1995) and Orlando Patterson (2008). Both authors have produced comprehensive studies that aim to provide far-reaching definitions of slavery. Patterson's scope is broader, as he crosses historiography, anthropology, and sociology to conceptualize slavery as a universally applicable model. This makes considerable sense, as slavery—albeit in varied forms, which Patterson describes—has existed in numerous human societies across four continents. Meillassoux's work, though more modest in scope, remains extensive, focusing specifically on precolonial slavery in West Africa. Both works develop complex arguments supported by detailed and dense empirical evidence, which will not be reproduced here in full. Unlike some of the other authors discussed, Meillassoux emphasizes the individual dimension of domination. He views the legal framework and comparisons between slaves and domestic animals as a "contradictory and unsustainable fiction". Nonetheless, his central category is depersonalization, which stems from alienability, whether through war or market forces—the two primary structures producing captives. Meillassoux identifies a fundamental opposition within African domestic or subsistence slavery: the distinction between kin and strangers, with the slave epitomizing the non-kin, the "stranger" or the other. Using kinship theory, he positions the slave outside the system of roles and *statuses* that allow kinship to serve as a tool for social and, primarily, economic reproduction. The slave, therefore, is a stranger integrated into the family nucleus but from outside the lineage structure. This explains why slaves could not establish descent or be recognized by ancestors: "[...] we discover here a characteristic that will appear in all forms of slavery, a feature that is its very essence: the social incapacity of the slave to reproduce socially, that is, the legal incapacity to be kin" (Meillassoux, 1995, p. 28).

While Meillassoux's Marxist anthropology seeks to explain the articulation of social group reproduction with the production of social conditions for such reproduction—echoing Engels's tradition of considering family and kinship as elements of political economy—Patterson adopts an explicitly Weberian approach. Patterson focuses on the ritualistic and symbolic dimensions of human social life and the grim complementarity between slavery and freedom, an idea rooted in Hegel's dialectic of master and slave (Hegel, 2002). Patterson, however, prefers the term "parasitic" complementarity, where the slave's dishonor fuels the honor and freedom of the master.

Patterson examines slavery through the lens of power relationships. In his words, relations are based on inequality and domination. Slavery, as the most extreme and, in some sense, paradigmatic form of domination, exhibits three key characteristics: (1) singularity or the maximum intensity of power, reflecting the historical manifestation of Hegel's master-slave dialectic; (2) the role of violence as the primordial political act in stratified societies, with the whip and lash serving as cruel yet essential tools of material and symbolic social control; and (3) the individualized domination of the conditions of slavery.

Slavery appears as an alternative to violent death in war, although the market remains the other "womb" of slavery—as we can also see studying other authors. Once sold, the slave becomes "res" (thing), governed by contractual and economic law that obliterates their Humanity. As a conditional exchange—life for freedom—enslavement produces a non-person, what Meillassoux calls the anti-kin, someone entirely alienated and alienable, stripped of natal roots. The slave is thus socially dead (devoid of rights and claims, a "genealogical isolate" who possesses a past, but which is not a legacy. This alienation renders the slave the perfect human tool: malleable, available, and capable of fulfilling any role, a plasticity simultaneously human and amplified by the contradiction between thing/person.

In modern times, or even in classical antiquity, it was only through the denial of the slave's Humanity and independent social existence that "men of good standing" could justify the glaring injustice of slavery. Enslavement rituals, akin to anthropological rites of separation, served to remove the individual from their social and genealogical place, leading to absolute depersonalization. This depersonalization became transmissible, manifesting in the perpetual and hereditary loss of freedom. In summary, slaves were generally dishonored individuals devoid of names (and thus honor), they only had to protect the honor of their masters. The symbolic and status-related aspects of slavery, rather than its economic dimensions, are what impart its universal character. Nevertheless, economic factors remained central to modern African slavery and colonial systems.

The structural significance of slavery, beyond its historical manifestations, emerges through common attributes—though not exclusive—to the *plantations* of the United States: (1) the direct and insidious violence; (2) namelessness and invisibility; (3) the endless personal violation; and (4) the chronic and inalienable dishonor. Slavery, therefore, can be understood as the permanent and violent domination of individuals, the loss of honor, and its relation to the loss of power (Patterson, 2008).

It is largely through critical readings of Patterson and Frantz Fanon that Frank Wilderson (2010) develops his critique of historical materialism. He describes the slave's positionality as the matrix of Blackness in the modern world—defined primarily by a libidinal economy—"the economy, or distribution and arrangement, of desire and identification, of energies, concerns, points of attention, anxieties, pleasures, appetites, revulsions, and phobias—the whole structure of psychic and emotional life—that are unconscious and invisible but that have a visible effect on the world, including the money economy" (_____, 2017, p. 7). This perspective challenges the traditional prioritization of political economy and displaces class primacy over race. Wilderson interrogates the nature and destiny of Black suffering in the afterlife of slavery. Unlike more absolutist authors, who view anti-Black racism as the structuring element of all human history in the Old World (Moore, 2010), Wilderson is more cautious, situating his analysis within the modern anti-Black world, particularly within the context of the United States (Wilderson, 2010).

Karl Marx and historical materialism made numerous references to racism and colonialism, as I have discussed in this book, though usually as metaphors—what Matory (2018) calls a "pedestal" for the oppression of the European working class. Marx often viewed slavery as a stage in Humanity's violent and inexorable progress, driven by contradictions between social relations of production and technological development (Marx, 1998, 2011). These contradictions, as we know, are resolved through violent transformations, as human history is a history of struggle, massacres, violence, and revolutions. In "Capital", discussing the "convenience of the normal workday", Marx compares "free" workers to slaves in Georgia, saying: "For slave-trade read labour-market, for Kentucky and Virginia, Ireland and the agricultural districts of England, Scotland, and Wales, for Africa, Germany" (Marx, 1998, p. 308). Similarly, in "Kindred", the character Dana compares the employment agency where she finds work—and where she met her husband—to a "slave market" (Butler, 2019, p. 85).

Thus, slavery is often depicted metaphorically as the ultimate example of exploitation and violence. In "Grundrisse", Marx (2011) further states that:

> In the relations of slavery and serfdom this separation does not take place; rather, one part of society is treated by the other as itself merely an inorganic and natural condition of its own reproduction. The slave stands in no relation whatsoever to the objective conditions of his labour; rather, labour itself, both in the form of the slave and in that of the serf, is classified as an inorganic condition of production along with other natural beings, such as cattle, as an accessory of the earth. (p. 401)

Clearly, the enslaved person is not a subject for themselves, as they cannot objectify themselves under the social and historical conditions of society's reproduction. However, Wilderson does not invoke the figure of the slave merely as a worker or capital. Instead, this being—whom Aimé Césaire (2020) describes as "the famine-man, the insult-man, the torture man/ You can grab anytime/ Beat up, kill—no joke, kill—without having to account to anyone/ Without having to make excuses to anyone" (p. 1).

Conversely, the figure of the enslaved is better described through the libidinal economy, which specifically demands gratuitous violence, fetishization, terror, and desire. Wilderson, however, does not outright reject Marxism; rather, he challenges its primacy or exclusivity in formulating an answer to the question: "What is a Black? A subject? An object? A former slave? A Slave?" (Wilderson, 2010, p. 11). In an interview, he states:

> I'm sometimes misunderstood to be saying that I have left Marxism. I'm sometimes misunderstood to be saying that the cognitive map that Marx gives us should be thrown out. That's not what I'm saying. How do you throw out

a cognitive map that explains political economy so well?
(Wilderson, 2017, p. 17)

The problem, however, is that political economy does not explain everything. It fails to account for what Fanon (1983) suggests as the difference between social oppression and structural suffering. Nor does it allow for the fundamental task of theorizing the (ontological) impossibility of Blackness, based on the "ruse" of analogy that assumes Black people exist within the "world". According to Fanon, there is instead an essential incompatibility between Blackness and the "world". In this sense, Fanon points to what has already been described above as a grammar of (Black) suffering, which is definitively irreconcilable with civil society. This is because Black men and women exist outside the "world" due to what Fanon refers to as "phobogenesis", or the fact of Blackness: "I am the slave not of the 'idea' that others have of me but of my own appearance" (Fanon, 1983, p. 96). This produces the well-known impossible dilemma for Black people: to be means not to be Black. Indeed, as in the condition of criminal subjection, it is violence that repositions Black individuals into the void of a historical movement that has no analogy with the ontologically living. Gratuitous violence against Black people constitutes the primary ontological instance of our existence. Wilderson (2010) provides a striking comparison: Jews entered and exited Auschwitz as Jews—a human holocaust. Africans, however, entered the slave ships and exited as Blacks—a metaphysical holocaust:

> The violence which turns a body into flesh, ripped apart literally and imaginatively destroys the possibility of ontology because it positions the black in an indefinite and indeterminately horrifying and open vulnerability, an object made available (which is to say fungible) for any subject. (Wilderson, 2010, p. 38)

For Fanon, and as we also see in Marx, Blackness serves as a comparison—a means through which Humanity recognizes itself in the Other who is not. This other is defined by gratuitous violence and social death, which would require a thanatology: Blackness becomes the embodiment of impossibility, incoherence, and incapacity. This perspective allows us to distinguish between the structural antagonism that governs Black existence in the anti-Black world and the conflictual harmony that characterizes competing political currents within the white world, or the "zone of being" (Grosfoguel, 2012). The coherence essential to whiteness in modernity lies in this immunity to genocide (if not as a concrete historical experience, then as a mode of positioning). White populations, of course, can experience genocide, but genocide does not constitute them; it is not what makes white people white (that is to say, human). A radically different phenomenon occurs with Black people, who are defined precisely through the middle passage or the experience of being born into the market or war, not as humans but as non-humans, strangers, anti-kin, or the socially dead. Black people are recognized or read only as this accursed "inorganic part" or as capital goods. While the (white) worker labors upon the commodity, the Black individual is the commodity itself (fungible in this sense). However, and this is fundamental, a commodity can—and, as we shall see, does—resist.

THE SCENE OF OBJECTION: PERFORMANCE AND SOCIAL DEATH

Over seven thousand kilometers apart, the city of New Orleans, Louisiana, and the Recôncavo region of Bahia—more specifically, the district of Acupe, part of the municipality of Santo Amaro da Purificação—are connected through the global dynamics of the slave trade and the colonial *plantation* economy. The external, economic, and historical face of colonial expansion and the slave trade conceals a powerful undercurrent of cultural invention and subjectively materialized forms of resistance.

In the previous sections of this chapter, we revisited, from new perspectives, the question posed in Chapter 1 regarding the subjectivity, "personhood", and agency of Africans enslaved in the New World. This analysis occurs within the paradigmatic framework of social death, countered by the vibrant structures of resistance operating under the sign of Africa. Slave narratives reveal a limit, akin to the "Black border", to the representation of the self or the production of a subject within stable and self-recognizable frameworks. This impossibility is at once historical and epistemological, because the voice of the black subject, which reflects on the harsh objectivity of the social order, can only exist through the negation of its ontological and epistemological autonomy. The construction of the enslaved subject in autobiographical narratives—mediated by "transcribers", "sponsors", or conventional narrative formulas—therefore embodies a contradiction: the self that speaks of itself within this structure simultaneously negates itself and any autonomous epistemological or cultural capacity to "be". This process involves movement between the place of negation and opacity as a slave and the subsequent conversion—through the denial of their value as a thing—into their value as a subject or person. The white, anti-Black world and its masks are thus integral to the invention of the Black subject, as discussed in Zózimo Bulbul's film "Alma no Olho". It represents a structural and structured limit—one that we cannot pinpoint with accuracy.

Blocked from "being" in literary narratives, the Black subject, whose personhood exists as a legal possession, arbitrated by the state and infused with the fungible ontological density of the market, emerges within materialist ontology through the definition of their "social being". The enslaved individual's thingness—an apparent contradiction—reflects the essential ambiguity of Brazil's slave-based superstructure. Slaves are recognized as an active consciousness yet denied the status of a moral person, citizens, or foundational members of the *polis* (Campello, 2018; Vargas, 2017). At once movable property and a human being, the slave remains trapped in this tension between non-being and being nothing, an object of interchangeable value, tradeable and negotiable. Paradoxically, it is precisely due to this essential ambiguity—between flesh and "value"—that the slave, as the subjective agent of labor and as a commodity, produces society, in the material point of view, by producing their own negation as a person. This negation of the person is, in fact, the very production of society. Slaves thus enact a negation not located in some utopian future but within the layers of the colonial-slave order itself. Or in the scene of objection.

On February 25, 2020, the last day of Mardi Gras, I had the fortune to witness a "practice" or performance by one of the elusive Mardi Gras Indian Tribes. This occurred on a corner—or crossroads—of Henriette Delille Street and Governor Nicholls Street, near Louis Armstrong Park and Congo Square, a sacred and ancestral territory of Afro-diasporic traditions in New Orleans. Further along Henriette Street lies the Backstreet Cultural Museum, a vital center for the preservation and resistance of Black traditions in the city. Henriette Street runs parallel to the bustling North Rampart Avenue, which separates the historic French Quarter—with its beautiful architecture attesting to the city's French and Spanish past—from the Tremé neighborhood, a traditional African American territory. Today, the French Quarter, particularly Bourbon Street, is a "landscape of power" dominated by the commodification and tourism-driven marketing of the city's "Creole" traditions. Tremé, meanwhile, has undergone post-Katrina gentrification,[48] which has transformed the city, as will be explored further below. Running parallel to North Rampart but relatively hidden, the museum is indeed located on the backstreet—an urban-spatial metaphor for the marginalization of the city's Black population. For someone like me, coming from Salvador, Bahia, it is impossible not to draw comparisons between the two cities. One striking aspect, that I noticed from my very first days, was the visible Black presence in public spaces, alongside the clear subalternization of Black individuals, who occupy undervalued roles everywhere—bus drivers, McDonald's cashiers, or people cleaning streets and buildings. This stood in sharp contrast to the predominantly white population concentrated in Uptown and at Tulane University, where I spent part of my days working.

I knew very little about the Mardi Gras Indians when I arrived in New Orleans, and even less about the performance I was about to witness. Prior to Carnival, I had attended two Indian practices—specifically of the Wild Magnolias Tribe—on Dryades Street, at the Sportsmen Corner bar, and another location, the Handa Wanda. Despite my initial ignorance, the impact was profound when I encountered the Black crowd: young men, women, children, and elders, moving with grace to the percussive sound of antiphonal music—the call-and-response style—so familiar to anyone accustomed to samba, capoeira, and other Afro-Brazilian cultural forms.

During Carnival, however, I was able to witness a performance of the Indians in full regalia. Emerging one by one from a garage, the participants of this performance-procession-ritual filled the street, competing for space with a crowd of photographers and videographers. It is no surprise that some "chiefs" demand financial recognition for the immense and passionate labor involved in creating their incredibly elaborate and extravagant costumes, which they refer to as "suits"—appropriately described as "performative objects of cultural mediation" (Becker, 2013, p. 36). As I mentioned, they appeared one by one: the Spyboy, the Flagboy, the Big Chief, and the exuberant, dreamlike procession of Black men adorned with iridescent feathers, beads, and sequins. Their suits featured mystical, ancestral iconography, depicting Plains Indians from North America and, in this particular case, symbols of African ancestrality—something I later learned is not as common among other "tribes". Notably, the use of the mask stood out as an innovation.

---

[48] In 2005, Hurricane Katrina struck the city, leaving thousands homeless and causing millions of dollars in damages. The city has yet to fully recover from the trauma, and the memory of despair and destruction remains present in every conversation and at every moment.

At the time, I did not know that the group I was watching perform on the "backstreet" was the Spirit of Fi Yi-Yi and the Mandingo Warriors—the group credited with "Africanizing" the performance of the Mardi Gras Indians. The Fi Yi-Yi tribe was founded in 1984 by Victor Harris, a former Flagboy of the Yellow Pocahontas Tribe. The Yellow Pocahontas group holds a central place in the Mardi Gras tradition due to the immense contributions of its legendary Big Chief, Alison "Tootie" Montana, who is credited with numerous aesthetic innovations and with transforming the groups' traditional aggression and territorial disputes into ritualized, aesthetic competitiveness. Montana's death in 2005 was both tragic and heroic: he collapsed during a testimony at the New Orleans City Council while addressing yet another incident of police violence against the Indigenous people. This particular episode had occurred on March 15, Saint Joseph's Day, a significant date when they also perform in the streets of the city's Black neighborhoods (Wehmeyer, 2010).

Harris explains that he founded the Spirit of Fi Yi-Yi through the direct spiritual intervention of an entity that instructed him to make the Indigenous people more African. In that moment, this was precisely my impression—my emotional response—that Africa had been reterritorialized there. I felt the same way on Dryades Street, even if the Wild Magnolias did not present themselves in such an overtly Africanized manner. Much like the samba and/or pagode gatherings I had attended or the paredões in Cachoeira, I felt transported to another place or temporal dimension. The combination of percussive music, the massive presence of Black bodies, the dancing, the laughter, and the alcohol created an atmosphere of profane sacrality. At Mardi Gras, in front of the masks adorned with cowries, clearly referencing the West African tradition that sacralizes/monetizes the shells—as embodiments of both wealth and the dead—the African heritage was undeniable to me. Moving sinuously among the photographers, the masked figure, like a depersonalized Egungun, led the way into a transtemporal space mediated by the resignification of death.

Image 11 — The Spirit of Fi Yi
Source: Author's image, 2020.

Wearing an Indian suit is a form of embodiment that often facilitates entering "into the spirit." Drums, chants, tambourines, and cadenced rhythms are all associated with Mardi Gras Indian performance, which is reminiscent of spiritual, shamanic, and trancelike states from other traditions. "Masking" permits the expression of dissent. (Ehrenreich, 2004, p. 117)

The spiritual, or mystical, dimension of the Indians is evident. The practice is seen as connecting to spiritual or mystical dimensions, such that Tootie Montana, according to his son, refused to perform at a major jazz festival because of the desecration it would represent (Becker, 2013). VanSpanckeren (1990) also emphasizes how the Indians—Inju—view their practices as religious. Spiritual connections between Indigenous and African Americans in New Orleans, as well as between Afro-Brazilians and Indigenous peoples (Caboclos), are well-documented (Santos, 1995; Pinto, 2014).

Stephen C. Wehmeyer discusses these connections from a historical and mythical perspective regarding the Spiritual Church, a syncretic denomination with dozens of communities in New Orleans. Although Christian, this spiritualist church prominently venerates the spirit of Black Hawk, a Suak Fox Indigenous hero who fought alongside the British in the War of 1812, when the British supported Indigenous nations against the Americans. Later, in 1832, he led the resistance against the U.S. Army in the Black Hawk War, ultimately being defeated the following year. In 1883, Black Hawk published his autobiography, and after his death, he became a sacred figure, a spirit. Today, he is viewed by some in New Orleans as an invisible force controlling the streets (Wehmeyer, 2010; Lipsitz, 1988). These same streets, contested and reinvented by the performative agency of the Indians, serve as marginal spaces possessed by rites of deterritorialization, which, as George Lipsitz states, demonstrate how a "fictive" identity can give voice and place to deeper beliefs and values (Lipsitz, 1988, p. 102).

Two main versions circulate to explain the emergence of the Mardi Gras Indians in New Orleans. One emphasizes a maroon (quilombola) connection or descent among Indigenous peoples, Africans, and Afro-descendants during the colonial period. Mystical and spiritual interpretations often converge on this view, which is more mythopoetic than historical, though mythopoetry itself is part of history. As discussed in the context of slave memory retold in narratives, mythopoetry indeed constitutes history. These interpretations emphasize African heritage and the continuity of traditions, seen, for instance, in the use of feathers and plumes, which are purportedly inherited from the Kongo kingdom. As a form of atoning for the trauma of the Middle Passage, such analyses "purposefully emphasize an African connection, even if such connection cannot be proven historically" (Becker, 2013, p. 40). From another perspective, many Indians emphasize not only spiritual but also familial connections. As Breunlin (2009) explains: "Lil Walter Cook, Big Chief of the tribe, disputes this claim, arguing that oral histories passed down in his family trace their involvement in the masking tradition to at least the 1830s" (p. 66). This periodization contrasts with another set of more historical versions, which attribute the creation of the Mardi Gras Indians to the founding of the first "tribe", the Creole Wild West, following the influence of Buffalo Bill's "Wild West" show in New Orleans in 1884–1885. This tribe was created by Becate Batiste, born into a Creole family of Martinican origin and the great uncle of Big Chief Allison "Tootie" Montana. This connection also suggests ties between the Mardi Gras Indians and Caribbean traditions found in Martinique, Haiti, and other Caribbean islands with strong African or Kongo presence (Becker, 2013).

The 1880s, therefore, represent the historical context of the Indians' creation, marked by intense racial segregation and violence. As in Brazil, particularly in Bahia and Rio de Janeiro, racial segregation and its accompanying violence shaped the history of Carnival in New Orleans. As Christopher Dunn's (2008) excellent review summarizes, during this period in Brazil, authorities sought to repress pre-carnival celebrations or Shrovetide and the "boisterous amusements" of black drumming by introducing Carnival balls and "Venetian-style" public parades imported as a celebration of the civilization. Similarly, in New Orleans, Anglo-American elites asserted their cultural and political hegemony by creating Krewes in the newly Anglicized Uptown neighborhoods.

Younger than Salvador or other urban agglomerations in the Recôncavo region, New Orleans was founded in 1699 by the French, incorporated by the Spanish in 1764, and finally sold to the Americans in 1803. Between 1809 and 1810, the city's population doubled with the arrival of refugees from Saint-Domingue, who came via Cuba after the Haitian Revolution. These refugees were divided into three groups: French-origin whites, free people of color, and enslaved Blacks (Dunn, 2008). This rich and complex history continues to shape the city's cultural identity—now commodified (Perry, 2015)—and solidifies its place in the American imagination as an exotic, "European" city. This is something I heard repeatedly during my visit—from the Uber driver, the cashier at CVS, and others—along with the notion that New Orleans is relatively more racially tolerant due to its history of racial mixing. Cultural disputes between Anglos and Creoles also influenced the assertion or creation of whiteness through Carnival. Krewes such as "Bacchus" and "Endymion" played a significant role in this narrative, particularly during the period of the so-called "reconstruction",[49] when the relative racial ambiguity and unique position of free people of color were threatened by the biracial order imposed under Jim Crow laws. Segregation also extended to Carnival, contributing to the development of an "aristocratic" mythology, symbolized by the peculiar practice—at least from my perspective—of throwing bead necklaces and other trinkets to the audience, the "vulgus profanus". These spectators passively watch but do not participate in the Krewes's parades, which continue to dominate the streets during Carnival with monumental floats and satirical costumes.

These Krewes, which emerged in the 19th century, were also aligned with the supremacist and eugenicist ideals of the time, as Dunn (2008) thoroughly documents. This same period marks the creation of the Indians, establishing an evident structural and formal contrast: while the Krewes are white, the Indians are Black; while the Krewes parade for a mesmerized audience along the city's main streets—primarily Uptown— through highly scripted performances with aristocratic, classical, literary, or Greco-Roman references, the Indians follow no predetermined script. Instead, they involve the entire local community in neighborhoods like Tremé or the 9th Ward through spontaneous and unannounced "appearances". These appearances, much like the Nego Fugido ritual in Acupe, which will be discussed later, are organized around ritualized dialogues that transcend racial violence and terror, reterritorializing the streets— what can be described as "border spaces" under the control of "nomads" (Wehmeyer, 2010, p. 429).

In a widely cited work, Joseph Roach draws on the tradition of the Indians to critique the Eurocentricity of performance and theater studies. He seeks to "re-interpret the American culture as a series of political boundaries both marked and contested by performances" (ROACH, 1992, p. 462). This is a perspective to which I express profound solidarity. The "practice"—what Perry (2015, p. 95) terms the "performative spheres of Black vernacular culture"—of the Indians unfolds in the contested and liminal space of the streets, particularly in the "backstreets". Improvisational yet grounded in the abundant frameworks of African or Kongo tradition and epistemology, this practice is "fugitive" (Harney & Moten, 2013). It displaces conflict, struggle, pain, and violence into the liminality of the street or the crossroads, spaces where I myself encountered the Spirit of Fi Yi-Yi and the Mandingo Warriors.

---

[49] The period following the American Civil War (1861–1865), marked by the reintegration of the Confederate States of the South into the Union, or the United States of America, along with the subsequent, yet ultimately frustrated, attempts to integrate formerly enslaved people, is known as Reconstruction.

As Marc Perry highlights when discussing the duality of Black presence in post-Katrina New Orleans, the disposability of Black bodies and individuals who do not conform to the commodification of culture and bodies is a structured and articulated device. The predisposition to the killing of certain Black bodies absorbs the "surplus", the "accursed share" that does not fit within exoticized, sexualized, and fetishized narratives of Black culture. The fugitivity of the Indians—who adhere to a strict script of improvisational performative practices with their characters, such as Flagboys, Spyboys, and chiefs, much like the Nego Fugido with its "nêgas" and "hunters"—improvises and reinterprets Blackness at the razor's edge, on the mortal line that separates the zone of being from the zone of non-being.

> I suggest that black New Orleanians are often figured within two seemingly competing frames of racialized spectacle that impact social fields of opportunity and the broader vitality of black working-class New Orleans. The first of these is predicated on commercially assimilable and therefore "good" black subjects as instrumental facets of New Orleans' tourist-driven cultural industry; the other tied to those deemed unassimilable and hence deviantly "bad" and dispensable. (Perry, 2015, p. 95)

In other words, the social forms that social death assumes in this context—so local yet so diasporic—take on a duality: either disposability, through physical death, dispossession, erasure, indignity, and demise; or self-conversion into commodity and stereotype. The Black body, in this case, achieves a form of survival if it "makes sense" within the exoticized narrative of Creole New Orleans, mixed-race, Latin, or European. The horrific tragedy of Hurricane Katrina made this reality starkly evident, as Perry discusses with numerical precision, demonstrating the demographic changes and the racialized class topography within which the Indians must maneuver. The contrast and comparison with Salvador—and the Recôncavo region—is even more striking given the vast differences in the history of the two regions. Yet, as Christen Smith (2016) describes, Salvador experiences a very similar paradox or duality: the celebration and exaltation of Black culture alongside the genocide of Black people.

From a performative standpoint, I emphasize, as do other authors, the relationship between performance and the "street" as a producer of scenes that theatricalize social death and ancestrality in ways that are at once in-credibly creative and flamboyant, grounded in African epistemology. For this tradition, both the street, or the crossroads, and secrecy are essential dimensions. "The streets, as urban 'frontier space', are the natural environ-ment for manifestations of the Indian spirits" (Wehmeyer, 2010, p. 434).

Commenting on the unpredictable script of the Indians' "appearanc-es" in the streets, Larry Bannock, Big Chief of the Golden Star Hunters, says: "The map has to be in our heart" (Roach, 1992, p. 471). The map in the heart allows for the reconquest, repossession, and reclamation of the physical territory of the streets as a space over which ancestral spirits hold power—notably, the power to resist the conquest of hearts and territories by white supremacy and social death.

For my approach to the Nego Fugido ritual of Acupe, in the Recôncavo of Bahia, I rely heavily on the work of Monilson dos Santos Pinto, an organ-ic intellectual of the Nego Fugido, himself a brincante (player/performer) and academic researcher in the field of performing arts. Monilson is from Acupe, a district of Santo Amaro da Purificação, a city that, like others in the Recôncavo Baiano, serves as the backdrop for various manifestations of African—or Améfrican—traditions in the colonial Brazilian territory.

In his original master's thesis, "Nego Fugido: Teatro das Aparições", de-fended at the Graduate Program in Performing Arts at São Paulo State University (UNESP), Monilson navigates performing arts, anthropology, history, memory, and poetry to interrogate the Nêgo Fugido and his own formation as a critical subject: performer, researcher, activist, and "native". At just 8 years old, he first encountered the apparitions that invade the dis-trict of Acupe in July, when fishing and shellfish harvesting—foundations of the local quilombola economy—pause for the season.

> I saw a mysterious figure, face painted black, shotgun in hand, and blood dripping from his mouth, moving through the festive commotion in the streets of the Acupe district on a Sunday afternoon in July. That day, early in the morning, as the frantic beats of atabaques echoed from the caboclo festivals in the candomblé terreiros, I heard rumors about performances by capoeira groups, samba de roda, and masked apparitions running through the streets, attempting to whip people. There were screams and groans from women wrapped in sheets, figures with oversized heads and short legs who invaded the streets of

the community to create a commotion. (Monilson, 2014, p. 1)

Amid this fantastic, dreamlike, and mythical atmosphere that erupted in the streets of Acupe, the author's initial interest in these "apparitions" emerged—first as a performer (brincante) and later as a researcher and activist.

In summary, Nego Fugido is a tradition of popular dramatic performance that occurs spontaneously in the Acupe district and tells the story of enslaved people's struggle and liberation in a way that differs from how it appears in History books. In Nego Fugido, the "nêgas"[50]—usually young boys who portray enslaved men—are pursued by the "hunters", with faces painted black and mouths painted blood-red. Other key characters include the "King of Portugal", assisted by "soldiers", and the godmother Dona Santa. This traditional set of characters forms the basis of the performance. The performance, or dramatic dance, follows a predefined script within which the brincantes improvise, interact with, and provoke the audience. The hunters, acting as capitães do mato,[51] chase the fugitive slaves, the "nêgas", and the entire pursuit is marked by Artaudian paroxysms—characters throw themselves to the ground, scream, and contort, begging for money to "purchase" their freedom while the hunters attempt to sell them. The scene escalates into a rebellion—a subversion within the scene of objection—as the slaves kidnap the King, demanding freedom for all as his ransom. This is a total subversion of the official narrative: There is no passive granting of freedom by Princess Isabel and the Golden Law. Instead, what unfolds is a revolt, an uprising that mimics, through dramatic stages, a narrative subversion of history itself.

---

[50] As Maria José Villares Barral Villas Boas (2019) discusses, it is striking that the enslaved characters are referred to as "nêgas" in the feminine form, even though, traditionally and still today, they are mostly performed by male participants.

[51] T.N.: The term "capitão do mato" (literally "captain of the woods") refers to a historical figure in colonial Brazil and the early post-colonial period who was tasked with capturing escaped enslaved people, known as "negros fugidos". Capitães do mato often worked as agents for plantation owners or local authorities.

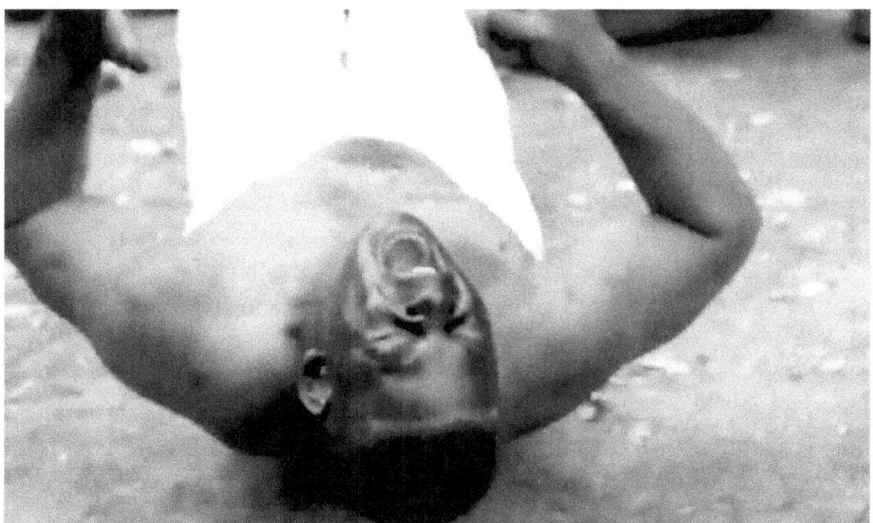

Image 12 — Still from the video "Nego Fugido de Acupe – da Bahia para o Centro de São Paulo"
Source: SESC São Paulo, 2018.

As Monilson reminds us, this performance parallels other manifestations that the author refers to as "quilombola dramatic dances". Examples include the "dança dos quilombos" in the city of Limoeiro de Anadia, Alagoas, and the "lambe-sujo" of Laranjeiras, Sergipe (Reis, 1996).[52] While differences exist in the script or dramatic structure, the ritualized or dramatized remembrance of the experience of bondage remains a constant. The persistence of these manifestations in communities still recognized as quilombolas today reinforces the author's argument that the performance of an imagined past reflects the struggles and contradictions of the present. On a more radical level, it blurs the line between past and present through mythical and ritual evocations. The historical layers and political disputes involved in consolidating these performances are complex. For example, in the Lambe Sujo, where enslaved quilombolas are defeated by Indigenous figures, Demian Reis suggests a moralizing manipulation—an intervention in the dramatic narrative—to transform it into a kind of auto (didactic play) that teaches conformity to formerly enslaved people (Idem).

In Acupe, however, the slaves—the "nêgas"—emerge victorious, as the King grants freedom to all amidst the rhythms of batuque and the ecstatic performance, often culminating in a state resembling trance among the brincantes. Monilson highlights the connections between the Nego

---

[52] And I suspect there are others. During Carnival in 2008 or 2009, while visiting the beach of São Tomé de Paripe, in the Subúrbio Ferroviário of Salvador, I came across a group of young Black men with their faces painted black and ropes tied around their necks.

Fugido and local religious traditions, particularly the worship of Xangô. He also draws attention to the near-trance states experienced by the nê-gas during the performance. The terreiro dedicated to Xangô, located in the Vai-quem-quer community—a site of central importance to Acupe's quilombola identity—sits at the base of Alto do Cruzeiro hill. For many years, this terreiro was led by Vovó Loriana, who passed away in 1997 at an uncertain age. Some claimed she was 123 years old at the time and that she remembered the abolition of slavery. It is said that she once recounted that: "When freedom came, I was a little girl. I heard many fireworks and shouts of joy; it was a party!" (Pinto, 2014, p. 25). As with the Mardi Gras Indians, the connection between these performances and religious traditions is clear, and perhaps even more structurally significant in Acupe.

Regarding trance, Monilson draws on the ideas of Antonin Artaud, for whom trance constructs a "body without organs", subverting the prerogatives of linear, disembodied reason.[53] In Artaud's view, theater erupts into life—either within or outside of it—destroying and demolishing the distance between representation and existence. In doing so, it realizes the utopia of a life re-enchanted by art and a theater that, cruelly, serves as a means to insert the extraordinary, the phantasmagorical, the oneiric, and the uncommon into life—something that allows for "the appearance of a ghost on stage" (Artaud, 1987, p. 71). In this theater, the scenic resources allow a "double" to detach from the actors and the performance—a fantastic and terrifying other that is not a "representation" of reality but its virtuality, paroxysmally achieved. As with the intersection of history and fiction discussed in the case of Black narratives, the imagination, in a moment of danger, tears the subject away from their fixation in the historical time of coherence between body–subjectivity–identity. This process produces the subject as the Other of oneself, promoting an anti-Maussian synthesis between person and character, in an argument similar to the one developed by Augras (2008).

> Duality constitutes the permanent structure of being. It is play, dance, theater, the revelation of the one and the many, the manifestation of the double, the shadow, the fraternal stranger or the anguishing reflection—an image of God or the devil. (2008p. 22)

---

[53] Regarding the body without organs, a concept originally coined by Antonin Artaud, Deleuze and Guattari state in "A Thousand Plateaus": "the body without organs is not a dead body but a living body all the more alive and teeming once it has blown apart the organism and its organization" (1996, p. 43).

As Bastide (2016) states, "The mask is the substitute for the gods" (p. 97). In this same vein, Monilson interprets the body painting of the nê-gas not as Blackface, but as the production of a duality that detaches the subject from the historical time–space and propels them toward mythical, communal, and non-linear time, where contradictions and masks of iden-tity can be experienced and, in this sense, contested and subjected to the material test of mythical performance in the Nego Fugido ritual on the streets of Acupe (Pinto, 2017).

The district of Acupe is a small community of approximately 7,000 in-habitants, located on the shores of the Baía de Todos os Santos (All Saints Bay) in the Recôncavo region of Bahia. Surrounded by mangroves, it is part of the municipality of Santo Amaro da Purificação, as previously men-tioned. The community, with Black and Indigenous origins, is said to have emerged from the settlement of formerly enslaved people who left plan-tations such as Engenho Murundu, Engenho São Gonçalo, and Engenho Acupe. It is considered by many a quilombola territory, as freed and eman-cipated Black individuals established their communities there after 1888, in the interstices of the plantation-based slave order. The community is permeated by various narratives that reference the era of slavery, the time of bondage, and the "other world", where enchanted beings, giant snakes, eguns, and fantastic apparitions are part of everyday life.

One of the community's central narratives recalls the figure of the cru-el slave master, Francisco Gonçalves, who now survives as a ghost. Tia Neném tells that:

> the residents of Acupe always heard, at the crack of dawn, an anguished and mournful sound like the trot of a horse passing through the community's streets. On horseback rode an imposing old man dressed in a black tailcoat and top hat. It was the tormented soul of Senhor Francisco Gonçalves. (Monilson, 2014, p. 18)

As Monilson insists, the fantastical narratives about Francisco Gonçalves and his cruelty toward enslaved people are part of a social memory device that keeps alive the extraordinary presence of "terror", an instrument of control over the enslaved population and a creator of a "zone of death" (Taussig, 1993). This terror materialized in the blood of tortured enslaved individuals, which, from time to time, is said to still seep from a banana grove growing in the very spot where enslaved people were buried.

Violence, "terror", and death are central characters in the community's narrative. Another fascinating story compiled by Monilson centers on Iku, the personification of death in Nagô cosmology. Iku is said to explain why, each year in July, the Nego Fugido and other fantastic entities—such as the Mundus and the caretas—appear on the streets of Acupe. According to one of Monilson's interlocutors, Paulo Henrique da Cruz, tatá of the Casa de Angola Inzo Tumbalê Junçara in Acupe:

> [...] The slaves from Engenho Acupe, who belonged to the Hausa nation, performed many rituals at the master's orders, even offering people as sacrifices to gain wealth and money. Eventually, the enslaved lost control of the situation because they performed too many rituals, and with no more people to offer, they stopped the offerings. Iku, death, became furious and cast a curse in the month of August. Since then, every year in that month, many people in the community began to die. Everyone feared the arrival of the month of tragedies. The priests of the time, says the tatá, came together and made an offering to drive the curse away from Acupe. The mandus, good spirits, began to walk the streets in July, a month earlier, to banish evil spirits and attract good ones, freeing the community from the curse of August. (Pinto, 2014, p. 37–38)

Once again, Monilson turns to Artaud to interpret the myth and the ritual as forms of a "total exorcism of the soul"—in this case, the soul of the community, haunted by ghosts and curses. Far from being dead, these forces are very much alive, returning every year to remind the community that death and absolute violence are embedded in the subterranean heart of Acupe, a foundation buried in the map-heart of the territory.

As Juana Elbein dos Santos and others emphasize, in Nagô cosmology and its mythical repertoire, the material world—the ayê—and the transcendental world—the orun—exist as parallel realities that mutually influence and interpenetrate each other. In this sense, the meaning of death should be reconsidered within this paradigmatic model, which is not exhausted by a phenomenology of the visible, even though it makes use of it. This is evident in the concept of "olharidade" proposed by Monilson, which aims to highlight the sensory aspects—visual, tactile, olfactory—for the phenomenology of social life in Acupe: "The theater of apparitions is the theater of 'olharidade,' a presentification of the senses that unmasks the darkest realities of life in society" (Pinto, 2014, p. 157). Death, however, takes on various forms and possesses an almost invincible power. It can be ritually addressed, but never denied.

Júlio Braga, in his book on the devotion to Babá Egum, cites William R. Bascom:

> Every four days, she descended from the sky and invaded the Ojalfé market; She killed, she and her people, as many people as she could, with the help of large staffs. Most of the inhabitants of Ifé were soon massacred. The survivors then turned to the orixás, invoking Lafogido (then called Oni), Oduá, Orixalá, Ijugbe, Alass and all other existing orixás, so that they would come to save them. But the orixás could do nothing against death. (Bascom. In: Braga, 1992, p. 106)

The narrative in question is one of the myths that explains how death—Ikú—was "domesticated" by a man named Ameiygun, who tricked death and dressed it in colorful cloths and mirrors. In this way, death—impersonal, collective, and irrational devastation—came to be venerated in the individualized form of the divinized ancestor, the egum, who, in Itaparica, Bahia, dances on sacred nights, dressed in the powerful, multicolored opá. Death, a terrible masculine scourge that bows to no one—not even to Exu—can, if not defeated, be transcended once it is symbolized, individualized, and effectively incorporated as masculine ancestral guardians (Prandi, 2001).

The old specter of death also appears in New Orleans, disguised as the "bone gangs"—groups of Black men dressed as skeletons who roam the streets, waking families in the early hours on the days the Indians parade. According to Helen Regis, this practice connects to similar manifestations found in Haiti, Trinidad, and among the Yoruba (Breunlin, 2009), once again revealing the Afro-Caribbean—diasporic—connections of Black culture in New Orleans. Despite the claims made by ADOS, we know that the Black experience in the United States has never been merely national. The fatal trauma experienced by African American lineages has a global scope.

Image 13 — Bone Gang
Source: Author's image, 2020.

Between June and July 2018, a collective of artists was selected through a grant from the Bahia State Government to carry out an artistic residency in the district of Acupe, with the intensive collaboration of Monilson dos Santos. The project, "Billy the Kid — Expedition III: Nego Fugido, Acupe/ BA", produced experiences, workshops, and records, which were compiled in the sui generis publication "Terra Quente", released in 2020, and which also informs this work. In this publication, Monica Santana (2020) describes the experience of witnessing the performance in the streets as "an appeasement of the forces of death" (p. 4), which, fundamentally for the argument of this book, is not produced as representation: "Orality is in the body, which materializes resistance—not as metaphor, but as a thing in itself" (Idem, p. 7). This, incidentally, aligns with Monilson's own reflections, as he recalls that, under the nêga mask, the rejoicing for the freedom attained strikes him with the force of a current, true, and complete experience—real, not as mere dramatization (Pinto, 2014). It is an "experience without organs", of such a nature or order that it incorporates the invisible and the fantastic. The poet Alex Simões (2020), acting as a kind of ethnographer, brings us closer to this "presentified" experience: "observe what is around. And what is around is visible and has the invisible surrounding it" (p. 14).

The Nego Fugido has attracted the attention of other artists beyond those involved in the Billy the Kid Project, notably due to Monilson Santos Pinto's academic and activist work, which bridges Acupe and São Paulo. As Monilson himself points out, he has conducted workshops based on his experiences and research with Nego Fugido for artists and researchers, developing collaboration with his advisor Marianna Monteiro and establishing a dialogue between performance/theater studies, and anthropology. Monteiro describes how her journey as an artist, researcher, and activist led her from work with social movements and urban popular communities to the Nego Fugido. This trajectory marks a theoretical shift, where: "the notion of representation gives way to the notion of presentification" (Abreu & Monteiro, 2016, p. 3). Like Monilson in his master's thesis, Mariana reflects on the Nego Fugido to relate critical perspectives on theater and dramatization to performance theory in anthropology. She draws on the tradition established between Victor Turner and Richard Schechner to advance toward a "new distribution of the sensible" (Monteiro, 2013, p. 382). The popular form of dramatic performance, closely aligned with ritual, as already highlighted, could pose new challenges for theatrical theories like those of Brecht and Artaud. This stems from the place of experience, which holds distinct yet convergent meanings for these two authors concerning the relationship between theatrical representation—or its implosion—and life.

For Brecht, life is understood in its social significance, mediated through the proposal of a "didactic" theater that challenges the distinction between audience and actors. Mariana cites Walter Benjamin to explain that, in didactic plays, each "spectator is simultaneously an observer and a participant" (Idem, p. 376). For Artaud, life takes on a more transcendental significance, where the goal is "to expand the boundaries of what we call reality to infinity" (Artaud, 1987, p. 22). The radical assumptions of artists as dense as Brecht and Artaud are, therefore, already embedded in this popular manifestation, produced and sustained by and for "people who have never been to the theater". The artistic vanguard of São Paulo, Paris, or Berlin has much to learn from Nego Fugido and the community of Acupe, which has consistently materialized radical artistic objectives that, ultimately, point to the dissolution of boundaries between life and art, subject and object, and the dramatic scene and its socio-historical setting.

As Diana Taylor suggests, the forms of producing, storing, transmitting, and manipulating knowledge in non-literate or "traditional/primitive" communities are rooted in performance, particularly in dramatic performances that constitute what she calls the "repertoire"—a mode distinct from, and perhaps opposed to, the "archive", the typical modality of knowledge objectification in literate societies with state structures (Taylor, 2003, 2006). For Victor Turner, as well as other scholars, the reflective and inventive dimension of performance, especially ritual, is central (Turner, 1982; Drewal, 1992). Through ritual and its dramatic forms, society confronts its contradictions and deepest values, staging or ritually mobilizing them through the incorporation of collective agents—transcendent beings embodied as mythical characters: "In other words, drama induce and contain reflexive process and generate cultural frames in which reflexivity can find a legitimate place" (Turner, 1982, p. 92). The focus on experience, particularly sensory and embodied experience, dissolves rather than reifies the individual as the subject of culture or understanding. This is because experience is based on the dissolution of the self into the malleable body of culture, permeated by powerful symbols that act to dismantle the boundaries between Self and Other, as in trance, and between past and present, as in myth. This subverts linear temporality and its Western irreversibility, as demonstrated in Nego Fugido and candomblé traditions. Within this ancestral cosmology, death is the passage, the fundamental threshold, which depersonalizes the individual, returning them to the undifferentiated domain of the ancestors, positioning them within a cycle of multiple levels and connections (Conceição, 2017).

The ritual and the performance produce a "scene" to establish their effectiveness—a scene which, as we have seen, unfolds on the street, navigating multiple levels of temporality and existence. This process confuses the past—the era of bondage—and the present, defined by racialized capitalism, while dissolving the dichotomy between observer and performer. What is the meaning of the "scene"? Diana Taylor speaks of "scenarios" as the codified form through which a narrative "grabs the body", inserting it into an interpretive framework. This enables the repertoire—performative and irreproducible, despite its reversibility—to be transferred to the archive, as seen in the historical scenes of discovery or the abolition of slavery. Codified and immobilized, the bundle of events, subjects, acts, symbols, and meanings takes on a legible form, constrained by the same principle of separation discussed by Clastres and revisited in Chapter 4. However, the scene of performance cannot be captured without losing something essential or transforming into something else. The experiential and multivocal performance, defined by "olharidade", becomes a record, a video, a lecture, or a book when it transitions from the repertoire to the archive. This transposition is a power operation that denies the immanence of African diasporic cultural forms by attempting to represent them.

Within the horizon of events unfolding in the fractal theater of operations of global antiblackness—simultaneously structural and multitemporal—slavery forms the backdrop of the primordial scenes. When the existential, political, and aesthetic resources of ancestrality take form, they act, as Joanice Conceição (2017) explains while discussing Yoruban cosmologies in Brazil, as forces that "repair social and spiritual order" (p. 59). This is evident in the Indians of New Orleans, who both court and reject the forces of History, or in Nego Fugido, which exorcizes social death in the Recôncavo of Bahia. Faced with gratuitous violence and the inconsistency of white masters—sometimes paternalistic, sometimes cruel, as seen in slave narratives—and in the face of the dehumanizing superstructure of colonial slavery and its historical cynicism, and the brutal phobogenic violence of the fact of blackness, the social death of the enslaved emerges as the ultimate alienation under white supremacy. This death finds its setting in the scene of slave torment, where a material/libidinal order takes root, imprisoning us in this harsh bondage.

As Saidiya Hartman explains, the slave subjectivity, which informs the objective forms of Black subjectivity in modernity, is circumscribed by violence—sometimes deferred but often direct, brutal, and with no guilt

(Hartman, 1997). In this sense, the experience of brutality, often beyond any formal signification, can find within performance a context for the collective enunciation of pain. This pain is exemplified in Frederick Douglass's recollection of his confrontation with the reality of slavery through the martyrdom of his aunt Hester (Hartman, 1997, p. 3). It is also reflected in paintings of enslaved individuals being whipped at the Pelourinho, such as those by Rugendas or Debret (Wood, 2014). The primordial scene of torment becomes the setting for the establishment of a codified order to regulate both the body and racialized experience. However, the insurgency within the scene produces an objection.

Fred Moten, revisiting the primordial scene of torment as narrated by Douglass, discusses the resistance of the "object"—slaves traded as commodities or movable property. Nevertheless, they can resist or object precisely because they have been objectified or captured within the material processes of enslavement. This is well-attested in discussions of enslaved subjectivity in Brazilian historiography. The enslaved could and did produce meaning, construct family relationships, and build a tradition that stood as an objection to their own objectification. However, the formation of their subjectivity, and of their "personhood", balances within violent tensions that disfigure the relationship between subjectivity—the possession of oneself as a subject—and personhood as a formal, juridical-state category. This tension allows us to consider a "force of resistance or objection that is always already in excess of the limits of subjection/subjectivity" (Moten, 2003, p. 242). The primordial scene of slavery, codified in established scenarios, provides the framework for the construction of a subjectivity in objection—a form of resistance often withdrawn from the normal world of bourgeois rational experience. In this context, performance becomes the most appropriate or possible means of reclaiming or repossession of oneself, the body, and the scene.

> This is what objection is, what performance is—an internal complication of the object that is, at the same time, her withdrawal into the external world. Such withdrawal makes possible communication between seemingly unbridgeable spaces, times, and persons. (Moten, 2003, p. 253)

A collective performance, like a repertoire, informs the scene of rebellion in the pagode of Bahia, which shows contempt for the bourgeois moral conventions that have historically—and in the present—constructed the Black body as hypersexualized, amoral, base, and dirty, and therefore so desirable. A scenario like the Dutch tropics, reimagined in Eckhout's "ethnological" series, which takes representation itself as an epistemological modus operandi, producing racialized alienation. An artistic trajectory like that of Musa Matiuzzi, which pierces through Black flesh to shatter the boundaries of representation and pain. All this, and much more, comprises the procession of tensions and resources through which social death is reincarnated into multiple transformations. These transformations form the same locus, infused with all the tension through which subjects free themselves from the captivity of representational codes—a form of denying meaning to what cannot be represented. It is an impossible subject, one that can only dream of eradicating its own and familiar bondage in the destruction of the world.

AFTERWORD:
TURNS AROUND THE WORD

Maria Dolores Sosin Rodriguez

"[...] blackness as matter signals ∞, another world: namely, that which exists without time and out of space, in the plenum."
— **Denise Ferreira da Silva (2019)**

This text will not stem from a lack. It will not summarize. It will not circumscribe the work within a defined and defining spectrum of, or by, a logic. It will not analyze the author's intent, nor will it dwell on defining, describing, or contesting him—except, perhaps, indefinitely, in a movement of nebulae of temporary meanings. Today seems like the perfect day to finally conclude it. Even though I had to put aside everything else I was doing to re-read Derrida and his idea of the supplement. In the glossary organized by Silviano Santiago, they say that a supplement is an addition—a signifier that adds itself to replace and compensate for a lack on the side of the signified, providing the excess that is needed. This sounds, to me, as if I have never truly understood the logic of Derridean supplementarity. What reassures me is what follows when they refer to the supplement as tied to the absence of center—our old acquaintance, then, is Derridean decentering. The idea of a postscript, perhaps, strikes me as a supplement. Even so, I refuse to imagine a center. To sniff out a center, to admit the possibility of its existence. I do not know if I am lying to myself. Perhaps what is needed is an eroticism of theory (Sontag, Pinho)—a refusal to circumscribe our desire. To leave desire pulsing, something akin to hunger and less close to a grammar that holds meaning. The ultimate meaning.

I will not say what the author meant to say, especially because the author is always hidden beneath some hybrid desire, between their own twilight and an apparently loud expectation.

At this very moment, it is 11:13 p.m. I have seventeen tabs open in my browser, and this is my sixth Word document. I have made abstract attempts and contortions that would demonstrate to the reader how I am the most qualified person to carry out this task. Yet I do not feel sufficiently certain of this myself. And saying so is corny. The thought that this too may seem frivolous, small, and failed comes me at this moment. I read about what a postscript [postface] is despite having read many of them at various points in my life. Many, often entirely unnecessary. This could be the very matter of my hesitation. A postscript can be whatever we want it to be. And this extensive negativity around it may simply be a curve in the drawing of my desire. After all, what do I want here? I considered adopting the form of a dictionary, a glossary, or keywords. What would be the insignia of this book? All are quite evident. I also refuse to name what I think should have been here but isn't. There is a truly admirable methodological clarity in this book by Osmundo Pinho, and it is fascinating to go through these pages with content so explicitly placed. In other circumstances, while reflecting on it, I wanted to speak about other characteristics of its methodological form. Rigor is one of them. I think about the urgent need to redefine what we take as scientific rigor. What theoretical-methodological mechanisms define or are associated with rigor?

What seems to most surprise people is the fact that Black experience appears and is claimed as important within academic productions. More than simply using the first person, speaking about our places of creation—particularly in terms of racial, gender, and sexual belonging—sounds, in many circumstances, like an excessively self-centered or inward-looking act. These issues appear as questions in "Bondage": "[...] These questions, repeated in various forms and registers here, seek to answer the question of who I am by interrogating where I come from" (Pinho, 2021, p. 128).

Reflecting a little on the meaning and place of experience, I think of *"Our Black Feminisms Revisited"*, where Luiza Bairros (1995) narrates:

> Once, in Salvador, Bahia, I saw a program about cooking on television. It was a morning program aimed at a female audience, where the host demonstrated how to prepare a dish, I no longer remember which one. At that moment, what captured my attention lay behind the immediately visible image on the TV screen. The setting was a kitchen, and the central figure was a hostess who did not stop giving instructions and advice. In contrast, a young Black

woman participated in the scene in complete silence. (p. 458)

She reflects on the concepts of (a) woman, (b) experience, and (c) personal politics. By bringing her own lived experience into her writing, she incorporates it as a preview of what she will discuss. The perception she offers regarding the silencing of Black women in the scene she observes carries a particular perspective—that of someone who theorizes but also lives the experience of silencing. The ability to distinguish the places and meanings assigned to each of the two women in the scene challenges the idea that experience alone can connect all women indiscriminately. Luiza Bairros exposes the inconsistency of such generalizations, questioning the univocal notion that all women share the same experiences and that women's oppression can be defined independently of other markers, such as race, class, territory, and sexuality, for instance. Equally significant is how Lélia Gonzalez begins "Racismo e Sexismo na Cultura Brasileira" with an epigraph. Gonzalez constructs a small narrative where the voice of a Black woman interrupts a charade hidden beneath an anti-Black imposed order. The breaking of silence is central to the story: Black people are invited to the launch of a book where whites will speak about Blacks, and: "[...] They were so busy, teaching all kinds of things to the Black folks in the audience, that they didn't even realize that if they squeezed in a bit, there was enough space for everyone to sit at the table together" (Gonzalez, 1980, p. 223).

The search for, or expression of, this voice seems to displease. We already know that constructing an identity no longer implies suspecting a centrality or unity, let alone an unaltered and singular form. To think about the Black experience is not to reduce it to a fixed space but to see it as one of multiplication and possibilities—difficult to synthesize, urgently alive, and inherently ambivalent, resisting closed meanings. We are interested in reflecting on dissents, distances, and approximations. Osmundo Pinho also shares this interest, revisiting his material to reassess it, sometimes drawing closer, sometimes further away, sometimes in disagreement, as he seeks what he calls theoretical profitability. This is not a profession of faith. In "Bondage", he shows extreme rigor by refusing to participate in the torrent of blindness that occupies debates both within and outside the academic world. Such debates often focus on electing new totems, crafting myths, pursuing easy resolutions, and projecting an overwhelming will to totalize all subjects, especially concerning Black knowledge production.

In the citations presented here, the recurrence of experience as a method becomes evident. Its importance extends beyond mere exemplification, as it brings forth the voices still relegated to silence and destabilizes the rigid core of scientific discourse. In "Feminismo Negro Diaspórico", Sônia Beatriz dos Santos conceptualizes the defining feature of Black feminisms in Afro-Latin America, the Afro-Caribbean, Afro-America, Black British feminism, and African feminism: a political and intellectual practice forged through the articulation of race, gender, class, and sexuality, produced and developed by Afro-descendant women—what she calls "the multiple dimensions of Black women's experiences with oppression" (Santos, 2007, p. 11). This intellectual production involves both an aesthetic-ethical construction and an inseparable connection between theory and practice. As the author explains: "In general, for Black women, thought and action are interconnected [...]." Thus, historically for Black feminists, "thought and action, or theory and practice, constitute part of the same process" (Santos, 2007, p. 16). She concludes that one of the greatest challenges for Black women intellectuals across the African diaspora is the denial of experience as a tool for knowledge production.

In the first month I began attending an Umbanda terreiro, a new format for consultations was introduced. These sessions occurred on specific days, and I was among the first to participate. The conversations took place with a preto velho who, from the first encounter, welcomed me and called me his goddaughter. Many reasons later distanced me from this religion. One was the realization that many of the entities and spirits considered more evolved by the leaders of the house were portrayed as white. The orishas, in turn, were understood as energies, without race, origin, or any connection to a specific people or place. Among these many incongruities, entities such as pretos velhos, pretas velhas, caboclos, and caboclas[54] were perceived collectively but viewed as less enlightened. They were understood as working to express their humility and adaptability amidst adversity—a way to connect with those who sought the terreiro while accelerating their own journey toward "spiritual enlightenment".

I often heard that the "preto velho is the psychologist of the poor". The dissents, the discrepancies in meaning between me and this experience, seem even more absurd to narrate now. And saying so feels corny. Many of the elements that surface almost as punchlines here, especially when placed alongside Osmundo Pinho's book, are directly relevant to his work. I could begin by commenting on the appearance of these meanings—apparently irreconcilable—and the dances of thought that brought me back to these memories from almost ten years ago. I remember a song that always caught

---

[54] T.N.: *Preto velho* or *preta velha* are spiritual figures of older Black enslaved men and women worshiped in Umbanda. *Caboclos* or *caboclas* are the spirits of Indigenous ancestors.

my attention when I was still part of the Umbanda faith and often felt, as I still do today, a bit distant, disconnected, and displaced in the world: "Vovô doesn't want coconut shells in the terreiro. Vovó doesn't want coconut shells in the terreiro, just so we don't remember the times of bondage, just so we don't remember the times of bondage...."[55] What brought this song to mind was not the coincidence between the bondage mentioned in the song and the title of Pinho's book, "Bondage", but its epigraph, also a song, signed by Seu Marujo. In it, bondage is once again invoked as a memory, as a kind of organizer of his experience.

There is here a bodily dimension that, strangely, fails to convince, even as it proves convenient for explaining certain conflicting realities and experiences in which the body appears camouflaged as something unimportant or secondary. This contradiction reflects precisely the impossibility discussed by the author that there is no Black experience outside the body. "The reduction of the Black individual, their body and personhood, to something non-human or sub-human, serves to confirm white Humanity" (Pinho, 2021, p. 112). I would say that no experience exists apart from this dimension because, as we know, believing otherwise is to assume the existence of the divine self, as explored by Grosfoguel:

Although Descartes never defines who this "I" is, it is clear that in his philosophy this "I" replaces God as the new foundation of knowledge and its attributes constitute a secularization of the attributes of the Christian God. For Descartes, the "I" can produce a knowledge that is truth beyond time and space, universal in the sense that it is unconditioned by any particularity—"objective" being understood as equal to "neutrality" and equivalent to a God-Eye view. (Grosfoguel, 2016, p. 28)

Thinking about this reminds me of a scene from the theatrical production "Pele Negra, Máscaras Brancas" [Black Skin, White Masks] by the School of Theater at the Federal University of Bahia, directed by Onisajé, co-directed by Licko Turle, and written by Aldri Anunciação. In the play, explicitly inspired by Fanon, there is a moment when the cast, composed entirely of Black performers, literally wear white masks. It is an aesthetically resolved moment. At that point, everyone on stage is dressed in white and sings in a unison that struck me as hypnotic and, at times, dissonant: "I, I, I, I, I, I, I, I". This categorical "I" dialogues with anti-Blackness, for as the author of "Bondage" states, alongside Fanon and Lewis Gordon, it speaks to "reification and the consequent unrepresentability of Blackness

---

[55] T.N.: The song in Portuguese: "Vovô não quer casca de coco no terreiro. Vovó não quer casca de coco no terreiro, só para que não nos lembremos dos tempos do cativeiro, só para que não nos lembremos dos tempos do cativeiro...."

and the Black subject" (Pinho, 2016). It is here that we can consider the body as a locality—as space, perhaps, as territory, as writing, as an existence that imposes itself.

This displacement, this impossibility of experience, is expressed as follows: "being outside the law—in the border or contact zones, positions us simultaneously within and outside the settler-created world of meaning and power. In this sense, we can only signify in a 'fugitive' way" (Pinho, 2021, p. 90). The Black body as prison of experience, however, finds disconformities, because there is a dimension often easily forgotten by the timid voices of Afro-pessimism: "But I am a Black Brazilian man, specifically from Bahia, and in my sociocultural experience, as for millions of other Afro-Brazilians and even Afro-Latin Americans and/or Caribbeans, the social horizon and the categories of intersubjective experience are full of references to Africa and elements of Africanity. There is no void" (Pinho, 2021).

The songs of pretos velhos and pretas velhas come to me as an epistemology that guides this incision of mine—or perhaps a suture, as Rosana Paulino names it. For these entities are, simultaneously, transcendent and immanent, spiritual yet tethered to a body and experience, by their own will, however. They could, theoretically, choose any reincarnate form but instead choose to carry the marks of bondage aboard slave ships. These marks ignite their significance, though it too remains captive to moralizing ontological traces rooted in Jewish-Christian traditions. For example, it seems inconceivable that an old Black man could be educated, refined, or even snobbish; to be a preto velho would necessarily involve a diminishing of meanings and possibilities, recreating bondage by mandating the figure of someone humble, illiterate, and suffering.

This is a conflicting duality that, in my view, does not produce the theoretical profitability sought by Osmundo Pinho, who sees Afro-pessimism and ancestrality as two forms or approaches that are not necessarily mutually exclusive or vengeful. The way I have always perceived Osmundo Pinho's work—before reading this book—has to do with something I notice in his style. I mean appetite. Like the fire of hunger. I think rigor can now be discussed in a less impossible way. And this may seem unwelcome at this moment. When I say rigor, I also mean hunger. Rigor means he allows himself to linger in seeing—less restrained than famished. Rigor means he refuses to abandon his hunger, rather than dance to silent songs. It is also necessary to know oneself to know if there is hunger, for many lose themselves clinging to the nearest life raft, just because someone says: "Come with me; we will escape the drowning, the flood." Promises.

In a class with Professor Florentina Souza, we read Lélia Gonzalez's "Racismo e Sexismo na Cultura Brasileira" (2020), and everything that seems obvious to me now was once new. I don't know if it was the magnitude of what she said. Perhaps less that and more the way she said it. Sometime later, what was said and how it was said no longer seemed like distinct things. Today, they seem to me the same. In truth, I don't remember who separated them for me. But I made a point of reuniting them when I realized the dimension of the false division they produced. The critique of representation is a critique of the desire to attribute truth—a truth that exists only in the fiction of depth, as opposed to the surface. It is the critique of the reduction of the body to what they say is the body's reduction. This critique is present throughout this book by Osmundo Pinho, but also in Denise Ferreira da Silva, when she writes "creative work > critique"; in Susan Sontag (1987), with her critique of the fiction of depth; and in Paul Valéry, who said: "The deepest is the skin." It is the body.

> If they ask you where everything comes from,
> answer:
> from the body,
> the body,
> the body.

The other day, I wrote about "Bondage" in one of my notebooks: "bondage in the songs of pretos velhos; historicize Osmundo's work by bringing in Ilê Aiyê and its efforts toward reaffirmation of African heritage, as well as other traces of his research and writings; the marujo's epigraph and the figure of the preto velho as those who inhabit not just two mythical worlds but conceptual ones (they exist within ancestrality but are bound to a temporal-historical paradigm—'not as dualities, but as metamorphosis'—Pinho, 2021). Would it be interesting to think from a narrative terreiro experience of my own?"

This writing, like all others, is done with the body. If we are able to understand that dance is discourse, just as capoeira and the samba circle are enunciations of knowledge—knowledge that sometimes resides in mystery, though no less legible for it—then the text, this craft upon which so many of us have drawn our lives, is also a making of the body.

What I want here, then, is to think about the vehement rejection of the structural division still imposed through the demand, the illusory premise, of a distinction between body and mind, body and spirit, or even mind and spirit. I want here to reincarnate the word, not just because I wish it, but because this is how things are, and this is how we perceive them: we, Black communities.

Perhaps what brings something new at this moment—though novelty itself is not a characteristic I value as essential for producing a work—is, so to speak, reclaiming the body as a complex instrument for writing and for the intellectual production that emerges through the word. Not just the word, of course. But it seems we have begun to reach a greater understanding of the body's intelligence, yet we remain less certain when we say that a poem, just like Osmundo Pinho's book and this very text, is made with the body, by the body. The body also appears in the artistic works discussed by Pinho. These works are not there to be deciphered, with a desire for exposure or the revelation of a secret.

This postface, engaging with the book "Bondage", is not an offering of a conclusion or a set of instructions, much less a prescription. Instead, it is an attempt to reflect on what I felt-thought while reading the book, striving to go a little further. I play with time, with the very idea of this textual genre—the postscript—drawing on what I know, what I know little about, and what I know nothing about, but am learning. Or perhaps unlearning. Even though the connections may have seemed difficult or even winding, this is what I have to offer at this moment. This is merely a text about a book that, after reaching this point, you—like me, just a reader of this work—understand that "Bondage" transforms the theoretical and critical landscapes, not only of the social sciences and anthropology but also, through its ties to the tradition of Black Radical Thought, to "African-American studies", and even to what Fred Moten proposes as "Black Studies". It points to streets, overpasses, and avenues (not just exits, as Itamar Assumpção[56] said, citing a poem by Paulo Leminski) for an undisciplined gaze at the themes it addresses.

---

[56]   See: https://www.brasildefato.com.br/2021/09/13/10-musicas-de-itamar-assump-cao-para-revelar-o-brasil/ Last accessed August 5th, 2025 at 3:29 pm.

REFERENCES

ABREU, Carolina; MONTEIRO, Marianna. Nego Fugido e trabalhadores da cultura: lições de agitprop para a antropologia. Paper presented at T087 — *"Artivismo, ação direta e ciber-protesto. Poéticas e performances políticas imaginando futuros"* during the *VI Congresso da Associação Portuguesa de Antropologia*, Coimbra, June 2–4, 2016. Available at: https://www.researchgate.net/publication/313634373_Nego_Fugido_e_Trabalhadores_da_Cultura_licoes_de_agitprop_para_a_antropologia. Accessed: Jan. 25, 2021.

ADJEI-KONTOH, Hubert. The tortured logic of #ADOS. *The Outline.* https://theoutline.com/post/8286/american-descendants-of-slavery-movement. 2019. Accessed: August 5, 2025.

AGAMBEN, Giorgio. O que é um dispositivo? *Outra travessia*, n. 5, Ilha de Santa Catarina, 2005, p. 9–16.

AIDOO, Lamonte. *Slavery unseen: Sex, power and violence in Brazilian history.* Durham; London: Duke University Press, 2018.

ALBUQUERQUE, Wlamyra. *O jogo da dissimulação: Abolição negra e cidadania negra no Brasil.* São Paulo: Companhia das Letras, 2009.

ALEIXO, Ricardo. In: _____; SIMÕES, Alex. *Trans Formas São.* Salvador: Organismo, 2018.

ALVES, Antônio Castro. *Navio Negreiro.* Livra Progresso Editora. Salvador. 1959.

ALVES, Castro. *Os Escravos.* Edições GRD. São Paulo. 1983.

ALVES, Jaime Amparo. From Necropolis to Blackpolis: Necropolitical Governance and Black Spatial Praxis in São Paulo, Brazil. *Antipode.* Vol. 46 No. 2 2013. pp. 323–339

AMAR, Paul. *The security archipelago: Human-security states, sexuality politics and the end of neoliberalism.* Durham: Duke University Press, 2013.

AMERICAN DESCENDANTS OF SLAVERY. Available at: https://ados101.com/. Accessed: Jan. 25, 2021.

ANDREWS, George Reid. Black political protest in São Paulo, 1888–1988. *Journal of Latin American Studies*, v. 24, part 1, Feb. 1992, p. 147–171.

ANUÁRIO BRASILEIRO DE SEGURANÇA PÚBLICA. *Fórum Brasileiro de Segurança Pública*, n. 7, São Paulo, 2013.

ARRAES, Jarid. Posfácio. In. ____ . JACOBS, Harriet Ann. *Incidentes na Vida de Uma Menina Escrava*. São Paulo. Todavia. 2019. Pp. 275-2282.

ARRUDA, Maria Arminda do Nascimento. Dilemas do Brasil Moderno: A Questão Racial na Obra de Florestan Fernandes. In . ____ . *Raça, Ciência e Sociedade*. MAIO. Marcos Chor & SANTOS, Ricardo V. Rio de Janeiro. Editora Fiocruz / Centro Cultural Banco do Brasil.1996, p. 195-206.

ARTAUD, Antonin. *The theater and its double*. São Paulo: Max Limonad, 1987.

AUGRAS, Monique. *The double and the metamorphosis: The mythical identity in Nagô communities*. Petrópolis: Editora Vozes, 2008.

AZZAN, Celso. *Anthropology and interpretation: Explanation and understanding in the anthropologies of Lévi-Strauss and Geertz*. Campinas: Editora da UNICAMP, 1993. BACELAR, Jeferson. *Ethnicity: Being black in Salvador*. Salvador: PENBA, Ianamá, 1989.

BACELAR, Jeferson. *Etnicidade. Ser Negro em Salvador*. Salvador. PENBA. Ianamá. 1989.

BAHIA MEIO DIA. Dezessete policiais são indiciados por sequestro, homicídio e ocultação do cadáver de Davi Fiúza, que sumiu em 2014. http://g1.globo.com/ba/bahia/noticia/2018/08/07/dezessete-policiais-sao-indiciados-por-sequestro-homicidio-e-ocultacao-do-cadaver-de-davi-fiuz%E2%80%A6/. Accessed: Sept. 29, 2001.

BAIRROS, Luiza. Orfeu e poder: Uma perspectiva Afro-Americana sobre a política racial no Brasil. *Afro-Ásia*, n. 17, 1996, p. 173–186.

BAKARE-YUSUF, Bibi. Yorubas don't do gender: A critical review of Oyeronke Oyewumi's *The invention of women: Making an African sense of western gender discourses*. *African Identities*, n. 1, v. 1, 2003.

BALDWIN, James. Relatório de um território ocupado. Translation for educational use: Osmundo Pinho, 2016. Available at: https://www.scribd.com/document/331417682/Relatorio-de-um-Territorio-Ocupado.

Accessed: Jan. 25, 2021.

_____. *Terra estranha*. São Paulo: Companhia das Letras, 2018.

BANDEIRA, Júlio; LAGO, Pedro Correa. *Debret e o Brasil: Obra completa (1816–1831)*. 3rd ed. Rio de Janeiro: Capivara, 2009.

BAQUAQUA, Mahommah Gardo. *Biografia de Mahommah Gardo Baquaqua*. São Paulo: Editora Uirapuru, 2017.

BARATA, Danillo. *Narrativas em fluxo*. Cruz das Almas: Editora UFRB, 2016.

BARNET, Miguel. *Memórias de um Cimarron*. Testimony. São Paulo: Editora Marco Zero, 1986.

BASTIDE, Roger. *O candomblé da Bahia*. São Paulo: Companhia das Letras, 2001.

_____. *O sonho, o transe e a loucura*. São Paulo: Três Estrelas, 2016.

BATAILLE, George. *A parte maldita*. Rio de Janeiro: Imago Editorial, 1975.

BECKER, Cynthia. New Orleans Mardi Gras Indians: Mediating racial politics from backstreets to main street. *African Arts*, v. 46, n. 2, p. 36–49, summer 2013.

BELCHIOR, Douglas. Shopping Vitória: corpos negros no lugar errado. *Carta Capital*, Dec. 2, 2013. Available at: http://negrobelchior.cartacapital.com.br/2013/12/02/shopping-vitoria-corpos-negros-no-lugar-errado/. Accessed: Dec. 2, 2013.

BELLUZZO, Ana Maria de Moraes. *O Brasil dos viajantes*. São Paulo: Objetiva/Metalivros, 1994.

BENJAMIN, Walter. Sobre o conceito de história. In: _____. *Obras escolhidas: Magia e técnica, arte e política*. São Paulo: Editora Brasiliense, 1996, p. 222–234.

BHABHA, Homi. *O local da cultura*. Belo Horizonte: Editora UFMG, 1998.

_____. "A Questão do "Outro": diferença, discriminação e o discurso do colonialismo", in H. B. de Hollanda (org.), Pós- modernismo e Política. Rio de Janeiro, Rocco. 1992.

BLAISDELL, Bob. Introduction. In: GARVEY, Marcus. *Selected writings and speeches of Marcus Garvey*. Edited by BLAISDELL, Bob. New York: Dover Publications, 2004, p. 3–12.

BOURDIEU, Pierre. A casa kabyle ou o mundo às avessas. *Cadernos de Campo*, São Paulo, v. 8, n. 8, p. 147–159, Mar. 1999. Available at: http://www.revistas.usp.br/cadernosdecampo/article/view/52774/56619. Accessed: Jul. 2, 2018.

_____. Introdução a uma sociologia reflexiva. In: _____. *O poder simbólico*. Lisbon: DIFEL, 1989, p. 17–58.

BRAGA, Julio. *Ancestralidade afro-brasileira: o culto de Babá Egum*. Salvador: EDUFBA/Ianamá, 1992.

BREUNLIN, Rachel. *The house of dance & feathers*. New Orleans: Neighborhood Story Project, 2009.

BRIENEN, Rebecca Parker. Albert Eckhout: A Dutch artist in Brazil — Historians of Netherlandish Art Reviews. Nov. 2004. Available at: https://hnanews.org/hnar/reviews/albert-eckhout-dutch-artist-brazil/. Accessed: Apr. 6, 2019.

_____. *Visions of savage paradise: Albert Eckhout, court painter in colonial Dutch Brazil*. Amsterdam University Press, 2006.

BRUMANA, Fernando G. *Antropologia dos sentidos: Introdução às ideias de Marcel Mauss*. São Paulo: Brasiliense, 1983.

BUCK-MORSS, Susan. *Hegel e o Haiti*. São Paulo: N-1 Edições, 2017.

BUTLER, Judith. Tortura e a ética da fotografia: Pensando com Sontag. In: _____. *Quadros de guerra: Quando a vida é passível de luto?* Rio de Janeiro: Civilização Brasileira, 2015.

_____. O parentesco é sempre tido como heterossexual? *Cadernos Pagu*, n. 21, 2003a, p. 219–260.

_____. *Problemas de gênero: feminismo e subversão da identidade*. Rio de Janeiro: Civilização Brasileira, 2003b.

BUTLER, Kim D. Defining Diaspora, redefining a discourse. *Diaspora*, v. 10, n. 2, 2001, p. 189–219.

BUTLER, Octavia E. *Kindred: Laços de sangue*. São Paulo: Editora Morro Branco, 2019.

BUVELOT, Quentin. *Albert Eckhout: A Dutch artist in Brazil*. Royal Cabinet of Paintings Mauritshuis, The Hague: Waanders Publishers, Zwolle, 2004.

CACHOEIRADOC. Mostras especiais. Available at: http://cachoeiradoc.com.br/2017/mostras-especiais/. Accessed: Jan. 25, 2021.

CALDEIRA, Teresa P. R. 'I came to sabotage your reasoning!': Violence and resignifications of justice in Brazil. In: COMAROFF, Jean; COMAROFF, John (Eds.). *Law and disorder in the postcolony*. Chicago, IL: The University of Chicago Press, 2006, p. 102–149.

_____. *City of walls: Crime, segregation and citizenship in São Paulo*. Berkeley, CA: University of California Press, 2000.

CAMPELLO, André Barreto. *Manual jurídico da escravidão: Império do Brasil*. Jundiaí: Paco Editorial, 2018.

CAPRIGLIONE, Laura. Mesmo sem crimes, 'rolezinho' causou pânico e levou polícia a shopping de Guarulhos. *Folha de São Paulo*, Dec. 16, 2013. Available at: www1.folha.uol.com.br/cotidiano/2013/12/1386132-mesmo-sem-crimes-rolezinho-causou-panico-e-levou-policia-a-shopping-de-guarulhos.shtml. Accessed: Jan. 25, 2021.

CARDOSO, Hamilton. Zumbi: Memórias de São Paulo. In: _____. *Re(Vivendo) Palmares*. Araraquara: FECONEZU, 2000, p. 4–9.

_____. E agora? *Versus*, n. 23, Jul.–Aug. 1978.

_____. O resgate de Zumbi. *Lua Nova: Cultura e política*, v. 2, n. 4, Jan.–Mar. 1986, p. 63–67.

_____. Um pouco da história da esquerda. *Lua Nova: Cultura e política*, v. 1, n. 3, Oct.–Dec. 1984, p. 42–49.

CARDOSO, Marcos. *O movimento negro em Belo Horizonte: 1978–1998*. Belo Horizonte: Maza Edições, 2002.

CARNEIRO, Sueli. Enegrecer o feminismo: A situação da mulher negra na América Latina a partir de uma perspectiva de gênero. *Portal Geledés*, Mar. 6, 2011. Available at: https://www.geledes.org.br/enegrecer-o-feminismo-situacao-da-mulher-negra-na-america-latina-partir-de-uma-perspectiva-de-genero/. Accessed: Jan. 26, 2021.

CARVALHO, Victa. Dispositivo e experiência: Relações entre tempo e movimento na arte contemporânea. *Revista Poiesis*, n. 12, Nov. 2018, p. 39–50.

CASTRO, Alex. Apresentação. In: _____; MANZANO, Juan Francisco. *A autobiografia do poeta-escravo*. São Paulo: Hedra, 2015, p. 15–26.

CBN. Rolezinho do shopping traz medo e pânico à sociedade. *CBN Foz do Iguaçu Online*, Dec. 14, 2013. Available at: www.cbnfoz.com.br/editorial/brasil/15122013-60789rolezinho-do-shopping-traz-medo-e-panico-a-sociedade. Accessed: Dec. 14, 2013.

CÉSAIRE, Aimé. Caderno de um regresso ao país natal. *Buala*. Available at: https://www.buala.org/pt/mukanda/caderno-de-um-regresso-ao-pais-natal. Accessed: Jan. 25, 2021.
_____. *Discourse on colonialism*. New York: Monthly Review Press, 2000.

CHAGAS, Ledson. Corpo, dança e letras: Um estudo sobre a cena musical do pagode baiano e suas mediações. Master's Thesis. Universidade Federal da Bahia, Programa Multidisciplinar de Pós-Graduação em Cultura e Sociedade. Salvador, 2015.

CLASTRES, Pierre. *A sociedade contra o Estado*. Rio de Janeiro: Francisco Alves, 1990.

CLEVELAND, Kimberly L. *Black art in Brazil: Expressions of identity*. Gainesville: University Press of Florida, 2013.

CLIFFORD, James. Sobre a autoridade etnográfica. In: _____. *A experiência etnográfica: Antropologia e literatura no século XX*. Rio de Janeiro: Editora UFRJ, 2008, p. 17–58.

COHEN, Cathy. Deviance as resistance: A new research agenda for the study of black politics. *Du Bois Review*, v. 1, n. 1, 2004, p. 27–45.
_____. *The boundaries of blackness: AIDS and the breakdown of black politics*. Chicago: The University of Chicago Press, 1999.

CONCEIÇÃO, Joanice. *Irmandade da Boa Morte e culto de Babá Egum: Masculinidades, feminilidades e performances negras*. Jundiaí: Paco Editorial, 2017.

CORRÊA, Mariza. Sobre a invenção da mulata. *Cadernos Pagu*, v. 6–7, 1996, p. 35–50.

CUNHA, Olivia. " Bonde do Mal: Notas sobre Território, Cor, Violência e Juventude numa Favela do Subúrbio Carioca." In *Raça como retórica: a construção da diferença*, edited by Yvone Maggie, Claudia Rezende and Claudia Barcellos, 83–154. Rio de Janeiro: Civilização Brasileira, 2001.

CORREIO DA BAHIA. Tiroteio durante show de Igor Kannário deixa um morto e dez feridos em São Francisco do Conde. *Salvador INFORMAR CIDADE*. Available at: http://www.correio24horas.com.br/detalhe/noticia/tiroteio-durante-show-de-igor-kannario-deixa-uma-pessoa-morta-em-São-francisco-do-conde/?cHash=fcea643048c6f-84dc24cafc29e7ae613. Accessed: June 24, 2014.

COSME, Carmen L. La narrativa en la autobiografía de un esclavo de Juan Francisco Manzano. *Masters Theses 1911*. Available at: https://scholarworks.umass.edu/theses/198. Accessed: Jan. 25, 2021.

COSTA, Richard Santiago. Um pintor holandês no novo mundo: os tipos brasileiros de Albert Eckhout e a glorificação de Maurício de Nassau. *Revista Valise*, Porto Alegre, v. 1, n. 2, Dec. 2011.

COTTER, Holland. Brazil enthralls with an art show of Afro-Atlantic history. *The New York Times*. Oct. 12, 2018. Available at: https://www.nytimes.com/2018/10/12/arts/design/afro-atlantic-histories-sao-paulo-museum-of-art-tomie-ohtake-institute.html. Accessed: Jan. 25, 2021.

CUNHA, Olivia. Bonde do mal: notas sobre território, cor, violência e juventude numa favela do subúrbio carioca. In: MAGGIE, Yvone; REZENDE, Claudia; BARCELLOS, Claudia (Eds.). *Raça como retórica: A construção da diferença*. Rio de Janeiro: Civilização Brasileira, 2001, p. 83–154.

CUNHA, Olivia Maria Gomes da. Black movements and the "Politics of Identity" in Brazil. In: _____; ALVAREZ, S.; DAGNINO, E.; ESCOBAR, A. (Eds.). *Culture of politics, politics of culture: Re-envisioning Latin American social movements*. Westview Press, 1998, p. 220–251.

CUNNINGHAM, George P. Race, gender and the captive body. In: _____; BLOUNT, Marcellus; CUNNINGHAM, George P. (Eds.). *Representing black men*. New York; London: Routledge, 1996, p. 131–156.

DAMATTA, Roberto. O que Faz o Brasil, Brasil? , Rio de Janeiro, 1994.

_____. Carnavais, Malandros e Heróis. Para uma sociologia do dilema brasileiro. Rio de Janeiro. Zahar Editores. 3ª Edição. 1981.

DARKWAH, Kofi. Antecedents of Asante culture. *Transactions of the Historical Society of Ghana New Series*, n. 3, 1999, p. 57–79.

DAS, Veena. The signature of the State: The paradox of illegibility. In: _____; POOLE, Deborah. *Anthropology in the margins of the State*. Santa Fe: School of American Research, 2004, p. 225–252.

DEBORD, Guy. *A sociedade do espetáculo: Comentários sobre a sociedade do espetáculo*. Rio de Janeiro: Contraponto, 1998.

DEBRET, Jean-Baptiste. *Viagem pitoresca e histórica ao Brasil*. Tomo I, v. I–II; Tomo II, v. III. São Paulo: Biblioteca Histórica Brasileira; EDUSP; Editora Itatiaia Ltda., 1989.

DECLARAÇÃO UNIVERSAL DOS DIREITOS HUMANOS. Available at: https://www.ohchr.org/EN/UDHR/Documents/UDHR_Translations/por.pdf. Accessed: Jan. 25, 2021.

DELEUZE, Gilles; GUATTARI, Félix. *Mil platôs: Capitalismo e esquizofrenia.* v. 1. São Paulo: Editora 34, 1996.

_____; _____. *Nomadology: The war machine.* New York: Semiotext(e), 1986.

DERRIDA, Jacques. *A escritura e a diferença.* São Paulo: Perspectiva, 1995.

DIAWARA, Manthia. *In search of África.* Cambridge; London, 1998.

_____. The absent one: The avant-garde and the black imaginary in looking for Langston. In: _____; BLOUNT, Marcellus; CUNNINGHAM, George P. (Eds.). *Representing black men.* New York; London: Routledge, 1996, p. 205–224.

DOUGLASS, Frederick. *Narrative of the life of Frederick Douglass.* n.p., s.d.

DREWAL, Margareth T. *Yoruba ritual: Performers, play, agency.* Bloomington: Indiana University Press, 1992.

DUARTE, Eduardo de Assis. Úrsula e a desconstrução da razão negra ocidental. In: _____; REIS, Maria Firmina dos. *Úrsula: Romance.* Belo Horizonte: Editora PUC Minas, 2018, p. 209–236.

DUNN, Christopher. A Roma Negra e o Big Easy: Raça, cultura e discurso em Salvador e Nova Orleans. *Afro-Ásia*, n. 37, 2008, p. 119–151.

DURÃO, Santa Rita. *Caramuru: Poema épico do descobrimento da Bahia.* São Paulo: Martins Fontes, 2005.

DURKHEIM, Émile. *As formas elementares da vida religiosa.* São Paulo: Martins Fontes, 2003.

_____. Introduction. In: _____. *Afro-pessimism, an introduction.* Racked & Dispatched. Minneapolis, 2017, p. 7–14.

EHRENREICH, Jeffrey David. Bodies, beads, bones and feathers: The masking tradition of Mardi Gras Indians in New Orleans—a photo essay. *City & Society*, v. 16, 2004, p. 117–150.

EQUIANO, Olaudah. *The interesting narrative of the life of Olaudah Equiano, or Gustavus Vassa, the African.* n.p., s.d.

FALCON, Barbara; GARCIA, Carol. *Grafitti Salvador.* Salvador: Pinaúna, 2014.

FANON, Franz. *Os condenados da terra*. Juiz de Fora: Editora UFJF, 2005.
_____. *Pele negra, máscaras brancas*. Salvador: Livraria Fator, 1983.

FBSP; IPEA. *Atlas da violência 2018*.

FÉLIX, João Batista de Jesus. Pequeno histórico do movimento negro contemporâneo. In: _____; SCHWARCZ, Lilia M.; REIS, Letícia V. de S. (Eds.). *Negras imagens: Ensaios sobre cultura e escravidão no Brasil*. São Paulo: EDUSP, 1996, p. 211–216.

FERGUSON, Roderick A. *Aberrations in black: Toward a queer of color critique*. Minneapolis: University of Minnesota Press, 2004.

FERNANDES, Florestan. *A integração do negro na sociedade de classes*. 2 v. São Paulo: Editora Ática, 1978.
_____. *Significado do protesto negro*. São Paulo: Cortez Editora, 1989.

FERREIRA, Viviane. Cinema novo e cinema negro: Da estética da fome à estética do faminto no Brasil. *Expressão, Memória*. Available at: http://nobrasil.co/cinema-novo-e-cinema-negro-da-estetica-da-fome-estetica-do-faminto/. Accessed: Jan. 25, 2021.

FIGARI, Carlos. @s Outr@s Cariocas: *Interpelações, experiências e identidades homoeróticas no Rio de Janeiro, séculos XVII ao XX*. Belo Horizonte/Rio de Janeiro: Editora UFMG/IUPERJ, 2007.
_____. Diversidade sexual. In: *Enciclopédia Latinoamericana*. Available at: latinoamericana.wiki.br/verbetes/s/sexual-diversidade. Accessed: Apr. 6, 2020.

FIGUEIREDO, Marcus Faria & CHEIBUB, José Antonio Borges. A Abertura Política de 1973 a 1981: Quem disse o que e quando – Inventário de um debate. Bib. <u>O que se Deve Ler em Ciências Sociais no Brasil 2</u>. São Paulo. ANPOCS/CORTEZ. 1986-1987. Pp. 243-263.

FLAUZINA, Ana Luiza Pinheiro. As fronteiras raciais do genocídio. *Direito*, UnB, v. 1, n. 1, Jan.–Jun. 2014, p. 119–146.
_____. *Corpo negro caído no chão: O sistema penal e o projeto genocida do Estado brasileiro*. Rio de Janeiro: Contraponto, 2008.

FLOR, Anatércia Lopes Vila. Salvador: Um novo espaço de cidadania negra? Master's Thesis. Master's in Social Sciences, Universidade Federal da Bahia. Salvador, 1992.

FONTAINE, Pierre-Michel. Blacks in the search for power in Brazil. In: _____. *Race, class and power in Brazil*. Center for Afro-American Studies, University of California, Los Angeles, 1985, p. 56–72.

FOUCAULT, Michel. *História da sexualidade: 1 — A vontade de saber*. Rio de Janeiro: Edições Graal, 2003.

FRAGINALS, Manuel M. (Ed.). *África en América Latina*. Ciudad de México: Siglo Veintiuno, 1977.

FRANÇA, Jean Marcel Carvalho; FERREIRA, Ricardo Alexandre. Apresentação: Um livro setecentista sobre a escravidão. In: _____. ROCHA, Manuel Ribeiro da. *Etíope resgatado, empenhando, sustentado, corrigido, instruído e libertado*. São Paulo: Editora UNESP, 2017, p. 7–30.

FRAZER, James G. *O ramo de ouro*. Rio de Janeiro: Zahar, 1982.

FREITAS, Décio. *Palmares: A guerra dos escravos*. Porto Alegre: Editora Movimento, 1973.

FREITAS, Henrique. *O Arco e a Arkhé: Ensaios sobre literatura e cultura*. Salvador: Ogum Toques, 2016.

FREYRE, Gilberto. *Casa grande & senzala: Introdução à história da sociedade patriarcal no Brasil*. 30th ed. Rio de Janeiro: Editora Record, 1995 (1933).

_____. *Modos de homem & modas de mulher*. São Paulo: Global Editora, 2009.

_____. *Sobrados e mucambos: Decadência do patriarcado rural e desenvolvimento do urbano*. 12th ed. São Paulo: Editora Record, 2000 (1936).

FRY, Peter. O que a Cinderela Negra tem a dizer sobre a "Política Racial" no Brasil. <u>Revista USP</u>. No. 28. Dez. 1995. Pp. 122-135.

GARVEY, M. *Selected writings and speeches of Marcus Garvey*. Edited by BLAISDELL. Mineola, N.Y: Dover Publications, 2004.

GELL, Alfred. *Arte e agência: Uma teoria antropológica*. São Paulo: Ubu, 2018.

GILROY, Paul. *O Atlântico negro: Modernidade e dupla consciência*. São Paulo: UCAM/Editora 34, 2001.

_____. *There ain't no black in the union Jack*. London, 1987.

GLEICH, Paulo von. Afro-pessimism, fugitivity, and the border to social death. *E-International Relations*, 2017. Available at: https://www.e-ir.info/2017/06/27/afro-pessimism-fugitivity-and-the-border-to-social-death/. Accessed: Jan. 25, 2021.

GONÇALVES, Ana Maria. *Um defeito de cor*. Rio de Janeiro/São Paulo: Editora Record, 2016.

GONZALEZ, Lélia. *Por um Feminismo Afro-Latino-Americano: Ensaios, Intervenções e Diálogos*. Edited by Flavia Rios, Rio Janeiro: Zahar, 2020.

_____. A categoria político-cultural de amefricanidade. *Tempo Brasileiro*, n. 92/93, Jan./Jun. 1988, p. 69–82.

_____. O movimento negro na última década. In: GONZALEZ, Lélia; HASENBALG, Carlos. *Lugar de negro*. Rio de Janeiro: Editora Marco Zero Limitada, 1982, p. 11–66.

GORDON, Edmund T. Cultural politics of black masculinity. *Transforming Anthropology*, v. 6, n. 1–2, 1997, p. 36–53.

_____; ANDERSON, Mark. The African diaspora: Towards an ethnography of diasporic identification. *Journal of American Folklore*, n. 112 (445), 1999, p. 282–296.

GORDON, Lewis. *Bad faith and anti-Black racism*. Amherst: Humanity Books, 1999.

_____. Critical reflections on afropessimism. *The Brotherwise Dispatch*, v. 3. Available at: www.brotherwise.com. Accessed: Jan. 25, 2021.

GORENDER, Jacob. *A escravidão reabilitada*. São Paulo: Editora Ática, 1990.

_____. *O escravismo colonial*. São Paulo: Expressão Popular, 2016.

GREEN, James. *Além do Carnaval: A homossexualidade masculina no Brasil do século XX*. São Paulo: Editora UNESP, 1999.

GROSFOGUEL, R. Decolonizing political-economy and post-colonial studies: transmodernity, border thinking and global coloniality. In: GROSFOGUEL, R.; SALDÍVAR, José Davi; MALDONADO-TORRES, Nelson (Eds.). *Unsettling postcoloniality: Coloniality, transmodernity, border thinking*. [s.l.]: Duke University Press, 2007.

_____. El concepto de racismo en Michel Foucault y Frantz Fanon: ¿teorizar desde la zona del ser o desde la zona del no-ser? *Tabula Rasa*, Bogotá, n. 16, Jan.–Jun. 2012, p. 79–102.

HALL, Stuart. *Cultura e representação*. Rio de Janeiro: PUC/Apicuri, 2016.

_____. Race, articulation and societies structured in dominance. In: ESSED, Philomena; GOLDBERG, David Theo. *Race critical theories*. Malden: Blackwell Publishers Ltd., 2002, p. 38–68.

HANCHARD, Michael. *Orpheus and power: The movimento negro of Rio de Janeiro and São Paulo, Brazil, 1945–1988*. Princeton: Princeton University Press, 1994.

_____. Cinderela Negra?: Raça e Esfera Pública no Brasil. Estudos Afro-Asiáticos. No. 30. Dez. 1996a. Pp. 41-60.

_____. Resposta a Luiza Bairros. Afro-Ásia, no. 18, 1996b. Pp. 227-234.

HARNEY, Stefano; MOTEN, Fred. *The undercommons: Fugitive planning and black study*. Winvehoe/New York/Port Watson: Minor Compositions, 2013.

HARTMAN, Saidiya. *Scenes of subjection: Terror, slavery, and self-making in nineteenth-century America*. New York; Oxford: Oxford University Press, 1997.

_____. Venus in two acts. *Small Axe*, n. 26, v. 12, n. 2, Jun. 2008, p. 1–14.

HEGEL, G. W. *Fenomenologia do espírito*. Petrópolis: Editora Vozes, 2002.

HERÁCLITO, Ayrson. Arte, cosmovisões e rituais sagrados (entrevista). *Djumbaiala*. Available at: https://djumbaiala.com/arte-cosmovisoes-e-rituais-sagrados. Accessed: Jan. 28, 2020.

_____. Leia textos sobre o vídeo "Barrueco", da mostra "Memórias Inapagáveis". Available at: https://m.folha.uol.com.br/ilustrissima/2014/08/1507943-leia-textos-sobre-o-video-barrueco-da-mostra-memorias-inapagaveis.shtml. Accessed: Aug. 31, 2014.

_____. Segredos no Boca do Inferno: Quatro pressupostos sobre o açúcar — Instalações. In: *17° Encontro Nacional da Associação Nacional de Pesquisadores em Artes Plásticas — Panorama da Pesquisa em Artes Visuais*, Florianópolis, Aug. 19–23, 2008.

HOMEM, Renata. Arte e fé: sincretismo afro-brasileiro. *Revista Kaypunku*, v. 1, Dec. 2014, p. 41–55.

HOOKS, bell. We real cool: Black men and masculinity. *Identities*, v. 9, n. 2, 2003, p. 225–240.

JACOBS, Harriet Ann. *Incidentes na vida de uma menina escrava*. São Paulo: Todavia, 2019.

JAMES, C. R. L. *Os jacobinos negros: Toussaint L'Ouverture e a revolução de São Domingos*. São Paulo: Boitempo Editorial, 2010.

JAMESON, Fredric. *Marxismo e forma: Teorias dialéticas da literatura no século XX*. São Paulo: Hucitec, 1985.

KLOOSTER, Wim. *The Dutch moment: War, trade and settlement in the seventeenth century Atlantic world*. London: Cornell University Press, 2016.

KREPP, Ana. Vídeo mostra PMs agredindo jovens em 'rolezinho' dentro do Shopping Itaquera. *Folha de São Paulo*, Jan. 11, 2014. Available at: www1.folha.uol.com.br/cotidiano/2014/01/1396629-video-mostra-pms-agredindo-jovens-emrolezinho-dentro-no-shopping-itaquera-em-sp.shtml. Accessed: Jan. 25, 2021.

_____; SOUZA, Felipe. PM usa bombas e balas de borracha em 'rolezinho' em SP; dois são presos. *Folha de São Paulo*, Jan. 11, 2014. Available at: www1.folha.uol.com.br/cotidiano/2014/01/1396595-policia-usa-bombas-de-gas-e-balada-de-borracha-em-rolezinho-em-sp.shtml. Accessed: Jan. 25, 2021.

KWON, Miwon. One place after another: Notes on site specificity. *October*, n. 80, 1997, p. 85–110.

LATIN AMERICAN SUBALTERN STUDIES GROUP. Founding statement. In: BEVERLEY, John; ARONNA, Michael; OVIEDO, José. *The postmodernism debate in Latin America*. Durham; London: Duke University Press, 1995, p. 135–146.

LEACH, Edmund. *Cultura e Comunicação*. Rio de Janeiro: Editora Zahar, 1978.

_____. *As ideias de Lévi-Strauss*. São Paulo: Cultrix, 1973.

LEAL, Gabriela; MENASCE, Mario. No primeiro domingo da Operação Verão, ao menos 15 pessoas são presas por roubo e agressão. *O Globo*, Sept. 14, 2014. Available at: http://oglobo.globo.com/rio/no-primeiro-do-mingo-da-operação-verão-aomenos-15-pessoas-são-presas-por-roubo-agressão-13933271. Accessed: Jan. 25, 2021.

LEVI-STRAUSS, Claude. Introdução à obra de Marcelo Mauss. In: _____. *Sociologia e Antropologia*. São Paulo: Cosac Naify, 2003, p. [pages missing].

_____. A estrutura dos mitos. In: _____. *Antropologia estrutural*. Rio de Janeiro: Tempo Brasileiro, 1975, p. 237–265.

_____. *As estruturas elementares do parentesco*. Petrópolis: Vozes, 1982.

_____. *O pensamento selvagem*. Campinas: Papirus Editora, 1989.

LEVY-BRUHL, Lucien. *A mentalidade primitiva.* São Paulo: Paulus, 2008.

LIMA, Zélia Jesus. Lucas Evangelista: O Lucas da Feira, estudo sobre a rebeldia escrava em Feira de Santana. Master's Thesis. Department of History, Universidade Federal da Bahia, 1990.

LIPSITZ, George. Indians: carnival and counter-narrative in black New Orleans. *Cultural Critique,* n. 10, Popular Narrative, Popular Images, 1988, p. 99–121.

LOVEJOY, Paul. Identidade e a miragem da etnicidade: A jornada de Mahommah Gardo Baquaqua para as Américas. *Afro-Ásia,* v. 27, 2002, p. 9–39.

LOWE, Lisa. Autobiography out of empire. *Small Axe,* n. 28, v. 13, 2009, p. 98–111.

LUGONES, Maria. Heterosexualism and the colonial/modern gender system. *Hypatia,* v. 22, n. 1, 2007, p. 186–209.

M´BOKOLO, Elikia. *África Negra: História e Civilizações.* Casa das Áfricas. EDUFBA. 2008.

MACHADO, Arlindo. O efeito Zapping. In: _____. *Máquina e imag-inário.* São Paulo: EDUSP, 1993, p. 143–164.

Machado, Ricardo Emmanuel Santana Reina. *"Edson Gomes: A Trajetória De Vida De Um Ícone Do Reggae Nacional." Relações De Classe E Raça Na Formação Da Cultura Brasileira.* Dissertação De Mestrado.Universidade Federal Do Recôncavo Da Bahia Mestrado Em Ciências Sociais. 2015.

MAESTRI, Mario. A revolução copernicana de Jacob Gorender — A gênese, o reconhecimento, a deslegitimação. *Cadernos IHU,* year 3, n. 13, 2005.

_____. O Escravismo Colonial: A revolução copernicana de Jacob Gorender. In: _____; GORENDER, Jacob. *O escravismo colonial.* São Paulo: Expressão Popular, 2016, p. 13–45.

MALDONADO-TORRES, Nelson. Sobre la colonialidad del ser: Contribuciones al desarrollo de un concepto. In: CASTRO-GÓMEZ, S.; GROSFOGUEL, R. (Eds.). *El Giro Decolonial: Reflexiones para una diver-sidad epistémica más allá del capitalismo global.* Bogotá: Siglo Del Hombre Editores, 2007, p. 127–168.

_____. *Against war: Views from the underside of modernity.* Durham: Duke University Press, 2008.

MANZANO, Juan Francisco. *A autobiografia do poeta-escravo.* São Paulo: Hedra, 2015.

MARRIOT, David. *On black men.* New York: Columbia University Press, 2000a.

_____. Murderous appetites: Photography and fantasy. In: _____. *On black men.* New York: Columbia University Press, 2000b, p. 23–42.

_____. Black Narcissus: Isaac Julien. In: _____. *Haunted life: Visual culture and black modernity.* New Brunswick: Rutgers University Press, 2007, p. 106–132.

MARTINS, Leda Maria. *Afrografias da memória: O reinado do Rosário do Jatobá.* Belo Horizonte: Mazza Edições/Editora Perspectiva, 1997.

MARX, K. & ENGELS, F. *Sobre el Sistema Colonial del Capitalismo.* Buenos Aires. Ediciones Studio. 1964.

MARX, Karl. *Grundisse.* São Paulo: Boitempo Editorial, 2011.

_____. *O capital — Crítica da economia política.* Book 1, vol. 1. Rio de Janeiro: Civilização Brasileira, 1998.

_____; ENGELS, F. *Sobre el sistema colonial del capitalismo.* Buenos Aires: Ediciones Studio, 1964.

MASON, Peter. Troca e deslocamento nas pinturas de Albert Eckhout de sujeitos brasileiros. *Estudos de Sociologia,* Revista do Programa de Pós-Graduação em Sociologia da UFPE, v. 7, n. 1–2, 2001, p. 231–249.

MATHERON, François; POST, Erin A. The recurrence of the void in Louis Althusser. *Rethinking Marxism: A Journal of Economics, Culture and Society,* v. 10, n. 3, 1998, p. 22–37.

MATORY, J. Lorand. *The fetish revisited: Marx, Freud and the gods black people make.* Durham; London: Duke University Press, 2018.

MATOS, Gregório. *Antologia.* Porto Alegre: L&PM, 2006.

MATTOS, Carla. Da valentia à neurose: Criminalização das galeras funk, "paz" e (auto)regulação das condutas nas favelas. *Dilemas: Revista de Estudos de Conflitos e Controle Social,* v. 5, n. 4, Oct.–Dec. 2012.

MATTOSO, Kátia de Queirós. *Ser escravo no Brasil.* São Paulo: Brasiliense, 1990.

MAUSS, Marcel. Uma categoria do espírito humano: A noção de pessoa e a noção do "eu". In: _____. *Sociologia e Antropologia.* São Paulo:

Cosac Naify, 2003, p. 367–398.

_____. Ensaio sobre a dádiva. In: _____. *Sociologia e Antropologia*. São Paulo: Cosac Naify, 2003, p. 294–314.

MBEMBE, Achille. *Crítica da razão negra*. Lisboa: Antígona, 2014.

M´BOKOLO, Elikia. *África negra: História e civilizações*. São Paulo: Casa das Áfricas/EDUFBA, 2008.

McCLINTOCK, Anne. *Couro imperial: Raça, gênero e sexualidade no embate colonial*. São Paulo: Companhia das Letras, 2010.

McKAY, Claude. The desolate city. In: LEWIS, David L. *The portable Harlem Renaissance reader*. New York: Penguin Books, 1995, p. 294.

MEILLASSOUX. *Antropologia da escravidão: O ventre de ferro e dinheiro*. Rio de Janeiro: Jorge Zahar Editor, 1995.

MERCER, Kobena. *Travel & See: Black Diaspora Art Practices since the 1980s*. Duke University Press, 2016

_____. *Welcome to the jungle: New positions in black cultural studies*. New York; London: Routledge, 1994.

MIRANDA, Jader. Confusão no Shopping Vitória deixa clientes em pânico. *Gazeta*, Vitória, Nov. 30, 2013. Available at: http://gazetaonline.globo.com/_conteudo/2013/11/noticias/cidades/1470338-confusao-no-shopping-vitoria-deixa-clientes-em-panico.html. Accessed: Nov. 30, 2013.

MISKOLCI, Richard. *O desejo da nação: Masculinidade e branquitude no Brasil de fins do XIX*. São Paulo: Anablume, 2012.

MISSE, Michel. Autos de resistência: Uma análise dos homicídios cometidos por policiais na cidade do Rio de Janeiro (2001–2011). Research Report. Núcleo de Estudos da Cidadania, Conflito e Violência Urbana, Universidade Federal do Rio de Janeiro, 2011.

MNU. *Movimento Negro Unificado: 1978–1988, 10 anos de luta contra o racismo*. Salvador, 1988.

MONTEIRO, Marianna F. M. Nego Fugido, teatro didático e agit-prop. In: _____; DAWSEY, John C. et al. (Eds.). *Antropologia e Performance: Ensaios Napedra*. São Paulo: Terceiro Nome, 2013.

MOORE, Carlos. *O marxismo e a questão racial: Karl Marx e Friedrich Engels frente ao racismo e à escravidão*. Belo Horizonte: CENAFRO/Nandyala, 2010.

MORE, Anna. Necro-economics and the early Iberian slave trade. *Tepoztlán Institute for the Transnational History of the Americas*, 2018.

MORRISON, Toni. *A origem dos outros: Seis ensaios sobre racismo e literatura*. São Paulo: Companhia das Letras, 2019.

_____. *Amada*. São Paulo: Companhia das Letras, 2007.

MOTEN, Fred. Blackness and nothingness (mysticism in the flesh). *The South Atlantic Quarterly*, v. 112, n. 4, 2013, p. 737–780.

_____. *In the break: The aesthetics of the black radical tradition*. Minneapolis; London: University of Minnesota Press, 2003.

MOTT, Luiz. Relações raciais entre homossexuais no Brasil colônia. In:

_____. *Escravidão, homossexualidade e demonologia*. São Paulo: Ícone Editora, 1988, p. 19–48.

_____. Tortura de escravos e heresias na casa da torre. In:

_____. *Bahia: Inquisição e sociedade*. Salvador: EDUFBA, 2010, p. 63–97.

MOUTINHO, Laura. *Razão, "cor" e desejo*. São Paulo: EDUS/UNESP, 2004.

NASCIMENTO, Abdias do. *O negro revoltado*. (Ed.). Rio de Janeiro: Nova Fronteira, 1982.

_____. *O quilombismo: Documentos de uma militância pan-africanista*. 2nd ed. Brasília: Fundação Cultural Palmares, 2002.

_____. *O genocídio do black brasileiro: Um processo de racismo mascarado*. Rio de Janeiro: Paz e Terra, 1978.

_____; NASCIMENTO, Elisa Larkin. Reflexões sobre o movimento negro no Brasil, 1938–1997. In: GUIMARÃES, Antonio Sérgio Alfredo; HUNTLEY, Lynn (Eds.). *Tirando a máscara: Ensaios sobre o racismo no Brasil*. São Paulo: Paz e Terra/SEF, 2000, p. 203–236.

NASCIMENTO, Beatriz. O conceito de Quilombo e a resistência cultural negra. In: RATTS, Alex. *Eu sou Atlântica: Sobre a trajetória de vida de Beatriz Nascimento*. São Paulo: Instituto Kwanza/Imprensa Oficial, 2007, p. 117–124.

NEURATH, Johannes. Los libros de Piel de Venado. *Códices prehispánicos, Artes de México*, n. 109, 2013, p. 50–53.

NUNES, Zita Cristina. Race, "miscigenation" and the construction of a national identity: The modernist period in Brazil. Ph.D. Thesis. University of California at Berkeley, 1994.

OKONKWO, R. L. The Garvey movement in British West Africa. *The Journal of African History*, v. 21, n. 1, 1980, p. 105–117.

O'NEILL, Caitlin. "The Shape of Mystery": The Visionary Resonance of Harriet Jacobs's Incidents in the Life of a Slave Girl. *The Journal of American Culture* _ Volume 41, Number 1 _ March 2018

OLIVEIRA, Eduardo. *Cosmovisão africana no Brasil.* Fortaleza: LCR, 2003.

OMAR, Artur. Que são faces gloriosas? In: _____. *Antropologia da face gloriosa.* São Paulo: Cosac & Naify, 1997.

OMI, Michael; WINANT, Howard. *Racial formation in the United States: From the 1960s to the 1990s.* New York: Routledge, 1994.

O'NEILL, Caitlin. The shape of mystery: The visionary resonance of Harriet Jacobs's *Incidents in the Life of a Slave Girl. The Journal of American Culture*, v. 41, n. 1, Mar. 2018.

OYEWUMI, Oyeronke. *The invention of women: Making an African sense of western gender discourses.* Minneapolis: University of Minnesota Press, 1997.

PALOMBINI, Carlos. Mora na filosofia: putaria é lixo. *Rio Baile Funk*, 2011. Available at: http://www.proibidao.org/mora-na-filosofia-putaria-e-lixo/. Accessed: Feb. 19, 2016.

PATTERSON, Orlando. *Escravidão e morte social.* São Paulo: EDUSP, 2008.

PEDROSA, Adriano et al. *Histórias Afro-Atlânticas, Vol. 1.* Exhibition catalogue. Instituto Tomie Ohtake/MASP, 2018.

PEREIRA, Dulce. Hamilton Cardoso (1953–1999): Sensibilidade, inteligência e solidariedade na luta contra o racismo. *Portal Geledés*, 2009. Available at: https://www.geledes.org.br/hamilton-cardoso/. Accessed: Jan. 25, 2021.

PERRY, Marc. Who dat? Race and its conspicuous consumption in post-Katrina New Orleans. *City & Society*, v. 27, n. 1, 2015, p. 92–114.

PHILLIPS, Dom. "A devastating scenario": Brazil sets new record for homicides at 63,880 deaths. *The Guardian: International Edition.* Available at: https://www.theguardian.com/world/2018/aug/09/brazil-sets-new-record-for-homicides-63880-deaths?CMP=share_btn_fb. Accessed: Jan. 25, 2021.

PIERSON, Donald. *Brancos e pretos na Bahia.* 2nd ed. São Paulo: Companhia Editora Nacional, (1942) 1971.

PIGNATARI, Décio. *Informação, linguagem, comunicação.* São Paulo: Editora Perspectiva, 1969.

PINHO, Osmundo de Araújo. A Bahia no fundamental: Notas para uma interpretação do discurso ideológico da baianidade. *Revista Brasileira de Ciências Sociais,* v. 13, n. 36, São Paulo, 1998, p. 109–120.

_____. O efeito do sexo: Políticas de raça, gênero e miscigenação. *Cadernos Pagu,* n. 23, Jul.–Dec. 2004, p. 89–119.

_____. "O sol da liberdade": Movimento negro e a crítica das representações raciais. *ComCiência: Dossiê O Brasil Negro.* SBPC/LABjor, 2003. Available at: http://www.comciencia.br/dossies-1-72/reportagens/negros/15.shtml. Accessed: Apr. 2, 2020.

_____. "Putaria": Masculinidade, negritude e desejo no pagode baiano. *Maguaré,* v. 29, n. 2, Jul.–Dec. 2015, p. 209–238.

_____. The black male body and sex wars in Brazil. In: _____; LEWIS, Elizabeth Sarah et al. *Queering paradigms IV: South–north dialogues on queer epistemologies, embodiments and activisms.* Oxford: Peter Lang, 2014, p. 301–319.

_____. Tiroteio: Violência e subjetificação no pagode baiano. In: _____; VARGAS, João H. C. *Antinegritude: O impossível sujeito negro na formação social brasileira.* FT/Editora UFRB/UNIAFRO, 2016, p. 121–142.

_____; ROCHA, Eduardo. Racionais MC's: Cultura afro-brasileira contemporânea como política cultural. *Afro-Hispanic Review,* v. 30, n. 2, 2011.

_____; VARGAS, João H. C. *Antinegritude: O impossível sujeito negro na formação social brasileira.* FT/Editora UFRB/UNIAFRO, 2016.

_____. África, signo da liberdade: Marcus Garvey, o carnaval da Bahia e o brado africano em Moçambique. *Maguaré,* v. 10, n. 20, Jul.–Dec. 2015, p. 497–509.

_____. Etnografias do Brau: Corpo, masculinidade e raça na reafricanização em Salvador. In: _____. *Olhares feministas.* 1st ed. Brasília: SECAD/UNESCO, 2006, v. 1, p. 345–372.

_____. O sacrifício de Orfeu: Masculinidades negras no contexto da antinegritude em Salvador. In: _____; CAETANO, Marcio; MELGAÇO, Paulo (Eds.). *De guri a cabra-macho: Masculinidades no Brasil.* Rio de Janeiro: Lamparina, 2018a, p. 146–173.

_____. Black bodies, wrong places: Rolezinho, moral panic and racialized male subjects in Brazil. In: _____; SIEGEL, Micol (Ed.). *Panic: Transnational cultural studies and the affective contours of power.* New York: Routledge, 2018b, p. 158–178.

PINTO, Monilson dos Santos. A dialética da máscara negra: Nego Fugido contra o blackface. *Revista Aspas*, v. 7, n. 1, 2017, p. 153–164.

_____. *Nego Fugido: O teatro das aparições.* Master's Thesis. São Paulo: Universidade Estadual Paulista Júlio de Mesquita Filho, Instituto de Artes, Programa de Pós-Graduação em Artes, 2014.

PINTO, Regina Pahim. Movimento negro e etnicidade. *Estudos Afro-Asiáticos*, n. 19, 1990, p. 109–124.

PIRES, Thula Rafaela de Oliveira. Estruturas intocadas: Racismo e ditadura no Rio de Janeiro. *Revista Direito Práxis*, Rio de Janeiro, v. 9, n. 2, 2018, p. 1054–1079.

POLITO, Ronald. Introdução. In: _____; DURÃO, Santa Rita. *Caramuru: Poema épico do descobrimento da Bahia.* São Paulo: Martins Fontes, 2005, p. 11–48.

PRANDI, Reginaldo. *Mitologia dos orixás.* São Paulo: Companhia das Letras, 2001.

PRATT, Mary Louise. Arts of the contact zone. From *Profession 91.* New York: MLA, 1991, p. 33–40. Available at: http://l-adam-mekler.com/pratt_contact_zone.pdf. Accessed: Jan. 25, 2021.

QUARCOOPOME, Nii Otokunor. Art of the Akan. *Art Institute of Chicago Museum Studies*, v. 23, n. 2, *African Art at The Art Institute of Chicago*, 1997, p. 134–147, 197.

QUIJANO, Aníbal. Colonialidad del poder y clasificación social. In: _____; CASTRO-GÓMEZ, Santiago; GROSFOGUEL, Ramón (Eds.). *El giro decolonial: Reflexiones para una diversidad epistémica más allá del capitalismo global.* Bogotá, 2007, p. 93–126.

RACISMO NÃO PASSARÁ [YouTube]. Racismo dentro do Shopping Vitória (Racism in Vitória Shopping Mall). *YouTube Video.* Available at: www.youtube.com/watch?v=WoLa1Rw42b8. Accessed: Jan. 25, 2021.

RADCLIFFE-BROWN, A. R. *Estrutura e função nas sociedades primitivas.* Lisboa: Edições 70, 1989.

RATTS, Alex. *Eu sou Atlântica: Sobre a trajetória de vida de Beatriz Nascimento.* São Paulo: Instituto Kwanza/Imprensa Oficial, 2007.

REGIS, Helen A. Skeletons. In: _____; BREUNLIN, Rachel (Eds.). *The house of dance and feathers*. New Orleans: Neighborhood Story Project, 2009, p. 177–189.

REIS, Demian Moreira. Dança dos Quilombos: Significado de uma tradição. *Afro-Ásia*, n. 17, 1996, p. 159–171.

REIS, João José (Ed.). *Escravidão e invenção da liberdade: Estudos sobre o negro no Brasil*. São Paulo: Brasiliense, 1988.

_____; GOMES, Flávio dos Santos (Eds.). *Liberdade por um fio: História dos Quilombos no Brasil*. São Paulo: Companhia das Letras, 1996.

_____; SILVA, E. *Negociação e conflito: A resistência negra no Brasil escravista*. São Paulo: Companhia das Letras, 1989.

REIS, Maria Firmina dos. *Úrsula: Romance*. Belo Horizonte: Editora PUC Minas, 2018.

RIBEIRO, Djamila. *O que é lugar de fala?* Belo Horizonte: Letramento/Justificando, 2017.

RIBEIRO, Luciana. Arte do corpo. *A Tarde. Muito*, Aug. 21, 2017. Available at: http://atarde.uol.com.br/muito/noticias/1887965-arte-do-corpo. Accessed: Jan. 25, 2021.

RICOEUR, Paul. *Interpretação e ideologias*. 4th ed. Rio de Janeiro: Francisco Alves, 1990.

RISERIO, Antonio. *A utopia brasileira e os movimentos negros*. São Paulo: Editora 34, 2007.

_____. *Carnaval Ijexá*. Salvador: Corrupio, 1981.

ROACH, Joseph. Mardi Gras Indians and others: Genealogies of American performance. *Theatre Journal*, v. 44, n. 4, *Disciplines of Theatre: Theory/Culture/Text*.

ROCHA, Manuel Ribeiro da. *Etíope resgatado, empenhando, sustentado, corrigido, instruído e libertado*. São Paulo: Editora UNESP, 2017.

RODRIGUES, Jacinto. Joseph Beuys — Um filósofo na arte e na cidade. *Millenium*, May 15, 2019. Available at: https://www.ipv.pt/millenium/Millenium25/25_24.html. Accessed: Jan. 25, 2021.

RODRIGUES, João Jorge dos Santos. *Olodum estrada da paixão*. Salvador: Grupo Cultural Olodum/Fundação Casa de Jorge Amado, 1996.

ROMO, Anadelia. *Brazil's living museum: Race, reform and tradition in Bahia*. Chapel Hill: The University of North Carolina Press, 2010.

ROSENTHAL, Dália. Joseph Beuys: o elemento material como agente social. *ARS*, v. 8, n. 18, 2011, p. 110–133.

RUBIN, G. O tráfico de mulheres: notas sobre a "Economia política" do sexo. *SOS Corpo*, [1975] 1993.

RUBIN, Gayle. Thinking sex: Notes for a radical theory of the politics of sexuality. In: _____; NARDI, Peter M.; SCHNEIDER, Beth E. (Eds.). *Social perspectives in lesbian and gay studies: A reader.* London; New York: Routledge, 1993, p. 100–133.

SALGADO, Gabriela. Leia textos sobre o vídeo "Barrueco", da mostra "Memórias Inapagáveis". Aug. 31, 2014. Available at: https://m.folha.uol.com.br/ilustrissima/2014/08/1507943-leia-textos-sobre-o-video-barrueco-da-mostra-memorias-inapagaveis.shtml. Accessed: Jan. 25, 2021.

SAMAIN, Etienne. "Ver" e "Dizer" na tradição etnográfica: Bronislaw Malinowski e a fotografia. *Horizontes Antropológicos*, Porto Alegre, year 1, n. 2, Jul.–Sep. 1995, p. 23–60.

SANTANA, Monica. Nego Fugido, performance negra e a liberdade yardia. In: _____. *Terra Quente: Projetil Billy the Kid — Expedição Acupe.* Salvador: Tanto Produções Compartilhadas, 2020, p. 1–9.

SANTOS, Jocélio Teles dos. Divertimentos estrondosos: batuques e sambas no século XIX. In: _____. SANSONE, Livio; SANTOS, Jocélio Teles dos. *Ritmos em trânsito: Sócio antropologia da música baiana.* Salvador: Dynamis Editorial/Programa a Cor da Bahia/Projeto Samba, p. 17–38.

_____. *O dono da terra: O caboclo nos candomblés da Bahia.* Salvador: Sarah Letras/Programa a Cor da Bahia, 1995.

_____. Caramuru e Catarina Paraguaçu: mito fundante, dilema nacional e onde o negro está ausente. In: _____. *Ensaios sobre raça, gênero e sexualidades no Brasil. Séculos XVIII–XX.* Salvador: EDUFBA, 2013, p. 169–177.

SANTOS, Juana Elbein. *Os Nagô e a morte: Pàde, Àsèsè e o culto Égun na Bahia.* Petrópolis: Vozes, 2017.

SCHECHNER, Richard. "Pontos de contato" revisitados. *Revista de Antropologia*, v. 56, 2013, p. 23–66.

SCHWARCZ, Lilia Moritz. Imagens da escravidão: o outro do outro (séculos 16 a 19). In: _____; PEDROSA, Adriano et al. (Eds.). *Histórias Afro-Atlânticas, Vol. 2: Antologia.* MASP, 2018, p. 524–538.

SCHWARTZ, Stuart B. *Segredos internos: Engenhos e escravos na sociedade colonial.* São Paulo: Companhia das Letras, 1995.

SCOTT, David. Introducción: Sobre las arqueologías de la memoria negra. *Small Axe*, n. 26, Jun. 2008, p. 5–16.

SEXTON, Jared. Afro-pessimism: The unclear word. *Rhizomes: Cultural Studies in Emerging Knowledge.* Available at: www.rhizomes.net/issue29/ sexton.html?fbclid=IwAR3yJdGicu357i-CpmXd0bzHXkZMX3jqEzm-T7rrq7zN1mYwGb65F1g2U9Vg. Accessed: Jun. 15, 2019.

_____. *Amalgamation schemes: Antiblackness and the critique of multi-racialism.* Minneapolis: University of Minnesota Press, 2008.

_____. On black negativity, or the affirmation of nothing. *Society & Space.* Available at: http://societyandspace.org/2017/09/18/on-black-negativity-or-the-affirmation-of-nothing/. Accessed: Jun. 22, 2018.

_____. The social life of social death: On Afro-pessimism and black optimism. *Tensions Journal*, n. 5, 2011.

SHARPE, Christina. The wake. In: _____. *In the wake: On blackness and being.* Durham: Duke University Press, 2016, p. 1–24.

SILVA, Denise Ferreira da. *A dívida impagável.* São Paulo: A Casa do Povo, 2019.

SILVA, Jônatas. História das lutas negras: Memórias do surgimento do movimento negro na Bahia. In: _____; REIS, J. J. (Ed.). *Escravidão e invenção da liberdade: Estudos sobre o negro no Brasil.* São Paulo: Brasiliense, 1988, p. 275–288.

SILVA, Maria Palmira. Anexos: Entrevistas. In: _____. *Bloco Afro Ilê-Aiyê - Seus protestos e sua beleza: Um estudo psicossocial das minorias ativas na constituição da identidade negra na Bahia.* Master's Thesis. Social Psychology, Pontifícia Universidade Católica de São Paulo, São Paulo, 1995, p. 156–207.

SIMÕES, Alex. Excertos de notas do diário de campo da residência artística BTK: Acupe/Itapema. In: _____. *Terra Quente: Projetil Billy the Kid — Expedição Acupe.* Salvador: Tanto Produções Compartilhadas, 2020, p. 1–13.

_____. *Trans Formas São.* Salvador: Organismo, 2018.

SKIDMORE, Thomas E. Race and class in Brazil: Historical perspectives. In: _____; FONTAINE, Pierre-Michel (Ed.). *Race, class and power in Brazil.* Center for Afro-American Studies, Los Angeles: University of California, 1985, p. 11–24.

_____. Redemocratização: Novas esperanças, velhos problemas. In: _____. *Uma história do Brasil*. São Paulo: Paz e Terra, 1998, p. 267–328.

SLENES, Robert W. *Na senzala, uma flor: Esperanças e revelações na formação da família escrava*. Campinas: Editora da UNICAMP, 2011.

SMITH, Christen A. *Afro-Paradise: Blackness, violence and performance in Brazil*. Chicago: University of Illinois Press, 2016.

SONTAG, Susan. A imaginação pornográfica. In: _____. *A vontade radical — Estilos*. São Paulo: Companhia das Letras, 1987a, p. 41–76.

_____. Contra a interpretação. In: _____. *Contra a interpretação*. Porto Alegre: L&PM, 1987b, p. 11–23.

SOUZA, Mateus Raynner André de. Entre o sêmen e o dendê: Aproximações do orixá Exu na fotografia de Ayrson Heráclito. *Arteriais. Revista do PPGArtes, ICA, UFPA*, n. 5, Dec. 2017.

SOUZA, Raquel Luciana de. Ethnographic notes from a war zone: Surviving and resisting. *Lasaforum*, v. 48, 2017.

SPILLERS, Hortense J. Mama's baby, papa's maybe: An American grammar book. *Diacritics*, v. 17, n. 2, *Culture and Countermemory: The "American" Connection*, 1987, p. 64–81.

SPIRITO SANTO. Guerreiro africano 1641: Quadro de Albert Eckhout. Available at: https://spiritosanto.wordpress.com/2011/04/24/guerreiro-africano-1641-quadro-de-albert-eckhout/. Accessed: Apr. 6, 2019.

SPIVAK, Gayatri. *Pode o subalterno falar?* Belo Horizonte: Editora UFMG, 2014.

STOLER, Ann Laura. *Race and the education of desire: Foucault's history of sexuality and the colonial order of things*. Durham; London: Duke University Press, 1995.

STOLKE, Verena. O enigma das interseções: Classe, raça, sexo, sexualidade. A formação dos impérios transatlânticos do século XVI ao XIX. *Estudos Feministas*, n. 1, v. 14.

STRATHERN, M. *The gender of the gift: Problems with women and problems with society in Melanesia*. Berkeley: University of California Press.

SUNDIATA, Ibrahim. *Brothers and strangers: Black Zion, Black slavery, 1914–1940*. Durham: Duke University Press, 2003.

TAUSSIG, Michael. *Xamanismo, colonialismo e o homem selvagem: Um estudo sobre terror e cura*. São Paulo: Paz e Terra, 1993.

TAYLOR, Diana. *The archive and the repertoire: Performing cultural memory in the Americas*. Durham; London: Duke University Press, 2003.

TELLES, Edward. *Racismo à brasileira: Uma nova perspectiva sociológica.* Rio de Janeiro: Relume-Dumará, 2003.

TERREFE, Selamawit D. The pornotrope of decolonial feminism. *Critical Philosophy of Race*, v. 8, n. 1–2, 2020, p. 134–164.

_____; WILDERSON, Frank B. Afro-Pessimism — African American Studies. *Oxford Bibliographies*. Available at: https://www.oxfordbibliographies.com/view/document/obo-9780190280024/obo-9780190280024-0056.xml. Accessed: Feb. 4, 2020.

TESSITORE, Mariana. Ayrson Heráclito, um artista exorcista https://artebrasileiros.com.br/sub-home2/ayrson-heraclito-um-artista-exorcista/ . 27 de junho de 2018

TODOROV, Tzvetan. *A conquista da América: A questão do outro*. São Paulo: Martins Fontes, 1993.

TRAPP, Rafael Petry. Eduardo de Oliveira e Oliveira sobre a USP: "nós temos direito a essa instituição". *Portal Geledés*, 2017. Available at: https://www.geledes.org.br/eduardo-de-oliveira-e-oliveira-sobre-usp-nos-temos-direito-essa-instituicao/. Accessed: Jan. 25, 2021.

_____. Intelectuais negros no Brasil: Uma proposta de análise a partir de Eduardo de Oliveira e Oliveira. Paper presented at the *7º Encontro Escravidão e Liberdade no Brasil Meridional*, Curitiba (UFPR), May 13–16, 2015.

TREVISAN, João Silvério. *Devassos no Paraíso*. São Paulo: Max Limonad, 1986.

TROUILLOT, Michel-Rolph. *Silenciando o passado: Poder e a produção da História*. Curitiba: Huya, 2016.

TURNER, Victor. *From ritual to theater: The human seriousness of play*. New York: PAJ Publications, 1982.

_____. *O processo ritual: Estrutura e anti-estrutura*. Petrópolis: Vozes, 1974.

VARGAS, J. H. Costa. *Never meant to: Genocide and utopia in black diaspora communities*. Lanham: Rowman & Littlefield Publishers, Inc, 2010a.

_____. A diáspora negra como genocídio: Brasil, Estados Unidos ou uma geografia supranacional da morte e suas alternativas. *Revista da ABPN*, Florianópolis, v. 1, n. 2, Jul.–Oct. 2010b, p. 31–65.

_____. Gendered antiblackness and the impossible Brazilian project:

Emerging critical Brazilian studies. *Cultural Dynamics*, v. 24, n. 1, 2012, p. 3–11.

_____. Por uma mudança de paradigma: Antinegritude e antagonismo estrutural. *Revista de Ciências Sociais*, Fortaleza, v. 48, n. 2, Jul.–Dec. 2017, p. 83–105.

VAZ, Henrique Claudio de Lima. Apresentação — A significação da fenomenologia do espírito. In: _____. HEGEL, G. W. *Fenomenologia do espírito*. Petrópolis: Editora Vozes, 2002, p. 11–22.

VIDEOBRASIL. Ayrson, Heráclito & Danillo Barata: Parceria entre artistas é motivada pelo legado do tráfico negreiro. Available at: www.videobrasil.org.br/news/1787633. Accessed: Apr. 16, 2020.

VIGOYA, Mara Viveros. La sexualización da la raza y la racialización de la sexualidad en el contexto Latinoamericano actual. Available at: http://www.derechoshumanos.unlp.edu.ar/assets/files/documentos/la-sexualizacion-de-la-raza-y-la-racializacion-de-la-sexualidad.pdf. Accessed: Jan. 25, 2021.

VILAÇA, Sérgio Henrique Carvalho. A música no cinema revolucionário de Santiago Alvarez. *Encontro Nacional de História da Mídia*, Ouro Preto, 2013.

VILLAS BOAS, Maria José Villares Barral. Masculinidade entre crianças negras — Uma reflexão sobre raça e gênero no Nêgo Fugido em Acupe/BA. *Cadernos de Gênero e Diversidades*, v. 5, n. 2, Apr.–Jun. 2019.

VIVEIROS DE CASTRO, Eduardo. *Metafísicas canibais*. São Paulo: Ubu/N-1, 2018.

_____. Posfácio: O intempestivo, ainda. In: _____; CLASTRES, Pierre. *Arqueologia da violência*. São Paulo: Cosac Naif, 2014, p. 299–366.

WADE, Peter. *Race and sex in Latin America*. New York: Pluto Press, 2009.

WAGNER, Roy. *Símbolos que representam a si mesmos*. São Paulo: Editora UNESP, 2017.

WAISELFISZ, Julio Jacobo. *Mapa da violência 2013: Os jovens do Brasil*. Rio de Janeiro: FLACSO Brasil, 2014.

WALCOTT, Derek. *Omeros*. São Paulo: Companhia das Letras, 1990.

WARREN, Calvin. *Onticide: Afropessimism, queer theory, & ethics*. 2015.

WEHMEYER, Stephen C. Feathered footsteps: Mythologizing and ritualizing black Indian processions in New Orleans. *Social Identities*, v. 16, n. 4, 2010, p. 427–445.

WILDERSON III, Frank B. Gramsci's black Marx: Whither the slave in civil society? *Social Identities*, v. 9, n. 2, 2003.

_____. Afro-pessimism & the end of redemption. *The Occupied Times*. Available at: https://theoccupiedtimes.org/?p=14236. Accessed: Jun. 17, 2018.

_____. The vengeance of Vertigo: Aphasia and abjection in the political trials of black insurgents. *InTensions Journal*. Toronto: New York University, 2011.

_____. Blacks and the master/slave relation. In: _____. *Afro-pessimism: An introduction*. Racked & Dispatched. Minneapolis, 2017, p. 15–30.

_____. *Red, white & black: Cinema and the structure of U.S. antagonisms*. Durham: Duke University Press, 2010.

WILLIAMS, Linda. Skin flicks on the racial border: Pornography, exploitation and interracial lust. In: _____; WILLIAMS, Linda (Ed.). *Porn studies*. Durham; London: Duke University Press, 2004, p. 271–307.

WILLIAMS, Raymond. *Marxismo e literatura*. Rio de Janeiro: Zahar, 1979.

WYNTER, Sylvia. Unsettling the coloniality of being/power/truth/freedom. *The New Centennial Review*, v. 3, n. 3, 2003, p. 257–337.

WOOD, Marcus. Slavery and the romantic sketch: Jean-Baptiste Debret's visual poetics of trauma. *Journal of Historical Geography*, n. 43, 2014, p. 39–48.

WRIGHT, Richard. The color curtain. In: _____. *Black power*. New York: Harper Perennial, 2008.

YOUNG, Robert J. C. *Colonial desire: Hybridity in theory, culture and race*. London; New York: Routledge, 2002.

YOUNGBLOOD, Stephanie. A writing of nothing: Intercession and the autobiographical subject in Ouladah Equiano's interesting narrative. *Callaloo*, v. 36, n. 2, 2013, p. 414–429.

YÚDICE, George. Testimonio y concientización. *Revista de Crítica Literaria Latinoamericana*, n. 36, *La voz del otro: Testimonio, subalternidad y verdad narrativa*, 1992, p. 211–232.

ZMÁRIO, José Mario Peixoto Santos. Ayrson Heráclito: Performances, espaços e ações. *eRevista Performatus*.

About The Author

DR. OSMUNDO PINHO

Osmundo Pinho is from Salvador da Bahia. He has a PhD in Social Sciences (UNICAMP, 2003). He works in the undergraduate and post-graduate courses in Social Sciences at the Federal University of Recôncavo da Bahia and in the Postgraduate Program in Ethnic and African Studies at the Federal University of Bahia, in Salvador. He is an associate researcher at the Institute of African Studies at the Federal University of Pernambuco (UFPE) and coordinator of the Territoriality, Violence and Heritage Group in the Recôncavo da Bahia (UFRB/CNPq). He was a visiting scholar in the Department of African and Diaspora Studies at the University of Texas at Austin (2014) and a Richard E. Greenleaf Fellow at the Latin American Library at Tulane University in New Orleans (2020). Co-organizer with Joao H. Costa Vargas of "Antinegritude: The Impossible Black Subject in the Brazilian National Formation" (2016) and author of "Captivity: Antinegritude and Ancestrality" (2021), in addition to other books, articles and essays.

About The Translator

AYALA TUDE

English Teacher. Translator. Master's student in Literature and Culture at the Federal University of Bahia – UFBA. Member and associate researcher of the group Traduzindo no Atlântico Negro [Translating in the Black Atlantic]. Responsible for international communications at Diálogos Insubmissos de Mulheres Negras. Co-founder of the English course in an afro diasporic approach @afrodiasporaconnect.

About The Book Cover Artist

Khadija Jahmila (b. 1993, Maryland) is an Afro-Caribbean mixed-media artist, creative entrepreneur, and art educator whose work blends hand-cut paper and digital collage to explore Afrofuturistic themes and surrealism. Her vibrant creations celebrate the humanity, beauty, intersectionality, and otherworldliness of the African diaspora, merging the speculative with the fantastical to create immersive visual narratives.

In addition to her artistic practice, Jahmila teaches mixed-media art to young students and leads art classes for adults with intellectual and developmental disabilities. She also facilitates creative workshops that encourage playful exploration of collage and visual storytelling.

To explore more of Khadija Jahmila's work and stay updated on her latest projects, visit KhadijaJahmila.com and follow her on Instagram @khadija.jahmila.

Digital Cover Art Created by Khadija Jahmila
Artwork Title: Bondage Created in 2025
For more information, visit KhadijaJahmila.com

www.ingramcontent.com/pod-product-compliance
Lightning Source LLC
Chambersburg PA
CBHW060137130626
46556CB00006B/2390